IN THE ABSENCE OF TOWNS

Geographical Perspectives on the Human Past

General Editor: Robert D. Mitchell,
University of Maryland, College Park

Derelict Landscapes: The Wasting of America's Built Environment
by John A. Jakle and David Wilson

The American Environment: Interpretations of Past Geographies
edited by Lary M. Dilsaver and Craig E. Colten

In the Absence of Towns: Settlement and Country Trade in
Southside Virginia, 1730–1800
by Charles J. Farmer

Upstate Arcadia: Landscape, Aesthetics, and the Triumph of Social
Differentiation in America
by Peter J. Hugill

IN THE ABSENCE OF TOWNS

*Settlement and Country Trade in Southside Virginia,
1730–1800*

Charles J. Farmer

Rowman & Littlefield Publishers, Inc.

ROWMAN & LITTLEFIELD PUBLISHERS, INC.

Published in the United States of America
by Rowman & Littlefield Publishers, Inc.
4720 Boston Way, Lanham, Maryland 20706

British Cataloging in Publication Information Available

Library of Congress Cataloging-in-Publication Data

Farmer, Charles J.
In the absence of towns : settlement and country trade in
Southside Virginia, 1730–1800 / Charles J. Farmer.
p.   cm. — (Geographical perspectives on the human past)
Includes bibliographical references (p.) and index.
1. Virginia—Historical geography. 2. Virginia—Commerce—
History—18th century. 3. Virginia—Economic conditions.
I. Title. II. Series.
F229.F37   1993   975.5'03—dc20   93-2808   CIP

ISBN 0-8476-7795-8 (cloth : alk. paper)
ISBN 0-8476-7796-6 (paper : alk. paper)

Printed in the United States of America

The paper used in this publication meets the minimum requirements of
American National Standard for Information Sciences—Permanence of
Paper for Printed Library Materials, ANSI Z39.48–1984.

Contents

List of Figures

List of Tables

Preface

In an inventory and prospect essay on the domestic economy of colonial America during the eighteenth century (in Jack Greene and J. R. Pole's *Colonial British America*, published in 1984), Richard Sheridan states that "As key units in the network of trade, country stores and storekeepers should be studied more systematically, using probate and other records and the techniques of historical geographers." The primary "technique" of historical geography is to place the country store in its proper context of settlement evolution: the change over time from decentralized settlement to an urban network, with its morphological and functional hierarchy of places. Because country stores were the primary components of the early decentralized landscape, they must be considered in the context of urbanization. In the absence of towns—that is, when an urban network failed to develop—the country store assumed the functions if not the morphology of the urban place. Country stores were not unique institutions. They were critical parts of evolving settlement systems and should be approached in terms of geographical theory.

Professor Sheridan is quite correct when he suggests that inquiry should focus on local backcountry sources. The country store trade of the southern backcountry has long been common knowledge among students of early American history, but their perspective has been gleaned primarily from outside sources, from account books and personal correspondences of merchants based in Great Britain, Philadelphia, Norfolk, or Richmond—rarely from the perspective of the backcountry. The operation of that trade and the context of its development and persistence may be found in a variety of backcountry county records. It requires settling in for an extended stay.

Research for this study began over a decade ago at the Halifax County Courthouse. Mr. J. C. Sizemore, Clerk of Circuit Court, gave me access to all those fragile court judgments with only one condition. He handed me scissors and a quantity of ribbon, and indicated that he would be grateful if I would replace any worn ribbons or cords that bound these loose records. I eagerly accepted the challenge. I shall always be grateful to that fine gentleman for permitting me to tie those ribbons. Along the way, other depositories have also been generous with their materials, time, and staff. I wish to express my appreciation to the following: The Virginia State Library in Richmond; The Virginia Historical Society, also in Richmond; Perkins Library of Duke University; Alderman Library of the University of Virginia; the Southern Historical Collection of the University of North Carolina, Chapel Hill; the Manuscripts Division of the Library of Congress; the Library of Hampden-Sydney College; and the Colonial Williamsburg Research Center.

I am also indebted to numerous individuals who were critical to the completion of this study. At the Virginia State Library, Conley Edwards brought both the "British Mercantile Claims" and the Mutual Assurance Society records to my attention. Alice Moskowitz saved the project at its fledgling stage by constructing the original maps used in my dissertation, "Country Stores and Frontier Exchange Systems in Southside Virginia During the Eighteenth Century," from which much of this current study is derived. Scott Spiker did the line work and patterns for the current maps. In order that Scott's reputation not be tarnished, I must admit to the design and lettering of all maps and other figures and to the actual construction of four maps, the identities of which are all too obvious. Despite her overwhelming duties as Geography Department secretary at Frostburg State University, Gale Carney typed all the tables. Special thanks go to Bebe Elrick for her most generous technical and moral support, especially her generosity with time and talent during the final stages of production and editing.

I especially wish to express my gratitude to Professor Robert Mitchell for his support. For more than a decade, he has been friend, teacher, and adviser. He directed this study in its dissertation form at the University of Maryland, edited earlier versions of the present manuscript, and provided stimulating criticism at appropriate times. He also suggested the title, *In the Absence of Towns*, as usual guiding me toward the forest, away from all the many trees.

Generous support and guidance were provided by the staff of

Rowman and Littlefield. I am most indebted to Jonathan Sisk, editor in chief, and to Lynn Gemmell, production editor.

I wish to thank the American Council of Learned Societies for providing a grant for further research during the summer of 1987. Their generosity made possible much of the work on the post-Revolutionary War period of the eighteenth century and all of the analysis of the nineteenth-century context.

Certain aspects of this study were presented in "Country Store Trading Patterns in Backcountry Southern Virginia During the Eighteenth Century," in *The American South*, ed., Richard L. Nostrand and Sam Hillard, Geoscience and Man, vol. 25, Baton Rouge, Department of Geography and Anthropology, Louisiana State University, and in "Persistence of Country Trade: The Failure of Towns to Develop in Southside Virginia During the Eighteenth Century," *Journal of Historical Geography,* vol. 14. I wish to thank the publishers of these journals for permission to use these materials. There are some points of clarification that will facilitate the reader's understanding of this work. For those not familiar with the previous (nondecimal) British currency system, twelve pence equals one shilling and twenty shillings make a pound. Local customs are followed in the identification of county records. County order books are designated as such except in Halifax County, where they are identified as "pleas." In Pittsylvania County, will books are "accounts current"; in Charlotte County, judgments are "court cases"; and in Mecklenburg County, "loose papers." With the exception of the Halifax County judgments, all county records are on microfilm in the Virginia State Library in Richmond. Finally, the term "backcountry" that is used throughout this study is a general and functional reference to the interior frontier regions, primarily the Piedmont region, of Tidewater Virginia. This designation is not to be confused with the more specific "Backcountry" region of the Appalachian Mountains in David Hackett Fischer's recent innovative work, *Albion's Seed.*

1

In the Absence of Towns

At the beginning of the eighteenth century, there were only five large towns in the thirteen colonies of British North America. Reflecting the short settlement history of the colonies, the concentration of population along the Atlantic coast, and the strong trading connection with England, all five places were port towns. Boston, with 7,000 inhabitants, was the major commercial center of New England and the largest town in all the colonies.[1] Newport, Rhode Island, had a population of over 2,500 and, like several other smaller ports in that region, was a trading satellite of Boston. New York City, over a century away from controlling the vast and wealthy North American interior, and Philadelphia, in existence for less than twenty years and only beginning to penetrate the richest hinterland of the Atlantic coastal region, had populations of 5,000 each. Charleston, South Carolina, belying its position as the only major town in the vast southern region, contained barely 2,000 inhabitants.

The 70,000 inhabitants of the Chesapeake region in 1700 continued to be dispersed. The full complement of navigable waterways, the rise of the powerful rural-based tobacco planters, and English mercantile policy that discouraged colonial manufacturing worked in concert to create a trading system that was focused on decentralized plantation landings. The sites of Williamsburg and Annapolis had only recently been selected as capitals of their respective territories. Norfolk and Yorktown were developing, but it would be more than twenty-five years before the first of the fall-zone ports of Baltimore, Richmond, Petersburg, and Alexandria would be established.[2]

The eighteenth century was a period of town building as population and territorial expansion, together with economic development, provided the stimuli for the centralization of activities. New towns appeared both within the older settled areas of the seventeenth century and across the interior territories of the advancing eighteenth-century frontier that finally reached beyond the Appalachian Mountains into the Ohio Valley. Almost one hundred towns were founded in southeastern Pennsylvania alone between 1730 and 1800.[3] Deep in the interior of Virginia, the Shenandoah Valley contained twenty-seven towns and villages by the end of the century and 15 percent of the population of the more developed northern half of the valley lived in centralized settlements.[4] By 1800 Baltimore had grown to a population of 27,000 and ranked as the third largest town in the United States. Norfolk, with a population of 7,000, after recovering from British destruction during the Revolutionary War, and Richmond, Virginia's new capital, with 6,000 inhabitants, ranked eighth and tenth respectively. Even North Carolina, with one of the most dispersed populations in the new nation, had developed a threefold system of towns that included ports, midland linkage points, and interior places.[5] Amid this urban expansion, the original large ports of New York, Philadelphia, and Boston continued to dominate as the mercantile basis of town development continued to prevail. New York, emerging as the national metropolis, closed out the eighteenth century with a population of almost 70,000.

The importance of town development in settlement evolution initially appears to be greatly exaggerated since the urban population of the United States was no more than 10 percent of the total by 1800 and certain regions, primarily the American South, had relatively few towns. But the significance of towns went far beyond size and number. Towns were developed and maintained by the services they provided for large areas beyond their narrow municipal bounds. Towns determined the trading, political, and cultural structure for large numbers of people living in extensive geographic areas. Towns were places located at central points of convenience to large rural populations. Rural folk depended upon the town for the collection and distribution functions of trade, the provision of retail goods, the central authority of government, the interpretation and presentation of high culture, and the general dissemination of information. To the British in North America, as with other colonizing powers throughout the course of Western European overseas expansion, the development of towns was a symbol of the achievement of order on the new land. Towns represented the conquest of civilization over savagery.

The geographical structure of town development that evolved in early America was based on the relationship between population growth and economic development. By 1800 American settlement patterns had generally evolved from a frontier-mercantile pattern, based on a combination of key coastal service centers and numerous interior country stores that served pioneer rural populations, to an urban-dominated system, or central-place network, comprised of key coastal entrepôts; a variety of interior centralized places that included trading towns, county seats, and smaller service centers such as villages and hamlets; and declining numbers of decentralized country stores (Fig. 1-1). Increased urban development was a response to the trading requirements of a developing economy and a growing popu-

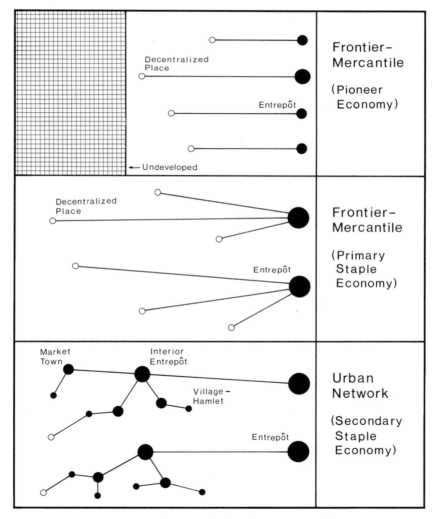

Figure 1-1. Settlement and economic development model.

lation. In a frontier-mercantile structure, a pioneer economy was served by long-distance trading activities. Frontier settlers exported natural products and small agricultural surpluses through country stores and backcountry towns to coastal entrepôts. From there, wholesale merchants exported interior products to overseas markets and imported manufactured goods for shipment to those same backcountry towns and stores for dispersal to local settlers. Local trade was predominantly country trade, with retail and service activities operating as much through country stores as towns and smaller service centers. In the later urban-dominated system of the late eighteenth century, supported by larger populations and extensive economic development, local towns and service centers increasingly took more control of internal trade. In this trading structure, country trade operated in a greatly reduced fashion in the shadow of the dominant centralized places.

This progression of settlement evolution, however, varied considerably in its level of structural intensity and completion. Nowhere was this more evident than in the southern Piedmont region of Virginia known as the Southside. In 1800, after a period of more than 130 years following initial exploration and resource evaluation, almost seventy years after the organization of the first county, and after the establishment of a population density and a level of economic development sufficient to support an urban system, this region of over 6,000 square miles and more than 127,000 residents located south of the Appomattox River had no towns or service centers.[6] The region still retained a frontier-mercantile trading structure. It remained a region of decentralized places where country stores continued to perform many of the functions generally ascribed to small towns.

Most of the literature on early American settlement has treated country-store trade either as a preliminary phase in the development of an urban system or as an activity peripheral to more important issues such as trade network formation, entrepôt origins and dominance, regional economic development, and population growth and spread. Country stores as components of settlement systems and as participants in settlement evolution have not been the focus of serious study. Their persistence in the Southside raises four critical questions. Why did urban places and an urban system fail to develop within the region? How was trade structured throughout such a large region in the absence of towns? To what extent did country stores organize both local and long-distance trading relationships? And what does the persistence of a store system tell us about existing theories of settlement evolution? The rest of this study is an attempt to provide answers to these questions and to place Virginia's Southside within the context of America's evolving settlement fabric. Its theoretical framework is based on three modes of explanation: central-place theory, the mercantile theory of trade and settlement, and the staple theory of settlement and economic development.

Southside Virginia

Southside Virginia appears to possess the necessary regional characteristics to provide the basis for an evaluation of country trade in the context of settlement evolution. It is a sufficiently large region to have undergone a prolonged frontier experience that led to an elaboration of cultural landscapes dominated by dispersed settlements (Fig. 1-2). Travelers disparate in time and purpose described with astonishing similarity the dispersed and sparse character of the Southside's population. To Pennsylvania Moravians traveling across its more developed eastern section in 1743, the great distances between settlers gave the region an inhospitable and even dangerous character. In 1753 other members of that religious group had great difficulty following the Great Wagon Road to the Carolinas in the wilderness conditions of the western part of the region.[7] Just before the onset of the Revolutionary War, on a journey that took him through the longer-settled eastern portion of the region, John Smyth stopped for the night at a "miserable house" that had no neighbors within five and eight miles on two separate sides of the property. Later in his travels, Smyth encountered few houses or travelers along an extensive area of the Virginia–North Carolina border and actually became lost in the dense woods and swamps in southern Halifax County.[8] Although the "wilderness" had disappeared in the wake of population growth and economic expansion, Congressman William Loughton Smith of South Carolina nevertheless observed a landscape that had strong vestiges of that earlier period as he traveled through the Southside in 1791.[9] True, the congressman was impressed with the fields of wheat and corn, but he also noted the great distances between plantations, the large amount of land still in forests, and the generally rough social character of the local inhabitants.

But the most profound association with an earlier period of settlement was the lack of towns, villages, or even hamlets. The congressman passed through no centralized places on a trip that followed the main road from Richmond through the counties of Amelia, Prince Edward, Charlotte, Halifax, and Pittsylvania to the North Carolina

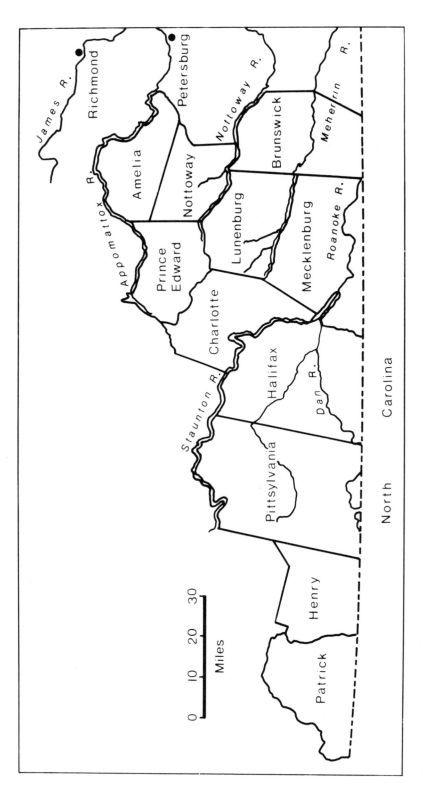

Figure 1-2. Southside Virginia.

border. In 1808 a band of peddlers traveled crude roads to service the still widely dispersed population of the region. The monthly meetings of the county courts were the only centralized gatherings of population of sufficient size to warrant their attention.[10]

The settlement character of Southside Virginia sprang from a Tidewater seedbed. The Southside, as the western expansion of Chesapeake society, was the recipient of the older region's tobacco economy and slave labor structure. Its large territory further enhanced the Tidewater's penchant for dispersed plantation sites as the dominant form of settlement. The Southside as a frontier modification of Chesapeake society has been captured in two important works with general but firm Turnerian interpretations. Both Michael Nicholls, in "Origins of the Virginia Southside, 1703–1753," and Richard Beeman, in *The Evolution of the Southern Backcountry*, portray a frontier society that emulated the older Tidewater society, but at greatly reduced levels of wealth, competence, and sophistication. They depict a fluid society built from primarily lower-level wealth groups who were crude individualistic seekers of economic opportunity, who were without a strong regional focus, and who lacked institutional orientation until the evangelical movements after midcentury.[11]

The lack of regional and institutional focus further suggests a highly dispersed society that functioned without benefit of an urban network. Although Southside Virginia, as a component of Chesapeake society, had less opportunity for town development because the export nature of tobacco placed little demand on the local infrastructure and the large slave population decreased the need for centrally located goods and services, the timing of settlement in conjunction with environmental realities and legal innovations was also an important factor in this persistence of decentralized trade. The fall zone, an area of rapids and falls where rivers pass from the slightly higher elevations and harder and older rock of the Piedmont to the lower elevations and unconsolidated materials that characterize the Coastal Plain, was not a barrier to population expansion into the interior. But as the clear terminus of the inland movement of ocean-going vessels in an era when waterborne trade usually determined the location of towns, it effectively blocked any opportunity for a large trading town in the Southside. As population expansion was initiated in the region during the 1720s and was accelerated during the 1740s, the landlocked Southside ironically became one of the primary supporters of town development at the fall zone. Responding to population growth and economic development in the interior, Richmond and Petersburg were chartered in 1742 and 1748 respectively. The initial irony, however, occurred earlier in 1733 when William Byrd actually conceived of the idea of fall-zone urban development during the course of an expedition deep into the heart of the Southside region.[12] Subsequent additions to the Tobacco Inspection Act of 1730, requiring Southside tobacco exports to be inspected and exported at the closest fall-zone port, completed what nature had provided and what contemporary ideas of economic development had nourished. The primary impetus for town development was never permitted to exist in the region. Petersburg and Richmond effectively preempted town formation in the Southside.

Although the eighteenth-century Southside possessed what is interpreted as an unusual settlement landscape, it also provides numerous clues to interpreting that landscape. The county court, as the primary focus of the local population, diffused intact from Tidewater to backcountry as did the strong sense of responsibility of its governing body. The justices of county courts, with their broad legislative, executive, and judicial powers, reflected the transfer of civic responsibility and public service of the planter class that in some instances developed into paternalism and opportunism. In a more pragmatic context, these gentlemen of the court, with a great deal of assistance from British and Union armies that marched elsewhere and with a great deal of luck that prevented the outbreak of fire, left behind for future researchers rich regional storehouses of primary public source materials. These include not only the frequently utilized court order books, deed books, and will books, but also the overlooked court judgments (loose court papers) that provide the details of mercantile activity and the rarely used legislative petitions that reveal the attitudes and concerns of the regional population.

Central-Place Theory and Settlement Patterning

Most discussions of urban networks have been considered in the context of central-place theory. Initiated during the 1930s by the German geographer Walter Christaller, further developed by the German economist August Lösch in the 1940s, and generously modified since the 1950s, central-place theory is concerned with both broad developmental and highly structured interpretations of urbanization.[13] The broader interpretation suggests that towns developed at geographic locations convenient to the greatest number of consumers in a given area. In this context the theory has replaced more traditional environmental explanations for town location and development. In its more structured aspects, central-place theory attempts to explain the distribution of urban places within a closed geographic system dependent on agriculture. This structure emphasizes the threshold size: the minimum population necessary to support a given function or a given place; the range of a good: the distance consumers will travel to purchase a particular good or obtain a particular service; and a nested hierarchy of places that is based on size, number, distribution, and functions of a place.

Central-place theory, despite its association with urban places and urban systems, has methodological significance for country trade in two contexts. First, although it is decentralized and is the lowest trade level in the urban network, country trade has hierarchical connections with higher-order places in the service system. Also, and more important, central-place theory can be used to evaluate certain aspects of the trade areas of country stores. These are the location and spacing of stores, the types of goods and services offered by stores, the geographic dimensions of their trade areas, the number of store customers, and the wealth characteristics of store clientele.

Although concerned only with establishing the basis for central places, Christaller did mention in passing dispersed places that were of too-narrow geographic orientation to possess the requisite level of centrality to be included in a complete regional settlement system.[14] These dispersed places were agriculturally based—the Southside for instance—where services were provided from the same place where agricultural production was carried out; resource-based, where services were narrowly focused on only specific locations that extracted localized natural products; and places that did not conform to either of the first two categories—for example, monasteries, home-based workplaces, and industrial settlements. Post-Christaller interpretations, with their more charitable views, have generally avoided methodological debate by incorporating these noncentral places into the fold of the entire regional settlement system above the level of individual, dispersed settlement.

However, whether for reasons of its emphasis on agricultural production, its lack of distinctive urban morphology, its lack of nonagriculturally oriented entrepreneurs, or its lack of modern credentials, the farm-plantation basis of service activities, or country trade, has continued to occupy the position originally assigned by Christaller. This study has no quarrel with that interpretation, choosing only to emphasize the importance of decentralized trade in a developing regional settlement system and the persistence of that trade in an export staple economy.

Studies of urban systems in historical context have paid little attention to country trade, choosing instead to focus on the later processes and phases of urbanization, particularly in the northern United States. In addition to developments in southeastern Pennsylvania and the Shenandoah Valley, southern New England had a well-developed urban system by the end of the eighteenth century, Vermont rapidly developed a central-place system during the late eighteenth century, and the Ohio Valley followed suit during the first quarter of the nineteenth century.[15]

Although there is no doubt that northern areas had considerably more urban development than southern areas during the eighteenth and nineteenth centuries, Max Schumacher's observation, in his study of northern agricultural markets, that "The most generally available agency for the collection of farm produce was the country store, the 'Noah's Ark of Commerce'" raises the question of whether most studies have been based on the realities of settlement evolution or biased in favor of identifying only urban forms and processes.[16] Joseph Wood, in the same revisionist context, has suggested greater significance to dispersed settlement in colonial New England by disproving the idea that the nucleated village dominated settlement in that region.[17] Bayly Marks has shown that, contrary to general beliefs on the evolution of a settlement system, centralized activities were actually reduced over time in St. Mary's County, Maryland, because of the increased activity and eventual dominance by Baltimore over the county's trading network.[18] Baltimore's trading hegemony supplanted the rapid development of industrial and craft activity and terminated the county's rapidly emerging central-place network.

Only Gregory Rose's study of the trade area of one store in Massachusetts during the mid-nineteenth century, Daniel Thorp's delimitation of the trade area of a combination tavern-store in the North Carolina Piedmont during the middle eighteenth century and his comparison of trade areas between rural and village-based stores, and my own analysis of two store trade areas in the Virginia backcountry during the eighteenth century have called attention to the geographic structure of country trade in the context of an urban network.[19]

Both Rose and I came to similar conclusions regarding the distance-decay effect of customer distribution in the trade area, the large trade areas of country stores, the variety of goods and services that the stores offered, the variations in consumer travel created by real-world situations, and the challenge of determining customer distribution in historical context. The primary division in our studies came from variations in the settlement systems of the respective study areas. Because the store in Rose's study was located in a small village that was part of a well-developed settlement system with places of similar and larger size, trade boundaries between places were determined both by mapping individual store customers and by using the predictions of the gravity model. But in a dispersed settlement system such as the eighteenth-century Southside, the delimitation of store trade areas was less precise because of greater impediments to determining location and, quite simply, the lack of a network of central places with its well-defined population and distance parameters. Thorp's study, based more in a frontier context, has more in common with decentralized trade in the Southside and will be discussed more thoroughly in Chapters 5 and 6.

Country trade has been given more attention in the study of urban networks in the American South because it persisted longer there than elsewhere. Studies of this persistence identify a variety of trading options that were available to settlers, but most attention has been focused on stores, ordinaries, taverns, mills, and inns located on plantations and farms and at crossroads and hamlets, and on itinerant merchants such as peddlers and wagon merchants. Robert Mitchell recognized that country trade still existed in more isolated areas of the Shenandoah Valley at the end of the eighteenth century.[20] Roy Merrens suggested even greater significance for country trade in the extensive and porous urban network of North Carolina during the colonial period.[21] Further, James O'Mara's study of urban evolution in the eighteenth-century Virginia Tidewater implied the importance of stores in settlement formation.[22] In constructing an urban system from a network of linkages between places at the macroscopic level, O'Mara included a number of small places at the bottom of the urban hierarchy that are usually not considered components of a traditional central-place network. His attempt to force a central-place framework on the region ironically revealed the importance of very small and decentralized places as significant points in the network of contacts within a relatively large region.

Karin Stanford used central-place methodology to determine consumer behavior at one country store in St. Mary's County, Maryland, during the 1820s.[23] She found that the wealth status of store customers was the primary explanation for variations in purchasing patterns and consumer mobility. Poorer consumers generally bought only small quantities of goods and did not have access to the financial services of the store. Middle-level wealth groups purchased a greater variety of goods on a more regular basis and were also permitted to borrow money and to meet external financial obligations through the store. Wealthier customers exhibited behavior similar to the middle-level group, but had greater access to the store's financial services and were able to purchase more expensive items in the limited store inventory. But the main characteristic of the wealthier consumer was the greater opportunity to bypass the local store and shop at distant, higher-order places within the urban network of the western shore of Chesapeake Bay. Mark's previously indicated study of the usurpation of the county's trading network by Baltimore suggests that the trading patterns revealed by Stanford were likely to continue for an extended period of time in Southern Maryland.

Studies by Lorena Walsh and Jean Russo, which utilize broad central-place principles in more rudimentary cultural landscapes, are more applicable to the system of decentralized places in Southside Virginia.[24] Walsh looked at spatial networks in a small area of St. Mary's County, Maryland, during the early frontier period of the seventeenth century. Focal points of human interaction ranged from local plantation-house living rooms and places of shared property boundaries to county courts, and beyond the bounds of the county to more centralized trading places. The causes of human interaction, whether individual or group, formal or informal, ranged from gossip, church, funeral, marriage, family gatherings, and mutual aid at the more local level to the wider arena of militia muster, court session, and long-distance merchant activity. The size of the spatial network was determined primarily by the sex, occupation, and status of the individual and by "physical geography," in this case usually where stream estuaries disrupted movement.

Russo incorporated local craftsmen into the network of decentralized activity in Talbott County, Maryland, during the first half of the eighteenth century. As the focus of the local business community, planter-merchants and innkeepers (ordinary-keepers) provided a great variety of services that included not only the usual sale of store goods and drink, but also products in great demand that were constructed by local artisans. These craftsmen, either indentured servants or slaves of the planter-merchant, or hired labor, made clothing, shoes, and barrels; sawed wood; constructed buildings; and repaired tools. These activities gave even more significance to important plantation locations, the "power points" in the decentralized settlement landscape, by becoming components of the local exchange system. In a trading system based primarily on a system of barter and book credit, artisan activity was sold, purchased, debited, and remitted among numerous individuals within the local exchange system. Although generally ignored by both historians and geographers, the prominence of the decentralized trading of services on the Eastern Shore of Maryland, which was also supported by the exchange system of Southside Virginia, suggests its widespread occurrence in frontier regions.

Staple Theory of Settlement and Economic Development

A staple interpretation of agrarian societies has been the primary conceptual approach to the economic history of North America. Recently, through the work of Carville Earle and Ronald Hoffman, that concept has been applied to the explanation of differential urban development in early America.[25] Earle and Hoffman have argued that towns are less likely to develop in areas dominated by a highly specialized primary staple, such as tobacco and cotton, than in areas where the economy is based on more diversified secondary staples, primarily associated with wheat production.

Because primary staples were exported in a raw state, there were few spread effects from their production. Both backward linkages (industries associated with the staple) and forward linkages (the development of new industries from staple input) were weak. For example, tobacco had little influence on the development of tertiary (service) and secondary (manufacturing) economic activities in the backcountry because it was exclusively exported, needed no special handling, and did not readily succumb to spoilage. Primary staple production required only plantation and port. As a result, in areas of primary staple production, settlement did not progress beyond the frontier-mercantile level and the simple trading structure of linear connections between entrepôt and decentralized points was extended in both space and time (Fig. 1-1).

Secondary staples, such as wheat and cattle, had a greater impact on backcountry settlement evolution because they were produced for both domestic and foreign markets and were more controlled by local entrepreneurs. Their stronger backward and forward linkages created a variety of secondary and tertiary activities that were centrally located within the region. Wheat and other grains were locally processed and consumed, required more specialized handling because of greater weight and spoilage potential, and created numerous activities beyond the primary economic sector—activities such as hauling, milling, road building, wagon construction, harness making, tavern keeping, tanning, baking, and brokerage. Towns emerged at crucial geographic linkage points in the infrastructure to service the demands of this economy.

Robert Baldwin contributed a critical societal component to the staple thesis.[26] He suggested that areas producing primary staples, or plantation societies, had few local retail and service needs because of reduced consumer demand created by labor-intensive production composed of unskilled workers (primarily slaves), uneven distribution of wealth, and reduced economic opportunity. By contrast, secondary staple-producing areas, or farming societies, had a more diverse society of skilled middle-income workers, who placed greater demands on the local area for centrally located goods and services.

Earle and Hoffman's interpretation of staple theory has only been applied directly at the local level in my own work on Southside Virginia, where I have indicated a strong correlation between the dominance of tobacco production and the lack of town development; and in Robert Mitchell and Warren Hofstra's study of Frederick County, Virginia, where they found no direct link between towns and the wheat and flour trade.[27] Mitchell and Hofstra show that town development was a more complex matter, with a variety of contributing factors that included reciprocity between town and rural areas, a diversified economy, local control of the import and export aspects of long-distance trade, and war. However, a large body of literature supports the tenets of Earle and Hoffman's theory by revealing distinctive regional settlement patterns in early America. Northern regions, which were more likely to have an economy based on secondary staples, had well-developed urban systems. Among the more illustrative works are James Lemon's study of southeastern Pennsylvania, Mitchell's work on the Shenandoah Valley, Edward Muller's investigation of the early Ohio Valley, and Morton Rothstein's comparison of the influence of wheat and cotton economies on settlement in the antebellum Midwest and South.[28]

By contrast, southern coastal and Piedmont regions, which were more likely to be producers of primary staples, had fewer towns and less complete urban networks. The largest volume of literature supporting the staple thesis, primarily concerned with eighteenth-century Virginia, supports in general fashion the more specific conclusions on tobacco and settlement systems made by my own research. Calvin Coulter and Robert Thompson have shown how trading activity took place within the context of a linear pattern of entrepôts and backcountry decentralized stores, supplemented by periodic administrative input from Williamsburg and county courthouses.[29] Jacob Price and James Soltow examined the dominance of externally based Scottish mercantile firms in the backcountry of the colony after the 1730s.[30] The establishment of the Scottish decentralized store system to collect tobacco in exchange for European manufactured goods dramatically revealed the lack of interior towns and the absence of local control of the trading network. Edith E. B. Thomson and Thomas Devine followed the operations of individual mercantile companies in this trading milieu, while Devine additionally placed Virginia within the context of a vast world economic system controlled from Western Europe.[31] Similarly, Robert Coakley has shown how the arrested development of a native Virginia merchant community, and by extension other native economic activities, was caused by the long-dominant position of British mercantile firms in the colony.[32]

Mercantile Theory and Trade Evolution

Because country trade is usually associated with early frontier or continuing prolonged frontier characteristics, James Vance's mercantile theory provides an appropriate conceptual structure.[33] This theory, also known as the wholesale model or the long-distance trade model, is concerned primarily with trade relationships in newly settled regions. In this context, entrepôts or, in the terminology of Andrew Burghardt, "gateway cities"[34] developed along contact zones between areas of differing intensities or types of production. Located on the margins of a frontier area that was undergoing settlement and economic development, the entrepôt functioned as a break-in-bulk center for manufactured and foreign goods destined for the interior and as collecting points for the raw materials and surplus agricultural products of the backcountry that were to be shipped to distant markets. Because population densities and economic productivity were not sufficient to support local towns, the country store was the primary focus of this backcountry trade. It was here that the final distribution of goods and the initial sequence of collection were carried out. The linear trading pattern between entrepôt and country store was relatively simple, but it was also part of a more complex international trading network.

Entrepôts developed in colonial areas and along developing national frontiers, especially in North America. The early contact zone between Europe and the North American interior was a series of ports along the eastern seaboard—Montreal, Boston, New York, Philadelphia, and Charleston. In Virginia, numerous small entrepôts developed on estuaries connected to the Chesapeake Bay and later along the fall zone between the Tidewater and the Piedmont frontier in the interior. In the lower Midwest during the early nineteenth century, the mercantile towns of Pittsburgh, Cincinnati, and Louisville, located along the Ohio River portal, functioned in a similar manner to the Atlantic coast ports. From their early entry locations on the Great Lakes, Cleveland, Detroit, and Chicago were to perform similar functions in the upper Midwest by the mid-nineteenth century.

Over time, in Vance's theory, the frontier region developed an interior regional entrepôt, or unraveling point, that provided both trade connections between the interior and the primary entrepôts on the periphery and, most importantly, was the base for the development of a regional urban system composed of a hierarchy of later-evolving central places (Fig. 1-1). This aspect of the mercantile model is based on criticism of central-place theory for failing to integrate local and long-distance trade. More appropriate to urban development in North America, Vance's urban system evolved from interregional trade and by a trickle-down process from the initially dominant entrepôt and country store trading structure. Since the central-place structure of Vance's model, once in place, is generally a replica of the system postulated by central-place theory, his contribution to this study will be limited to the critical frontier-mercantile trading structure that functioned without benefit of an urban system.

The breadth provided by the long-distance trading and exploitative contexts of the mercantile model suggests kindred viewpoints. Vance's model, emphasizing North American trade and settlement, appears to be a more narrowly oriented component of Immanuel Wallerstein's macroview of an evolving world-system economy.[35] In Wallerstein's interpretation, a dominant Western European core achieved economic hegemony over a distant, subservient periphery. Capital, technology, and decision-making were concentrated in the core, while the periphery supplied natural resources and agricultural products. By extension, backcountry regions such as Southside Virginia were further removed from the focus of power by a secondary core, represented by fall-zone entrepôts, that was not only a transfer point between core and periphery, but was also a powerful focus of capital concentration and decision making at the regional level.

Indeed, within the context of European colonialism, Edward Taaffe, Richard Morrill, and Peter Gould previously had developed an evolutionary transportation model that emphasized stages of settlement development from an initial base of dominant coastal entrepôts and backcountry posts and stations.[36] The earliest stages suggest scenes from the slave and ivory trade of the African interior depicted in

Joseph Conrad's *Heart of Darkness* and from the Indian trade and the European rivalry for territory in the early hinterland of Charleston, South Carolina, developed in Vernor Crane's *The Southern Frontier.*[37]

Studies of country trade in the context of the frontier-mercantile trading structure have emphasized country stores as the earliest places of mercantile-settlement evolution in newly settled areas. All of these perspectives directly or indirectly portray country trade as preliminary to the further elaboration of settlement and economy to be preempted by town formations. Mitchell's study of the Shenandoah Valley emphasized the formation of a well-developed urban network that emerged out of and had supplanted country-store trade in all but the most isolated areas by the 1790s.[38] Merrens suggested a long period of country trade dominance in North Carolina during the eighteenth century, which led eventually to town development in this highly rural colony.[39] Joseph Ernst and Merrens strongly emphasized the importance of decentralized trading places throughout the backcountry South during the eighteenth century, but they too succumbed to the pull of urban development by focusing on the backcountry town of Camden, South Carolina, rather than on the reciprocity between town-based and country-store-based trade.[40] Carville Earle's study of All Hallow's Parish in Maryland gave more attention to decentralized trade during the colonial period in a region of prolonged dispersed settlement, but the narrow geographic scale of the study and the close proximity to Annapolis evoke uncertainty in the applicability of his conclusions.[41]

Country-Store Historiography

Traditional works on country-store trade rarely place that trade within any perspective of settlement or economic development. Instead, they lean heavily on the store as a part of the unspecialized American frontier or as a lingering remnant of a romanticized past. The most common symbol of the latter perspective is the forced rusticity of the late twentieth-century "country store" near the interstate highway, where busloads of tourists sample regional food and other local fare in air-conditioned comfort. The true symbol of that genre is the long-abandoned, crumbling building on a back road in West Virginia that still retains a weather-beaten·sign that offers to purchase or trade for ginseng and animal skins. But this traditional approach to country-store trade has also given us important works that are placed in the perspective of a more historical reality, are methodological bridges between the more folksy aspects of traditional methodology and the settlement and economic structure of current research, and are highly stimulating to the student of dispersed settlement and decentralized trade. Studies by Lewis Atherton and Thomas Clark comprise a critical trilogy of formative works on country-store methodology.

Lewis Atherton's *Frontier Merchant in Mid-America*, published in 1939, emphasized country trade in a frontier-mercantile trading system and in a pioneer economy during the first half of the nineteenth century.[42] Although unstructured, anecdotal, and focused on the country merchant, Atherton's work is nevertheless useful because it focuses on country trade in its own time context rather than as a prelude to something else. In terms of frontier-mercantile trade, the main strength of the study is the analysis of contacts with distant wholesalers at entrepôt sites rather than with the study of local trade areas. Frontier country stores in the American Midwest, the geographic focus of his study, were in the wholesale trade areas of numerous gateway cities—St. Louis, New Orleans, Philadelphia, and several Ohio River sites. Distance and the unreliability of transportation created problems with availability of store goods, raised the prices of these goods, made difficult the long-distance marketing of local frontier products, and created problems with the transfer of remittances to distant wholesalers. Distance here, he argued, was more formidable than in early eastern frontiers.

Although not organized in an urban developmental structure, Thomas Clark's *Pills, Petticoats, and Plows: The Southern Country Store*, published in 1944, the second work in the trilogy of formative studies of country trade, must be considered in that context because of its late setting in the post–Civil War period.[43] The local country-store trade is used by Clark as the organizational focus of one of the most important portrayals of the human despair, economic retrogression, and increased geographic isolation and regional parochialism of rural backcountry Southern society during Reconstruction. Because of conditions that increased the friction of distance, the importance of country trade increased during this period, in his opinion, and this trade continued to be a viable component of retailing and service activity in many Southern areas into the first half of the twentieth century.

Atherton's *The Southern Country Store, 1800–1860*, published in 1949 and the final entry in the trilogy of country trade studies, developed some of the most important methodology for the study of relationships between country stores and their customers.[44] His primary objective was to emphasize the Southern backcountry and its farmers rather than the regional stereotypes of large planters and entrepôt-based cotton factors. But it was the dominance of the cotton economy, ironically, and its ties to traders in New Orleans, Mobile, and New York City, and to markets in Great Britain, that continued the frontier-mercantile trading pattern that was responsible for the enduring importance of the country stores at the local level in the backcountry. In the face of primary staple production, therefore, the settlement landscape was filled with large geographic holes that were partially served by country stores.

Regional Scale and Settlement Continuum

Two ideas, the importance of regional scale and the promise of a settlement continuum, have been at the center of previous discussion of settlement and economic theory, but have remained largely unfocused. Regional scale relates to the larger area that supports a system of places. This support is territorial, the recognition of boundaries that identify areas with a high degree of spatial and temporal homogeneity, and economic, the production that supports trade and ultimately settlement systems. The settlement continuum refers to the relative size of the components of a hierarchy of places and the assumption of a hierarchy of place functions commensurate with position in the system. It has been assumed that, because of the dominance of a primary staple economy, Southside Virginia had no central-place system with its settlement continuum of hamlet, village, and town. But verification that such a system did not exist must rest upon the pursuit of its existence. If it is confirmed that such a settlement system did not exist, then a decentralized settlement continuum must be discovered, perhaps a more variable network that included ferry, courthouse, plantation, store, ordinary, and tavern sites for service activities.

Previous discussion has strongly recommended the viability of Southside Virginia's regional scale. In an area of over 6,000 square miles, the more than 127,000 inhabitants by 1800 had experienced common economic, settlement, and environmental influences that had been active for approximately seventy years. It is apparent from this discussion that there is a critical linkage between trading and settlement systems, and that Southside Virginia during the eighteenth century exhibited characteristics that indicated a strong correlation between these two phenomena in creating the region's cultural landscape. The early Southside's pioneer economy was focused on distant ports. Later in the eighteenth century, with the development of a commercial economy, the expected evolution from a dispersed population to a regional settlement network focused on towns and service centers did not develop because of the dominance of tobacco, with its external market orientation and weak backward and forward linkages that continued the old frontier-mercantile trading structure. The region's rich store of primary source materials that are available to evaluate the precepts of this study provides the capstone of proof of the legitimacy of Southside Virginia as a viable regional identity.

Previous studies of early American economic and settlement systems, all cited in this chapter, have varied greatly in the strength of their regional frameworks. For example, the works of Merrens on North Carolina, Lemon on Southeastern Pennsylvania, and Mitchell on the Shenandoah Valley are based on relatively large regions that had high levels of similar internal character. By contrast, Earle's study of All Hallow's Parish in Maryland had weaker regional scale value because the dispersed settlement system he portrayed was based only on a portion of a county and did not take into account the larger settlement system of the western shore of Chesapeake Bay. Other studies of eighteenth-century trade, primarily by historians, have lacked distinctive regional context because of their formative character, the real and perceived limitations of primary source materials, and their lack of concern for a regional base.

In the traditional works on country trade, Atherton's study of frontier merchants was only generally focused on the lower Midwest and the economic and settlement contexts of the trade were not developed. His treatment of Southern country stores was more clearly defined as backcountry South, but examples ranged across areas of varied economy and settlement from Virginia to Louisiana. Although Clark's study was only broadly based in the Southern backcountry, the background of extensive economic and social retrogression after the Civil War provided a surprisingly strong relationship between subject and geographic context. This large and diverse area had acquired a new and stronger similarity of character.

The assumption of settlement evolution to a well-developed urban network, contrasted with the paucity of towns in the eighteenth-century South, has produced an emphasis on the town functions of a place to the neglect of urban form. This argument suggests that town functions occurred at numerous places despite the lack of commensurate town population and structures. Critics of this argument accept the existence and importance of traditional "urban" functions outside traditional "urban" forms, but are critical of the lack of division between town and country as expressed through distinctive urban morphology. Although it is critical to the evaluation of frontier and persistent rural societies to understand that a crossroads country store has the potential to provide the variety of goods and services found in larger, more centralized settlements, the functional approach invariably leads to a breakdown of distinction between central and decentralized places.

The seemingly amorphous nature of lower-level places is not solely the domain of the eighteenth century. The rural-urban continuum of the twentieth century also offers little distinction between its lower-level components. A town is larger than a village; a village is larger than a hamlet; and a hamlet is a collection of buildings and residents larger than a farmstead. The only clear distinction in the United States is the 2,500 population·threshold that is the division between urban and nonurban for census purposes. And, as in the eighteenth century, many nonurban places, primarily villages and hamlets, may perform as many functions as some places designated by size as "urban." Glen Trewartha sought to clarify the status of Midwestern hamlets in the 1940s, an important focus of local trading activity during that era.[45] Trewartha recognized hamlets as distinct from the countryside by their agglomeration of population, their nonfarm functions, a population range of sixteen to 150 people, and a maximum distance between buildings not exceeding one-quarter mile. Students of eighteenth-century settlement have also attempted to define the population of the components of the urban network. In more urban southeastern Pennsylvania, Lemon distinguished between towns and villages at a population of 300 and between villages and hamlets at 100 inhabitants. In addition, the hamlet was separated from the countryside by an agglomeration of activities—at least two nonagricultural operations such as some combination of store, mill, or tavern.[46] Mitchell defined town status in Virginia's Shenandoah Valley as statutory recognition and a population of at least 100 inhabitants, or twenty to twenty-five families living in close proximity.[47] Allan Kulikoff has placed the boundary between towns and villages at 500 inhabitants and between villages and hamlets at 250 in the Chesapeake region of Virginia.[48]

For the early Southern backcountry, the village designation does not seem relevant. The character of backcountry settlement does not warrant such a fine-tuning technique. Any place with 100 or 200 people was a town, probably an important town in the region. It is also difficult to establish a minimum population or number of houses for the town designation. Previous works on urban hierarchy in early America should be consulted as a guide, but individual places should be evaluated with both functional and morphological concepts in mind. For example, Lynchburg, on the James River just north of the study area, contained only a ferry and two or three houses in 1788. But in 1791, there were twenty houses, two tobacco inspection warehouses, and presumably at least that many taverns or ordinaries; by 1795 there were 100 houses.[49] Both in 1791 and 1795, Lynchburg was definitely a town. The Southern backcountry town at the end of the eighteenth century was probably somewhere between the following settlement distinctions in Illinois in 1832. Towns "include only such large towns, as have brick houses, paved streets, market houses, mayors, merchants, manufactuories and people of fashion." Villages were where "the forest trees are still growing in the streets, the birds warble out side windows, and the solitude of the country is all around."[50]

For Southside Virginia the problem is not identifying towns, villages, and hamlets, but differentiating low-level central places, or hamlets, from decentralized places, primarily plantations. Since most Southside trading activity was concentrated on plantations or located at some solitary site, it was rural or decentralized. Even though a plantation might have a store, a mill, and a tavern, or a solitary store might have multiple functions, sometimes as many as a hamlet or village, they were still rural in character. The level of clustering at some courthouse and ferry sites may have produced a few hamlets in the region, but they were not important compared to the more rural-based country trade. This study, therefore, focuses on the strong concentration of retail and service activities on plantations and at solitary sites, and their functional links with trade areas, but also subscribes to the important distinction between "rural" and "urban" as revealed morphologically. The structure of the work is defined by the four questions presented previously. Chapter 2 sets the stage by presenting the development of the region's decentralized settlement system. Chapter 3 evaluates the regional economy as the critical factor in the development of the settlement system. Chapters 4, 5, and 6 focus on various aspects of country-store trade. Specifically, Chapter 4 concentrates on merchants, store locations, and store structures over time; Chapter 5 explores what trading alternatives were available for consumers in a non-urban milieu; and Chapter 6 is concerned with the many functions of country stores, including the purchase and spatial patterns of store customers. A concern for settlement theory is a critical part of each chapter, but the final chapter evaluates the applicability of staple, central-place, and mercantile theories to the unfolding drama of America's settlement evolution.

NOTES

1. Population figures for 1700 are from Carl Bridenbaugh, *Cities in the Wilderness, The First Century of Urban Life in America, 1625–1742* (New York, 1971; originally 1938), 143.

2. The term "fall zone," used throughout this study, reflects the true geologic character of the boundary between Piedmont and Coastal Plain. In the context of settlement and economic development, it is the same geographic place and it functions in the same way as the more familiar term, "fall line."

3. James T. Lemon, *The Best Poor Man's Country: A Geographical Study of Early Southeastern Pennsylvania* (Baltimore, 1972), 118–49.

4. Robert D. Mitchell, *Commercialism and Frontier: Perspectives on the Early Shenandoah Valley* (Charlottesville, Va., 1977), 192, 198.

5. H. Roy Merrens, *Colonial North Carolina in the Eighteenth Century: A Study in Historical Geography* (Chapel Hill, N.C., 1964), 142–72.

6. The Southside, in its broadest extent, is defined as the region south of the James River. This delimitation also usually extends into the Coastal Plain south of the James River estuary. For the general boundaries of the region and the difficulties of delimiting it, see Landon C. Bell, *Sunlight on the Southside: Lists of Tithes, Lunenburg County, Virginia, 1748–1783* (Philadelphia, 1933), 9–12; Michael Nicholls, "Origins of the Virginia Southside: A Social and Economic Study" (unpublished Ph.D. thesis, The College of William and Mary, 1972), 4–8.

7. William J. Hinkle and Charles E. Kemper, "Moravian Diaries of Travel Through Virginia," *Virginia Magazine of History and Biography* 11 (1902–04): 380–81; 12 (1904–05): 275–77.

8. John F. D. Smyth, *A Tour in the United States of America* (New York, 1968; originally 1784) 1:173–76, 242–43.

9. "Journal of William Loughton Smith, 1790–91," *Massachusetts Historical Society Proceedings* 51 (1917–18) 67–71.

10. R. Beeman, ed., "Trade and Travel in Post-Revolutionary Virginia: A Diary of an Itinerant Peddler, 1807–1808," *Virginia Magazine of History and Biography* 84 (1976), 174–88.

11. Nicholls, "Origins of the Virginia Southside"; Beeman, *The Evolution of the Southern Backcountry: A Case Study of Lunenburg County, Virginia, 1746–1832* (Philadelphia, 1984).

12. William Byrd, "A Journey to the Land of Eden, Anno 1733," in *The Prose Works of William Byrd of Westover: Narratives of a Colonial Virginian*, Louis B. Wright, ed. (Cambridge, Mass., 1966), 388. Byrd is of course William Byrd II, but since his famous father, William Byrd I, and his well-known son, William Byrd III, are not part of this study, all references to this literary figure and planter will be "William Byrd."

13. Christaller, *Central Places in Southern Germany*, Carlisle W. Baskin, trans., (Englewood Cliffs, N.J., 1966); August Lösch, *The Economics of Location*, W. H. Woglom and W. F. Stolper, trans. (New Haven, 1954). For a

variety of applications of central-place theory, see Brian J. L. Berry, John B. Parr et. al., *Market Centers and Retail Location: Theory and Application* (Englewood Cliffs, N.J., 1988).

14.   Christaller, *Central Places in Southern Germany,* 16–17, 152–54.

15.   See, respectively, Douglas R. McManis, *Colonial New England, A Historical Geography* (New York, 1975), 41–85; M. J. Bowden, B. L. LaRose, and B. Mishara, "The Development of Competition Between Central Places on the Frontier," *Proceedings, Association of American Geographers* 3 (1971), 32–38; Edward K. Muller, "Selective Urban Growth in the Middle Ohio Valley, 1800–1860," *Geographical Review* 66 (1976), 178–99.

16.   Max G. Schumacher, *The Northern Farmer and his Markets During the Late Colonial Period* (New York, 1975; originally 1948), 81.

17.   Joseph S. Wood, "Village and Community in early Colonial New England," *Journal of Historical Geography* 8 (1982), 323–346.

18.   Bayly Ellen Marks, "Rural Response to Urban Penetration: Baltimore and St. Mary's County, Maryland, 1790–1840," ibid., 113–27.

19.   Gregory Rose, "Reconstructing a Retail Trade Area: Tucker's General Store, 1850–1860," *Professional Geographer* 39 (1987), 33–40; Daniel B. Thorp, "Doing Business in the Backcountry: Retail Trade in Colonial Rowan County, North Carolina," *William and Mary Quarterly* 3d Ser. 48 (1991), 387–408; Charles J. Farmer, "Country Store Trading Patterns in Backcountry Southern Virginia During the Eighteenth Century," *Geoscience and Man* 25 (1988), 57–65.

20.   Mitchell, *Commercialism and Frontier,* 153–56, 186, 189, 196, 210–13, 219, 236–37.   The reader is probably aware of the earlier use of the Shenandoah Valley in the discussion of northern settlement evolution.   In its settlement history and economic development, it is considered both northern and southern.

21.   Merrens, *Colonial North Carolina in the Eighteenth Century,* 167–72.

22.   James O'Mara, *An Historical Geography of Urban System Development: Tidewater Virginia in the 18th Century* (Downsview, Ontario, 1983), Atkinson College, York University Geographical Monograph No. 13, 193–204, 218–86.

23.   Karin B. Stanford, "A Country Store in Jacksonian America: A Study of Purchase Patterns in St. Mary's County, Maryland, in the 1820's," (unpublished M.A. thesis, George Washington University, 1976).

24.   Lorena S. Walsh, "Community Networks in the Early Chesapeake," in Lois G. Carr, Philip D. Morgan, and Jean B. Russo, eds., *Colonial Chesapeake Society* (Chapel Hill, N.C., 1988), 200–41; Jean B. Russo, "Self-Sufficiency and Local Exchange: Free Craftsmen in the Rural Chesapeake Economy," in ibid., 389–432.

25.   Carville V. Earle and Ronald Hoffman, "Urban Development in the Eighteenth-Century South," *Perspectives in American History* 10 (1976), 5–78.

26.   Robert E. Baldwin, "Patterns of Development in Newly-Settled Re-

gions," *Manchester School of Economic and Social Studies* 24 (1956), 161–79.

27. Charles J. Farmer, "Persistence of Country Trade: The Failure of Towns to Develop in Southside Virginia During the Eighteenth Century," *Journal of Historical Geography* 14 (1988), 331–41; Robert D. Mitchell and Warren R. Hofstra, "Town and Country in Backcountry Virginia: Winchester and the Shenandoah Valley, 1730–1800," *Journal of Southern History* 59 (1993), in press.

28. Morton Rothstein, "Antebellum Wheat and Cotton Exports," *Agricultural History* 41 (1967), 91–100.

29. Calvin B. Coulter, "The Virginia Merchant," (unpublished Ph.D. thesis, Princeton University, 1944), 27–100; Robert P. Thompson, "The Merchant in Virginia: 1700–1775," (unpublished Ph.D. thesis, University of Wisconsin, 1955). Also relevant to this issue is Ronald Grim, "The Absence of Towns in Seventeenth-Century Virginia: The Emergence of Service Centers in York County," (unpublished Ph.D. thesis, University of Maryland, 1977).

30. Jacob M. Price, "The Rise of Glasgow in the Chesapeake Tobacco Trade, 1707–1775," *William and Mary Quarterly* 3d Ser. 11 (1954), 179–199; James H. Soltow, "Scottish Traders in Virginia, 1750–1775," *Economic History Review* 2nd Ser. 12 (1959), 83–98.

31. Edith E. B. Thomson, "A Scottish Merchant in Falmouth in the Eighteenth Century," *Virginia Magazine of History and Biography* 39 (1931), 108–17, 230–38; Thomas W. Devine, "A Glasgow Tobacco Merchant During the American War of Independence: Alexander Speirs of Ellerslie, 1776–1781," *William and Mary Quarterly* 3d Ser. 33 (1976), 501–13; idem, *The Tobacco Lords, A Study of the Tobacco Merchants of Glasgow and Their Trading Activities, c. 1740–90*(Edinburgh, 1975).

32. Robert W. Coakley, "Virginia Commerce During the American Revolution," (unpublished Ph.D. thesis, University of Virginia, 1949). See also Richard M. Harrington, Jr., "The Virginia Merchant Community: A Case of Arrested Development, 1783–1789," (unpublished M.A. thesis, University of Virginia, 1972).

33. James E. Vance, *The Merchant's World: The Geography of Wholesaling* (Englewood Cliffs, N.J., 1970), 80–96.

34. Andrew F. Burghardt, "A Hypothesis About Gateway Cities," *Annals of the Association of American Geographers* 61 (1971), 269–85. For the origins of Virginia's fall-zone entrepôts, see Ronald E. Grim, "The Origins and Early Development of the Virginia Fall Line Towns," (M.A. thesis, University of Maryland, 1971).

35. Immanuel Wallerstein, *The Modern World-System: Capitalist Agriculture and the Origins of the European World-Economy in the Sixteenth Century* (New York, 1974); idem, *The Modern World-System II: Mercantilism and the Consolidation of the European World-Economy, 1600-1750* (New York, 1980).

36. Edward J. Taaffe, Richard L. Morrill, and Peter E. Gould, "Trans-

port Expansion in Undeveloped Countries: A Comparative Analysis," *Geographical Review* 53 (1963), 503–29.

37.   W. Crane, *The Southern Frontier: 1670–1732* (Durham, N.C., 1928), 3–46, 108–36.

38.   Mitchell, *Commercialism and Frontier*, 153–56, 186, 189, 196, 210–13, 219, 236–37.

39.   Merrens, *Colonial North Carolina in the Eighteenth Century*, 167–72.

40.   Joseph A. Ernst and H. Roy Merrens, "'Camden's Turrets Pierce the Skies!': The Urban Process in the Southern Colonies During the Eighteenth Century," *William and Mary Quarterly* 3d Ser. 30 (1973), 549–74.

41.   Carville V. Earle, *The Evolution of a Tidewater Settlement System: All Hallows Parish, Maryland, 1650–1783* (Chicago, 1975), University of Chicago, Department of Geography Series No. 170., 62–100.

42.   Lewis E. Atherton, *The Frontier Merchant in Mid-America* (Columbia, Mo., 1971; originally 1939).

43.   Thomas D. Clark, *Pills, Petticoats, and Plows: The Southern Country Store* (Norman, Okla., 1964; originally 1944).

44.   Atherton, *The Southern Country Store, 1800–1860* (New York, 1968; originally 1949).

45.   Glenn T. Trewartha, "The Unincorporated Hamlet: One Element of the American Settlement Fabric," *Annals of the Association of American Geographers* 33 (1943), 32–81.

46.   Lemon, *Best Poor Man's Country,* 144–45.

47.   Mitchell, *Commercialism and Frontier*, 195–96.

48.   Allan Kulikoff, *Tobacco and Slaves: The Development of Southern Culture in the Chesapeake, 1680–1800* (Chapel Hill, N.C., 1986), 126–27.

49.   Diary of Richard N. Venable, 1791–1792, Virginia Historical Society, Richmond; Isaac Weld, Jr., *Travels Through the States of North America and the Provinces of Upper and Lower Canada During the Years 1795, 1796, and 1797* (London, 1800) 1: 210.

50.   Quoted in Richard C. Wade, *The Urban Frontier* (Chicago, 1976; originally 1959), 311–12.

2

Settlement Organization, 1730–1800

Settlement organization is both temporal and structural. The temporal component is primarily concerned with the processes of initial settlement of a North American region by an expanding European population and the evolution of settlement over time. The temporal component is also comprised of regional and external factors that facilitate or hinder the settlement processes. Regional factors are primarily the disposition of environment and native population, whereas external factors provide the push that creates the population for the occupation of new territory. This interaction between regional and external factors over time gives rise to population growth, the third factor of the temporal component. Population growth provides the critical linkage between temporal and structural components. As population growth reaches certain levels, it can support a hierarchical system of centralized places with distinctive function and morphology.

The structural component of settlement organization, as the product of population growth within a regional context, includes a functional (or trading) component and a morphological (or place-form) component. In the early periods of settlement, or under conditions represented by the early stages of James Vance's mercantile theory, the small and scattered population did not support a regional hierarchy of places. The primary places of settlement were dispersed plantations or farms. At the same time, the focus of trade was on country stores. Over time, with population growth in numbers and expansion over space, a central place system developed. This hierarchy of places—towns, villages and hamlets—emerged in both functional and morphological contexts. Concerning the settlement organization of

Southside Virginia, there is one ultimate question: What were the settlement outcomes of eighteenth-century population growth and to what extent had towns emerged as part of the general settlement fabric by 1800? This question provides the basis for evaluation of the failure of an urban system to develop in the region, the identification of the trading structure in such a settlement system, the function of country stores in this trading structure, and the applicability of central-place theory.

The Temporal Component

Southside Virginia had an unusually long frontier period, and thus the interplay between settlement influences was rather subtle and drawn out over time. The time span between the first European encounter with the region in the mid-1600s and the agricultural settlement of the western sections was over a century, and strong frontier characteristics were still present as late as the post-Revolutionary period. The primary factors in the settlement of the Southside were its physical environment and aboriginal population, and the economic and population character of its immigrant source regions. However, no single factor was dominant; rather, each represented a variety of conflicting relationships.

Environmental Factors

There were three important environmental elements in the settlement of the Southside: the character of the rivers, the size of the territory, and the relative homogeneity of land across the region. These elements provided the basis for the many human decisions made concerning the settlement process.

The availability of water transport greatly facilitated the European settlement of North America in the seventeenth and eighteenth centuries. Building highways through heavily wooded areas was expensive and time consuming, and slowed both settlement and economic development. The numerous rivers, bays, and estuaries were critical factors in the development of Tidewater Virginia in the seventeenth century. Tobacco, the product that dominated the Virginia economy and was the basis for the accumulation of wealth, prestige, and power, was easily shipped from plantations to foreign markets because of the availability of these navigable waterways.[1]

There would also appear to be a psychological dependence on the many Tidewater Virginia waterways. They made the settlement process easier because they diminished the size of the early frontier by reducing distances. One has only to examine a map of Tidewater Virginia north of the James River estuary, with its numerous necks of land, to see that settlers were never very far from water. Although the population lived in a dispersed settlement pattern, the numerous large streams, by dividing up the territory, had the effect of bringing settlements closer together and softening the impact of living in a new and strange land. Even the settlement of a relatively small Tidewater area south of the James estuary in Surry County was delayed because six to nine miles from that major river was a drainage divide that took the streams in an opposite direction.[2]

Southside rivers, however, provided little aid in the development of settlement and trading systems in that region. The major Southside river systems, primarily the Appomattox in the north and the larger Roanoke in the south, had impassable falls and rapids in their lower courses and, in addition, the latter river flowed into the shallow Albemarle Sound in North Carolina (Fig. 1-2). This disrupted the settlement continuity that had been provided by the many navigable waterways in the Tidewater and made the transport of local products and imported foreign goods more difficult and costly. Considering the locations of colonial entrepôts as far up navigable rivers as possible, it is presumed that the Southside would have had a far different history had the falls of the Appomattox River been fifty miles farther upstream and had the Roanoke River flowed more agreeably and emptied into the lower James River near Norfolk.

By any measure, the abrupt disruption of navigation on the Appomattox and the lack of connection between the Roanoke and the Virginia Tidewater delayed the settlement process. But it was not just the obvious character of the main rivers that delayed settlement and made difficult economic development. To the early immigrant moving west or the later Southsider rolling or wagoning tobacco to fall-zone markets, the overland routes did not necessarily provide an escape from the vagaries of the river systems. In their generally eastern and western travels, they still had to cross the many tributary streams that primarily flowed north and south. Throughout the eighteenth century, Southsiders were often obsessed and were always preoccupied with fords, ferries, and bridges.

A second environmental factor was the large size of the Southside compared with the Tidewater. This was true for all of the Virginia interior, but especially for the southern Piedmont area. While the region extended as far as 150 straight miles and well over 200 travel miles from the fall zone and initially contained more than 8,000 square miles of territory, it was made even larger by the presence of the adjacent areas of the North Carolina Piedmont and much of that colony's inner Coastal Plain, which were essentially large territorial extensions of the Southside.[3]

With such a large territory available for settlement, and within the context of the limited number of potential settlers available, settlement was a slow process. The large territorial extent was also reflected in land prices. Many potential settlers from Pennsylvania and Maryland undoubtedly bypassed the Southside for the more distant Carolina backcountry, where land prices were considerably cheaper than in southern Virginia.[4] Of the 5,000 migrants who crossed the James River at one ferry during a period in the 1750s, it is likely that only a very few terminated their journey before reaching Carolina.[5] The size factor especially had a strong impact on the late settlement of the more interior areas west of the Staunton River and the continuation of the settlement process for an extended period of time. The far western counties of Henry and Patrick were chartered in only 1776 and 1791 respectively, the final date being almost sixty years after the organization of Brunswick, the first county.

Except for a few local areas, topography presented no problem to settlement or agricultural expansion. Although no region the size of Southside Virginia can be considered entirely homogeneous in its physical landscape, the area nevertheless deviated only slightly from a fairly continuous, uniform character. There was no juxtaposition of areas of strongly varied topography and potential productivity that characterized New England, eastern Pennsylvania, and the ridge and valley topography of western Virginia. This in part worked against important, unequal distributions of population in adjacent areas within the region.

Typical of the Piedmont region, the topography of the Southside was primarily a rolling and hilly upland surface on old, greatly reduced igneous and metamorphic rocks that increased in elevation and relief from east to west. All sections of the region, whether far west or near the fall zone, had extensive areas of relatively gentle relief. The areas with least slope were on some upland surfaces, in the two narrow Triassic Basins (small areas of younger sedimentary rocks) in parts of Pittsylvania, Charlotte, and Prince Edward counties, and in the floodplains of larger streams. Areas of greatest relief were along the majority of smaller streams throughout the region and especially in the foothills of the Blue Ridge Mountains in the west.

In the east, in eastern Brunswick and Amelia counties, elevations ranged from 150 feet above sea level in the stream valleys to 270 feet above sea level on the upland surfaces. In the more centrally located counties of Lunenburg and Prince Edward, elevations ranged from 300 to 600 feet above sea level. Farther west, in central Pittsylvania County, elevations varied from 600 to 900 feet, and along the Patrick and Henry counties' border, 800 to 1,000 feet. In the far west, and beyond the scope of this study, the crest of the Blue Ridge was about 3,000 feet on the western Patrick County line.

The soils of the region were not very fertile according to modern soil science. The parent material of igneous and metamorphic rocks and the climatic conditions of warm temperatures and high rainfall produce soils that are low in basic compounds, are easily weathered and eroded, and have large concentrations of iron and aluminum that give them their characteristic red and yellow colors. Even in an eighteenth-century context, Southside soils did not measure up to other regions of the Virginia backcountry. But their influence was limited not only to crop production. They probably had more of an influence on transportation than was exerted by the more familiar topography. The clay roadbeds completely halted all overland movement for brief periods, and Southsiders were aware of their influence at all times.

Despite the findings of modern soil science, parts of the region had relatively high-quality soil, especially the areas of hardwood forest, the bottom land of large floodplains, and the Triassic Basins. The Southside became Virginia's leading tobacco producer and also grew a variety of additional agricultural products, including corn, wheat, hemp, and cotton. Most of the high-quality soil during the early periods of settlement can be attributed to a lengthy time of stable conditions and a dense vegetation cover that made the influence of erosion insignificant. William Byrd, despite experiencing considerable rainfall on his two trips into the region, observed only one stream with turbid conditions. The availability of good soil probably existed throughout the eighteenth century for the region as a whole because of its large area, relatively slow settlement, and extensive land use. During this same period, with the removal of forests, the planting of row crops, and the lack of attention to conservation, many selected areas, primarily in the eastern sections, suffered the almost complete destruction of topsoil.[6]

Most important was the quality of Southside soil in comparison with the Tidewater soil, which had been damaged from years of overcropping with tobacco and corn. Many of the Southside settlers migrated from the Tidewater because of the reduced agricultural productivity of that region. The size of the Southside and its relatively undisturbed environment also encouraged the region to be perceived as productive. Because many settlers were escaping from areas of depleted soil resources, and considering that much of the agriculture was based on field rotation where productive land units were depleted of their productivity in three to five years, the amount of land available for initial cultivation and subsequent expansion was critical in this agricultural system.

The climate of the Southside did not present any new problems to settlers because the majority of them had already experienced similar climatic conditions from their stay in the Tidewater. Most importantly, the southern Piedmont had the potential, with its 200-day growing season, its relatively mild winters, and its rainfall totals in excess of forty inches annually, to produce the same crops grown in the Tidewater without modifications in long-standing agricultural practices. Tobacco did not physically need a 200-day growing season; that length of time was made necessary by the demands of linking the various stages of production. Although the seedbed was prepared in late winter or early spring, transplanting to the field may have taken as long as three months. According to the observations of John Smyth, tobacco plants were drawn from the seedbed and planted as early as the first rain after the vernal equinox.[7] But because the field needed sufficient moisture to guarantee the initial growth of the plant, planting may have continued until July. Plantings at this late date, or even in early summer, pushed the harvest period beyond late summer and into the autumn season. Additional factors such as unfavorable temperature and precipitation patterns during the growing period were also contributors to harvest extensions.

Early travelers in the Southside generally perceived the potential of the region in a favorable light. As early as 1650, almost eighty years before William Byrd traveled in this region, Edward Bland displayed a keen eye for evaluating the potential value of Southside resources. While exploring the southeastern section of the region, he noted rich soil, meadows, and grassland "very convenient for hogs and cattle," well-watered areas, and the presence of salt, copper, gold, silver, and iron. Bland prophetically suggested that tobacco would "grow large and more in quantity" than in the Tidewater.[8] Byrd saw great potential for development of the region's resources. Cattle, medicinal plants, sugar, silk, hemp, flax, cotton, rice, and wine were among the diversified products he envisioned for the Southside.[9]

This discussion of environmental factors has attempted to explain, in the context of the eighteenth century and on the basis of the evaluation of a variety of evidence, the significance of drainage, territorial size, climate and soil, and topography on the settlement of the

Southside. The regional drainage system, specifically the fall-zone disruption and the direction of flow, in part worked against the establishment of an early entrepôt in the region, which in turn was an important contributor to the failure of a town network to emerge. The large size of the region favored the continuation of the dispersed population and tobacco economy that diffused from the Tidewater. The benign climate and the abundance of new soil in the Southside also facilitated the transfer of Tidewater agricultural practices. The favorable topography in part ensured a relatively even distribution of population that varied primarily as a result of distance-decay from the fall zone.

Environmental factors of settlement should only be evaluated collectively and in the proper temporal context. Environmental factors as a group or any single aspect of environment, given the complexity of cultural and economic contributions, should never be offered as a grand design to explain regional settlement and development. Frederick Siegel has appeared to violate that axiom in *The Roots of Southern Distinctiveness*, a study that evaluates settlement evolution in Pittsylvania County over a period of eighty years, although prior events provide continuity that increase the time span to over 100 years.[10] With a minimum of evidence and debate, Siegel explained the lack of agricultural diversification and the difficulties of town development entirely in terms of climate. This grand design avoided the inertial aspects of tobacco cultivation and its slave-labor system that would appear to be a worthy consideration in any explanatory scheme. The credibility of the author's climatically based explanation was also considerably diminished by his apparent lack of basic knowledge of the American environment. Statements such as "the underlying sandy infertility of its soil" when referring to the early Southside and "the grassland soils of much of the Northeast" do not inspire confidence.[11]

The Aboriginal Factor

The Indians of the Piedmont had little direct influence on the European settlement of Southside Virginia. By the time that Tidewater settlers had begun to occupy land, Indian groups had been reduced to very small populations or had migrated from the region. Early Southside settlers did not suffer the hardships and loss of life that accompanied European confrontations with the Indians in the Tidewater region in 1622 and 1644, and along the fall zone in 1676. The Southside was more of a transient region and buffer zone between the larger and more powerful tribes of the north, primarily New York and Pennsylvania, and the Indians of the Carolinas. The local Indians—the Iroquoian-speaking Nottoway and Meherrin along the fall zone and the Siouan-speaking Occaneechi, Totero, and Saponi of the interior—had small populations and widely scattered distributions and occupied small villages along the larger rivers. One estimate places the total population of the Piedmont region as low as 1,000 in the 1670s.[12]

Only the Occaneechi Indians exerted any power in the region. From their base on the natural fortress of Occaneechi Island in the Roanoke River (present-day Mecklenburg County), they traded with both northern and southern Indians and were middlemen in the trade between European settlers in Virginia and the Carolina Indians. During the period of English contact, Occaneechi Island was the only important focal point of Indian trade in the region. This power base was destroyed in 1676 when Nathaniel Bacon, charismatic leader of the rebellion against Governor William Berkeley, and his followers killed many of the Occaneechi in a battle on the island and forced the remainder to flee to North Carolina.

The periodic raids from the Seneca Indians of the Iroquois Confederation of northern New York were the greatest menace to the stability of the Piedmont Indians. During their periodic war and trade forays into the southern Piedmont, the Seneca brought destruction to the weaker Indian tribes and fear to the Indians and Europeans alike who knew of their exploits. The Totero and Saponi were living with the Occaneechi in 1676, probably to gain greater protection from the Seneca, and the remaining population of these two small Indian groups had decided by 1701 to join with another small tribe to strengthen themselves against the menace from the north. Although there were no confrontations with Indians during the 1728 survey of the Virginia–North Carolina boundary, William Byrd and his party were quite anxious over the Seneca presence in the more western areas of the survey, where they discovered their fires that were set to drive game and their abandoned camp for dressing deerskins.[13]

Although the Indian population was greatly reduced in size and territorial range before settlement expansion, there were nevertheless instances when early settlers faced potential danger. Most of these occurred on the western frontier during the French and Indian War. The population on this western margin suffered great anxiety over potential raids from the Cherokee, and some settlers were victims of Indian atrocities. In 1755 George Washington reviewed the defense capabilities of the region and later expressed concern over the vulnerability to attack of one of the four forts constructed on the perimeter.[14] During this same period and in the same area of western Halifax County (present-day Pittsylvania or Henry), the execution of the robbery of a country store reflected the region's concern for potential Indian attack. The robbers darkened their faces and refrained from speaking so as to suggest that Indians were the culprits.[15] The Indian problem was likely the explanation for the reduction of population expansion during the 1750s. Population growth during the decade of the 1750s was less than 50 percent, compared to over 170 percent during the 1740s (Table 2-1).

The Cherokees once again penetrated the western areas of the region twenty years later during the period preceding the Revolutionary War. In the Smith River valley, traveler Smyth found that plantations were abandoned in favor of the protection of a nearby fort. Making his way toward the fort, Smyth traveled a distance with an Indian party, ate their food, and slept overnight at their camp under extraordinarily congenial circumstances. Hearing of Smyth's aid and comfort from the Indians, the cloistered settlers denied him entrance to the fort. As for the distraught Smyth,

> I continued to entreat for admittance until they threatened to fire upon me if I did not retire, which made me withdraw from the gate to consider what steps I must pursue, for I never found myself in so singular and unpleasant a predicament in my life.[16]

Although two towns were proposed for the protection of settlers during the French and Indian War, neither Peytonsburg, in Halifax County, nor Daltonsburgh, in Lunenburg County (present-day Charlotte County), functioned in that capacity.[17] Unlike Winchester, in the Shenandoah Valley, the Indian factor did not encourage permanent settlement concentration for protection of the population or for collection and distribution of army provisions.[18]

Population Source Regions

Southside settlers came primarily from Tidewater Virginia. It was the cultural baggage of these immigrants—corn, livestock, and tobacco economy; slave labor; rural settlement; strong county government; and the Anglican parish system—that defined the Southside. Tidewater emigrants settled throughout the region, but were more concentrated in eastern areas. Scotch-Irish from Pennsylvania, who settled in the region in large numbers after midcentury, were more concentrated in Prince Edward and Charlotte counties, and in the more western settle-

Table 2-1. Population Growth, 1735–1800

County	Tithables X 4						Census Count	
	1735	1740	1750	1760	1770	1780	1790	1800
Brunswick	3,876	5,636	7,920[b]	9,048	15,684	17,856	12,287[b]	16,339
(% increase for decade)		45	41	14	73	14		33
Amelia	2,352	4,376	11,136	10,953[a,b]	15,060[a]	15,909[a]	18,097	9,832[b,c]
		87	154	---	35	6		---
Lunenburg			8,476	13,124	6,732[b]	7,348	8,959	10,381
				55	---	9		16
Halifax				4,524	7,608[b]	10,852	14,722	19,377
					68	43		32
Prince Edward				3,270[a]	5,346[a]	6,537	8,100	10,962
					63	22		35
Mecklenburg					9,628	12,640	14,733	17,008
						32		15
Charlotte					6,440	8,880	10,078	11,862
						37		17
Pittsylvania					6,380	6,548[b]	11,579	12,697
						3		15
Henry						5,804	8,479	5,259[b,d]
Nottoway								9,401
Patrick								4,311
SOUTHSIDE	6,228	10,012	27,532	40,919	72,878	92,374	107,034	127,429
		61	175	48	78	27		19

Source: County order books; First Census of the United States; Second Census of the United States.

a. tithables X 3
b. loss of territory by creation of a new county (counties)
c. (19,233 and 7 if combined with Nottoway)
d. (9,570 and 13 if combined with Patrick)

ments on the Smith and Mayo rivers in Henry County, but were scattered throughout the area west of the Staunton River. Other distinct cultural groups were a few French Huguenots on the eastern border, a small number of Germans (or Swiss-Germans), who were either survivors from the ill-fated colonization scheme of William Byrd or migrants from coastal North Carolina, increasing numbers of African slaves, and a few immigrants directly from Great Britain.[19] But cultural variation within the region was insignificant. There were no immigrant groups that created variations in settlement, economy, or language. The institutions and experiences of Tidewater Virginia determined the course of regional development. The most apparent cultural variation, that of the Presbyterianism of the Scotch-Irish, was soon bated by the rapid emergence of a frontier Calvinist orientation that easily supplanted the veneer of Anglican authority and blurred theological distinctiveness.

Circumstances in the source regions were critical to the settlement of the Southside and to the backcountry in general. Before the 1690–1710 period, there was generally sufficient land in the Tidewater to support both a growing population and economic ambition. But during this period, the balance between population and resources was severely weakened by both tradition and change in tobacco production. The heavy demands made by tobacco on soil fertility had made necessary a system of shifting cultivation that demanded large quantities of additional land. The increases in tobacco cultivation brought on by continuing low prices prior to the turn of the century and the increased use of African slave labor required even larger landholdings. In an agricultural society with a growing population, this seriously decreased economic opportunity. As tenancy and poverty increased, moving to the Piedmont frontier was a means of recouping lost opportunity.[20]

Emigration from Pennsylvania resulted from the pressure of a growing population, especially increases in German and Scotch-Irish immigrants, on a finite amount of land. Variations in land availability and land prices between Pennsylvania and the southern Piedmont fueled the migration. In 1732 the price of fifty acres of land in Pennsylvania was £7 10s. During this same period, 400 acres of patented land could be acquired for £4 5s. in the Southside; in North Carolina the price of 100 acres was as low as 5s. as late as 1750.[21]

The character of Virginia source regions was an important factor in the late settlement of the Southside. Michael Nicholls has determined that Southside settlers came primarily from the fall-zone counties of Henrico, Hanover, Goochland, and Prince George.[22] These more interior source areas suggest a longer two-step migration between Tidewater and southern Piedmont. The availability of potential settlers from the adjacent Tidewater was also critical to the late settlement of the Southside. The James River estuary divided potential Piedmont immigrants into two groups. A much smaller population existed south of the James, the more likely source for direct migration to the Southside and the site of the county, Prince George, from which most of the Southside counties originated. In 1714 this area contained only 6,645 taxables. By contrast, the area north of the James had 23,000 taxables.[23] Inhabitants of the southern Tidewater counties could also move into adjacent areas of the North Carolina Coastal Plain. William Byrd's surveying party encountered several plantations and attracted small gatherings of people in the Coastal Plain area along the Virginia–North Carolina border as early as 1728.[24]

The failure of government efforts to sustain population expansion into the Southside is strong testimony to the lack of potential immigrants. In 1720 Governor Alexander Spotswood persuaded the Virginia Assembly to establish the frontier county of Brunswick, which included all the present-day Southside counties except Amelia, Nottoway, and Prince Edward, and to adopt a free land and no-tax policy for new settlers for a period of ten years, later reduced to seven years, and limited to 1,000 acres. This policy succeeded in increasing the number of land patents, but after its expiration in 1728 the number of patents decreased sharply.[25] Further, Brunswick County did not acquire sufficient population for recognition as a county until 1732. In 1738 a special government incentive program—in this instance, exemption from all taxes for ten years in exchange for settlement within two years—once again had to be devised to stimulate settlement in the region.[26] Whether in direct response to this decree or in combination with additional factors, immigration increased dramatically during the 1740s, especially from Pennsylvania.

Southside settlers were usually middle and lower wealth groups who initially purchased small quantities of land to support their individual families. This lack of extensive land speculation reduced the rate at which new settlers took up land and further strengthened the dispersed population distribution that was transferred from the Chesapeake. Michael Nicholls has stated: "By comparison with the rest of Virginia, the Southside did not have the spate of huge tracts issued to land companies and speculators in the Valley of Virginia or in the areas beyond the mountains."[27] For example, more than three-fourths of the 3,813 land patents issued between 1703 and 1753 were for less than 405 acres.[28] The modest wealth of early settlers is also suggested by Richard Beeman's study of the Southside elite. Beeman states that those individuals who became the local leaders came to the region with little wealth. They acquired their wealth and power in a period spanning ten to twenty years after their arrival.[29]

Despite the dominance of individuals occupying relatively small parcels of land, there was, nevertheless, considerable land speculation in the region. The scheme that had the greatest potential to develop the Southside was the plan of William Byrd. In 1735 Byrd petitioned the Council for 100,000 acres on the Dan River to settle Swiss-German Protestants. He was granted the land on the condition that he settle at least one family per 1,000 acres within a period of two years from the last day of October, 1736. His plans for a colony of industrious and community-oriented Europeans and their potential to develop a different settlement and economic system perished with most of the 250 Swiss who lost their lives in a shipwreck off the coast of Virginia in 1738.[30]

Speculation on the potential success of the Byrd project and its influence on Southside settlement and economy is most intriguing, but creates only more questions. Would a greater sense of community and settlement planning have generated centralized places and a settlement hierarchy? Would the Swiss settlers have introduced a new agricultural system or would they have succumbed to the economic addictiveness of tobacco production? And, in response to Frederick Siegel's environmental interpretation, would they have been forced to shelve their past experiences with a more diversified economy and its greater emphasis on a variety of grains, dairying, and viticulture because of the climatic imperative that would dictate the dominance of tobacco production? Although these questions hold great fascination to the student of the Southern frontier, they primarily emphasize the narrow reality of the westward extension of Chesapeake culture into the Southside frontier.

Population Growth

Despite its slow growth during the early period of settlement, the population of the Southside increased steadily and occasionally dramatically over the course of the eighteenth century. Using a conversion rate of four individuals to one taxable during the pre-census period, the region grew from about 6,200 people in 1735 to more than 127,000 in 1800 (Table 2-1).[31] The most rapid population growth occurred during the 1740s, with increases of 17 percent per year. After

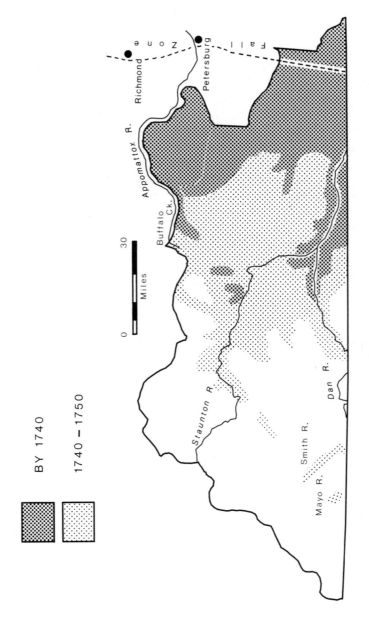

BY 1740

1740 — 1750

Figure 2-1. Settlement expansion by 1740, 1740–50. *Source:* County order books and deed books.

a sharp decline during the 1750s, primarily because of the French and Indian War and increased Indian hostilities on the western frontier, the population increased at an annual growth of 8 percent during the 1760s. However, during the last thirty years of the century, primarily because of reduced economic opportunity created by the growing dominance of plantation agriculture and the decline in relatively cheap land as new western frontiers were opened, growth slowed to just over 2 percent per year. But the growth had been sufficient to place three Southside counties—Halifax, Mecklenburg, and Brunswick—among the top ten in the state in total population.

The rapid western expansion of Southside population may be seen in the map of settlement for 1740 and 1750 (Fig. 2-1). This map shows areas of significant human activity such as road construction; petitions for road construction; establishment of churches, ordinaries, and grist mills; requests to view improvements on land; and heavy activity in land sales. These activities indicated that an area had been settled, was undergoing some degree of population growth, and perhaps possessed incipient forms of community development.

By 1740 settlement had proceeded a considerable distance up the Roanoke and Appomattox Rivers, and a lesser distance up the Meherrin River. The settlement process produced a generally continuous spread of population from east to west and to a distance of over eighty miles above the fall zone along the Roanoke's two major branches, the Dan and the Staunton; and to a distance of over fifty miles above the fall zone of the Appomattox. The more aggressive advance up the Roanoke was accomplished by less intensity of settlement. Settlers migrated westward, but left more unsettled land behind than in the Appomattox area. In the latter area, a smaller area with a more populous source region to draw from, the western movement was more conservative in that land was settled and community was developed before population advanced farther west.

Despite the advances into the interior, population was overwhelmingly concentrated along the eastern fringes. In Amelia County the areas of most intense human activity were along the many streams located between the Appomattox and the lower Nottoway River. The four new grist mills approved by the county court, the two new churches, and almost all the land sales took place within this area. In Brunswick County settlement was concentrated along the Nottoway and Meherrin Rivers and their tributaries. Nine of the eleven certified grist mills that could be located, two of the three churches that could be located, and the great majority of the land sales were well within the territorial confines of the relatively small area of the modern-day county. The locations of the courthouses for Brunswick and Amelia further confirmed the population concentrations in the extreme east. During a period when courthouses were located central to the population, both were located well to the east and within the areas of the modern-day boundaries of these two counties.

By 1750 settlers had penetrated the interior as far as the foothills of the Blue Ridge Mountains. In response to this western surge, a new county, Lunenburg, was established in 1746 and as a result inherited the great majority of the territory that formerly was Brunswick County. A very active settlement extension took place in the northwest on Goose Creek, Otter River, and Falling River (present-day Bedford County and in nearby areas of modern Charlotte County), tributaries of the Staunton River, and in the south along Difficult Creek and Banister River (present-day Halifax County), also tributaries of the Staunton. At least one grist mill was located in each of these areas. The most surprising development between 1740 and 1750 was the speed with which settlement spread to the far western areas of the valleys of Smith River and Mayo River (present-day Pittsylvania and Henry counties). The steady expansion up the Appomattox continued in western Amelia County (present-day Prince Edward County), especially in the Cub Creek area. The establishment of an Anglican Church, an additional Presbyterian Church, at least two mills, the construction of several new roads, and the licensing of two ordinaries took place within this area during the decade. The original area of western expansion along the Roanoke continued to grow in population and became the seat of the first courthouse of Lunenburg County.

Despite the impressive expansion of the outer zone of settlement between 1740 and 1750, the eastern counties of Brunswick and Amelia not only continued to contain most of the region's population, but also maintained impressive rates of population increase. Amelia's population increased by 154 percent and Brunswick, despite losing most of its territory by the creation of Lunenburg County, still increased its population by 41 percent during the ten-year period. By 1748 Amelia had almost 9,000 people and a density of eight persons per square mile; Brunswick contained over 7,000 people and had a density of over six persons per square mile (Fig. 2-2). In addition to the continuing growth of Amelia and Brunswick, another eastern area, essentially present-day Lunenburg County, displayed significant population increases between 1740 and 1750. During this period the area added at least six new grist mills.

The fifty years after 1750 were concerned with the filling-in process, settling a region that, despite its population expansion, still had large quantities of virgin land. The steady and continued growth of

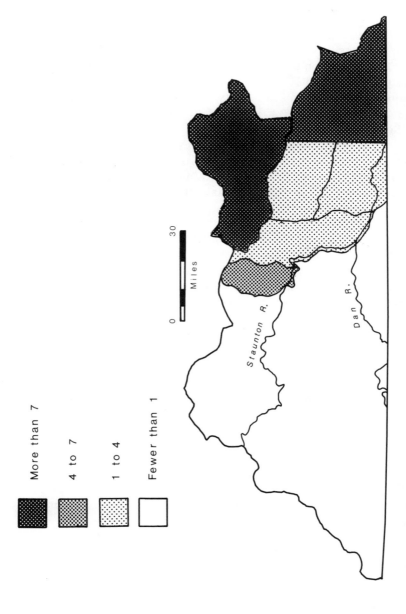

More than 7

4 to 7

1 to 4

Fewer than 1

Staunton R.

Dan R.

0   30

Miles

Figure 2-2. Persons per square mile, 1748. *Source:* Bell, *Sunlight on the Southside,* 58–86.

population in all areas of the region was reflected in the creation of several new counties. During the 1750s Halifax, Prince Edward, and Bedford were established, and Mecklenburg, Charlotte, and Pittsylvania were created in the 1760s. Henry County was chartered during the 1770s and the final two counties, Nottoway in the east and Patrick in the far west, came into being in 1789 and 1791 respectively. By 1770 the population density of Amelia reached almost thirty persons per square mile and Halifax County, the first county created west of Staunton River, reached a density of almost ten persons per square mile (Fig. 2-3). By 1800 the population densities of many areas of the Southside were similar to densities of counties in the Tidewater and in the Piedmont region north of the James River. The highest densities, just over thirty persons per square mile, were in the counties of Nottoway and Prince Edward, and the lowest density was in the far western and partially mountainous county of Patrick, with nine persons per square mile (Fig. 2-4).

Population Turnover

Despite the long period of population increase that would suggest a greater stability in the region, this did not always occur in the Southside. Whether from the close proximity of new frontiers on the western and southern borders, unfulfilled ambitions, the difficulties of purchasing land in a rapidly developing plantation economy, or flight to avoid payments of debts, people were constantly moving out of the region. This also created a situation where the remaining population was composed of an inordinately high percentage of recent arrivals. Richard Beeman has noted this phenomenon in Lunenburg County:

> During the years 1746–51, while Lunenburg's *total* population was increasing at the rate of sixteen percent annually, it was also losing its *existing* population at the rate of seventeen percent per year, a migration pattern that assured that over thirty per cent of the county's population would consist of individuals who had arrived only within the past year.[32]

This population instability was also present during the last quarter of the century. John Dorman has published in *Virginia Genealogist* several lists of claims by British merchants against Virginians for store debts incurred in the period just preceding the Revolutionary War.[33] During the time span of approximately twenty-five years (1770s to late 1790s), between the making of the debt and the attempts to col-

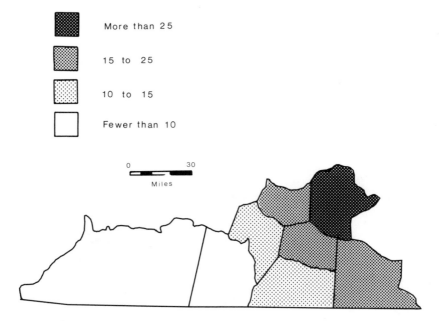

More than 25

15 to 25

10 to 15

Fewer than 10

0   30
Miles

Figure 2-3. Persons per square mile, 1770. *Source*: County order books.

lect, many of the debtors left the region. Of approximately 1,172 Southside entries, 495, or 42 percent, chose to emigrate during this period. Of that group of 495, 186 were traced to the Carolinas, sixty-six to Georgia, sixty-four to Kentucky, forty-two to other parts of Virginia, and eleven to Tennessee.

Slave Population

One of the primary factors in population growth in the Southside, especially during the latter half of the century, was the growth of the African slave population. Because the Southside was primarily an extension of the Tidewater economy and society, slaves were an important component of the southern Piedmont population. Although some of the earliest settlers brought slaves with them when they migrated into the region, most made their acquisitions later as tobacco cultivation spread and as planters became more affluent.

By 1790, the slave population of 48,165 made up 45 percent of the total regional population and 16 percent of all Virginia slaves (Table 2-2). Amelia County, where slaves comprised 60 percent of the total population, had more slaves than any other county in the state; Brunswick and Mecklenburg Counties also ranked in the top ten in that category. By 1800 the more than 62,000 slaves made up 49 per-

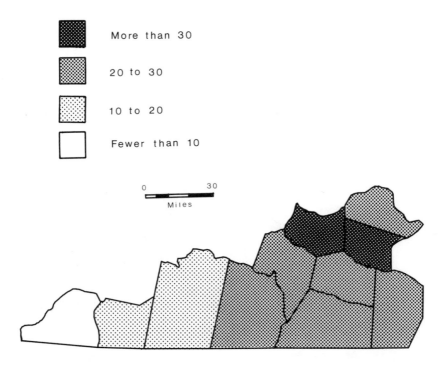

More than 30

20 to 30

10 to 20

Fewer than 10

0   30

Miles

Figure 2-4. Persons per square mile, 1800. *Source: Second Census of the United States.*

cent of the Southside population. This 30 percent increase from 1790 helped raise to five the number of counties with more slaves than whites in their population. Not only was the slave population growing faster than the white population, but the white population was actually decreasing in some counties. Amelia's white population, for example, declined by 8 percent between 1790 and 1800.

The distribution of slaves followed the same east to west pattern exhibited by the spread of population and tobacco from the Tidewater core area. The greatest concentrations were found in the eastern counties where tobacco had been produced for a longer period of time. As early as 1755, slaves accounted for 40 percent of the taxables of Amelia County and 33 percent of the taxables of Prince Edward. By 1800 slaves comprised over 50 percent of the population in all counties east of the Staunton River. Although slaves made up less than half the population in the western counties, they were increasing at high rates. The slave populations of Halifax and Pittsylvania, for example, increased at rates of 40 and 39 percent respectively between 1790 and 1800.

As part of the staple-theory interpretation of settlement and economic development, it was suggested earlier that the large slave population reduced consumer demand to below the level necessary to support urban development. The impact of the black slave population on urban development is revealed dramatically in Figure 2-5. The density of the white population in 1800 fell far short of the suggested population thresholds of twenty persons per square mile necessary to support urban development. The strong contrast between the population density of the whole population in 1800 (Fig. 2-4), with two counties having densities in excess of thirty persons per square mile and six additional counties with densities between twenty and thirty persons per square mile, and the population density of the white population, with no county above fifteen persons per square mile (Fig. 2-5), is strong evidence of the significance of tobacco production on settlement evolution. Given the relatively small number of settlers

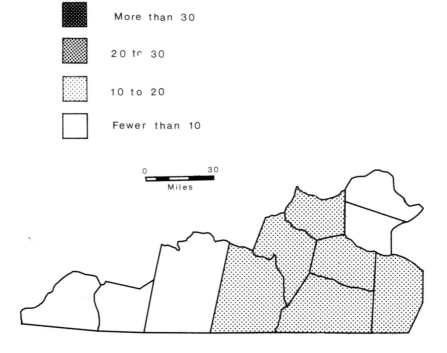

Figure 2-5. White persons per square mile, 1800. *Source: Second Census of the United States.*

Table 2-2.   Slave Population

County	Tithables 1755	Entire Population	
		1790	1800
Brunswick			
(# of tithables/persons)	976	6,776	9,422
(% of total population)	43	55	58
(% increase)			39
(% white increase)			26
Amelia	1,652	11,307	12,568[1]
			67
			11
			−8
Lunenburg	903	4,332	5,876
	43	47	57
			36
			−3
Halifax	141	5,565	7,911
	18	38	41
			40
			26
Prince Edward	410	3,986	5,921
	50	49	54
			49
			23
Mecklenburg		6,762	8,676
		46	51
			28
			5
Charlotte		4,816	6,233
		48	53
			29
			7
Pittsylvania		2,979	4,133
		25	33
			39
			−1
Henry		1,551	2,064[2]
		18	22
			33
			9
SOUTHSIDE	4,082	48,165	62,804
	46	45	49
			30
			9

Source: Greene and Harrington, *American Population Before the Federal Census of 1790,* 150–51; *First Census of the United States; Second Census of the United States.*

1. For purpose of computing population change from 1790 to 1800, Amelia and Nottoway are combined. Amelia's figures for first two categories are 6,585 and 70%. Nottoways are 5,983 and 64%.

2. For purpose of computing from 1790 to 1800, Henry and Patrick are combined. Henry's figures for first two categories are 1,414 and 27%. Patrick's are 649 and 15%.

within a large territory during the early stages of settlement and the rapid escalation of the slave population past midcentury, the fourteen persons per square mile in Prince Edward and Halifax counties represented the high-water mark for the white population density in the Southside during the eighteenth century.

Settlement Structure

The most important characteristic of the Southside population was its dispersed distribution. Despite rapid population growth from the 1740s to 1800, this characterization remained firmly intact. It is not surprising that William Byrd and Moravian travelers en route to North Carolina found the Southside of the 1730s, 1740s, and 1750s to be a region where human imprint had treaded very lightly. But more significant were Congressman Smith's observations during the early 1790s of the persistence of this decentralized cultural landscape. There was no central-place network in the region. There were no towns or lower-level service centers to accommodate the trading needs of the local population. But local places did provide these functions. The focal points in this decentralized society—plantation, ferry, and court-house—functioned as low-level service centers, but lacked the equivalent morphological identity.

Plantation Site

The primary focus for the decentralized population was the plantation. Because it was the functional base of tobacco culture and had a long use as the designation for general agricultural landholding in Virginia, the "plantation" reference was ubiquitous in the Southside. The designation "farm," with a strong association with wheat cultivation and positioned against the orientation of Virginia practice and tradition, had less usage in the region. The plantation did not necessarily have a certain minimum amount of acreage or house a designated number of slaves. It could even be little more than what would be designated a "hardscrabble" farm in backcountry New England or the Appalachian region. But in terms of functional significance in the Southside, the size of the holding and the prominence of the planter were crucial in making that plantation an important focal point.

Because of the absence of towns, plantations were the most important locations for relatively large and clustered populations and served as foci of decision making and commercial activity in the region. With planter, family, and slaves, a large plantation site might contain thirty to fifty individuals. In addition to their plantation duties, planters were the "movers and shakers" of regional society. They dominated the offices of the county court, county clerk, parish vestry, sheriff, county surveyor, and supervisor of road construction; served as trustees in various organizations and as advisors in a variety of contexts; and were the representatives to the House of Burgesses. Planters parlayed their capital derived from land speculation and agriculture, their external contacts, their ability to obtain long-term credit from distant wholesalers, and their control of strategic sites to dominate local business activities. Plantations were the dominant sites for country stores, taverns, ordinaries, mills, blacksmith shops, and wagoners.

Perhaps the most revealing evidence of the importance of the plantation as a focal point of service activity was the business strategy of several large Scottish mercantile firms. Recognizing the lack of an urban precedent in the region and needing to be close to the tobacco producers, these Glasgow-based operations, which supplanted the mercantile authority of local merchants during the fifteen-year period before the Revolutionary War, located several of their stores on working plantations. For example, the William Cunninghame and Company property in Mecklenburg County had forty of its 400 acres under cultivation in tobacco, wheat, and corn. In the same county, the Alexander Donald and Company plantation grew oats, corn, timothy, and clover, and held forty head of cattle, fifty head of sheep, and some hogs.[34]

Although Southside plantations functioned in the same regional context as Tidewater plantations, they were not at comparable levels. The great houses and their formal grounds were generally absent from the Southside. The wealth, power, work ethic, and genteel manners associated with Tidewater planters frayed considerably in the diffusion westward. Both people and structures were more likely to be crude on Southside plantations. Congressman Smith linked the endemic delinquency of plantation repairs to the planter's penchant for long sessions of male bonding at the local taverns. According to Smith, planters "have a great deal of leisure on their hands, which they spend in piazzas at taverns on the road, where a great number will collect and pass whole mornings in conversing about their geldings and 'mars' and relating anecdotes about their neighborhood and their own adventures."[35] Estate accounts often contained large debts to the ordinary- and tavern-keeper. Robert Munford's play, *The Candidates,* portrays Southside elections as spectacles with lots of drinking, brawling, and voter manipulation.[36] Representative of planter prominence and frontier crudity was the behavior of Matthew Marable. Marable was a leading merchant over several decades and a member of the county court and the House of Burgesses. But he was also a notorious character who bartered strong drink for votes and was also involved in numerous physical confrontations. For example, in 1766, only one of his many court appearances to defend his straying beyond the limits of accepted behavior, a William Connor accused the versatile Marable of severely beating him with "force and arms, to wit, with swords, clubbs, & knives fists and sticks."[37]

But *The Candidates* presents only part of the Marable personage. He was not just the egotistical, abusive, and manipulative individual depicted above. Although the frontier setting muted the genteel qualities and the sense of public service that was characteristic of the Tidewater planters, Marable, like the Tidewater planters, was a very successful and powerful individual in his region. He owned five separate plantations that contained over 7,500 acres and approached £10,000 in value.[38] He also owned a house and two lots in Petersburg, from which he based his tobacco-export business. His mercantile firm, with stores in Mecklenburg and Charlotte counties, was one of the few local businesses to thrive in the face of heavy competition from the dominant Scottish companies during the period immediately preceding the Revolutionary War. But of greatest significance to Southside settlement, specifically the matter of focal points in a decentralized society, was the location and structure of Marable's home plantation. It was located in a well-populated area of Mecklenburg County and was accessible by several roads. In addition to the six-room plantation house, the property contained separate store and ordinary buildings, tailor's shop, blacksmith's shop, lumber house, separate kitchen, dairy, meat house, barns, cribs, stables, slave quarters, overseers' houses, and school house. Although not possessing the requisite morphology and nonagricultural entrepreneurship of a central place, Marable's plantation had the functional capability and location of an active lower-level service center.

Although few plantations possessed the trading capability of the Marable property, the majority of plantations probably contained at least one service activity. Unlike the complex mixture of frontier character, emerging status, and Tidewater emulation found in the Southside planters, the role of the plantation as a regional focal point was much more straightforward. Country stores, ordinaries, taverns, mills, blacksmith shops, and wagoners were located on plantation land and were operated by planters or leaseholders of plantation property. For example, William Price of Charlotte County, John Wimbish, Jr., of Pittsylvania County, and William Worsham of Prince Edward County operated taverns on their plantations.[39] Price's business was located in a section of his large house. Robert Venable of Prince Edward, John Thomas and William Morton of Charlotte, William Baskerville of Mecklenburg County (Fig. 2-6), and William Cassells of Amelia County had stores on their plantations. Other plantations housed a variety of service functions. Parham Booker and John Jeter of Amelia (Fig. 2-7) each operated a store, tavern, and masonic hall on their plantations. James Towns, Jr., of Amelia had a tavern and a

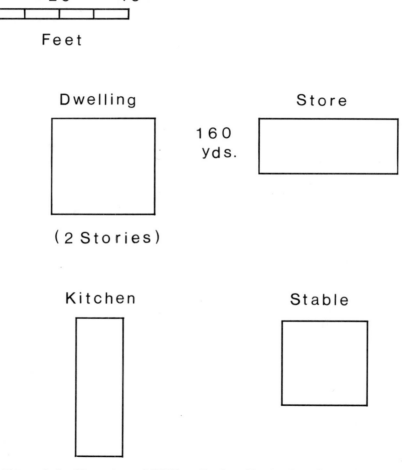

Figure 2-6. Plantation of William Baskerville (scale refers only to buildings, not to distances between buildings. *Source*: Mutual Assurance Society.

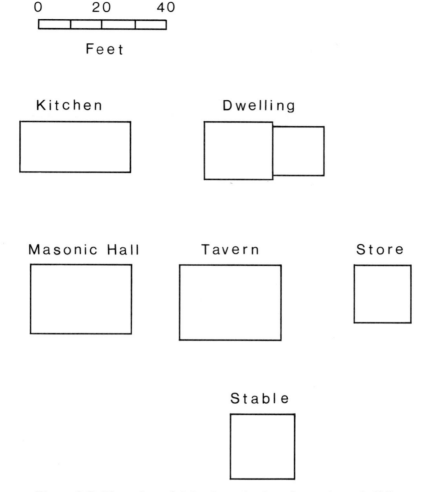

0   20   40

Feet

Kitchen

Dwelling

Masonic Hall   Tavern   Store

Stable

Figure 2-7. Plantation of John Jeter (scale refers only to buildings, not to distances between buildings). *Source*: Mutual Assurance Society.

masonic hall on his plantation, which was located adjacent to the county clerk's office (Fig. 2-8). As further evidence of decentralization, the county courthouse was located four miles to the southeast. John Royall of Amelia had a store and manufacturing mill on his plantation "Caxanata." Whether for locational identity or planter ego, or suggesting nascent service centers, other planters also gave proper names to their plantations. Jeter's plantation was called "Painville," and James Henderson of Nottoway County had separate store and counting house facilities on his property "Hendersonville" (Fig. 2-9).

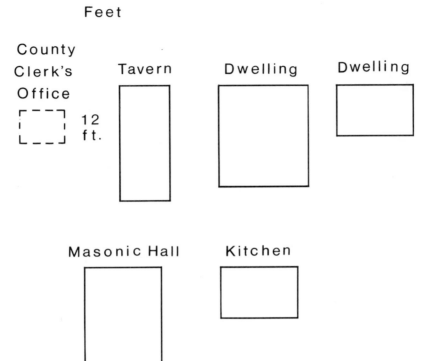

Figure 2-8. Plantation of James Towns, Jr. (scale refers only to buildings, not to distances between buildings). *Source*: Mutual Assurance Society.

   The location of more than one service activity on a plantation and the location of services on adjacent plantations gave rise to country clustering, the most important form of agglomeration in the Southside. The plantations of Henderson, Baskerville, Jeter, and Towns cited above, as well as the functions on the Marable site, were examples of the more intensive plantation clustering. Clustering as a result of activities on adjacent plantations, or the open-country neighborhood pattern, was in response to the proximity of important local focal points, primarily ferries and courthouses. Most major ferry and court-house sites had some combination of store, ordinary, tavern, and black-

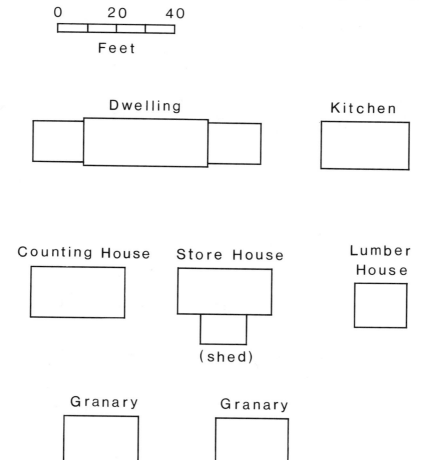

Figure 2-9. Plantation of James Henderson (scale refers only to buildings, not to distances between buildings). *Source*: Mutual Assurance Society.

smith shop in the general area. For example, at least one store and an ordinary were located within 200 yards of Taylor's Ferry on the Roanoke River in Mecklenburg County. At least one store, one ordinary, three carpenters, one tailor, a blacksmith, a wheelwright, and several wagoners were located in the vicinity of Booker's Ferry on Staunton River in Halifax County.[40] Twelve of the twenty-three Scottish stores that could be located were sited at or near ferry sites (Fig. 4-1). The Mecklenburg County courthouse had a tavern and ordinary at the site, two taverns less than a mile from the site, and five additional taverns within five miles.[41]

The Potential Urban Network

Despite the strong regional adherence to decentralized service points, several towns were legislated for the Southside. However, they generally made little impact on the region for their existence was either ephemeral or they were established very late in the century. Their existence in no way altered the fact that Southside Virginia was devoid of urban places in the eighteenth century and that country stores were the primary trading places.

Table 2-3.   Southside Towns

Name of Town	County	Date of Founding	Site
Peytonsburg	Halifax	1759	Security, courthouse
Daltonsburg	Lunenburg	1759	Security, later site of Charlotte Courthouse
Chatham	Pittsylvania	1769	Growth related to designation as courthouse in 1777
Cooksburg	Pittsylvania	1788	Trade
Saint Taminy	Mecklenburg	1791	Ferry, tobacco inspection
Martinsville	Henry	1791	Courthouse
Taylorsville	Patrick	1792	Courthouse
Danville	Pittsylvania	1793	Ferry, falls, tobacco inspection
South Boston	Halifax	1796	Ferry
Clementstown	Amelia	1796	Ferry, tobacco inspection
Jamestown	Prince 'Edward	1796	Tobacco inspection
Meadsville	Halifax	1798	Falls, tobacco inspection
Farmville	Prince Edward	1798	Ferry, bridge, tobacco inspection
Ligontown	Amelia	1798	Unknown
Little York	Mecklenburg	1797	Ferry

Source: Hening, *Statutes*, vols. 7, 8, 12, 13; Shepherd, *Statutes*, vols. 1, 2; legislative petitions.

Fifteen towns were chartered between 1759 and 1800 (Table 2-3 and Fig. 2-10). The three pre-Revolutionary War towns were created for defense and trade, and occupied central sites in their respective counties. The twelve post-Revolutionary towns primarily were established as trade and tobacco inspection centers, and were usually located at ferry sites on major rivers. Both sets of legislated towns held

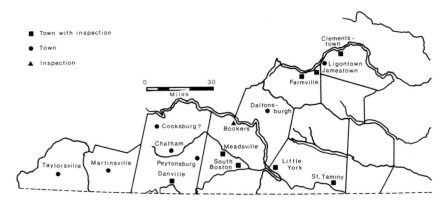

Figure 2-10. Southside towns and inspections, 1791–1800. *Source:* Hening, *Statutes*, vols. 7, 8, 12, 13; Shepherd, *Statutes*, vols. 1, 2: legislative petitions.

in common sites distant from the fall-zone entrepôts. Distance from these dominant ports would permit the interior towns, or potential "unraveling" points, to have their own trade areas and exist within the frontier-mercantile trading structure in this region where town-building contexts were very weak.

The earliest towns, Petytonsburg in Halifax County and Daltonsburgh in Lunenburg County (present-day Charlotte County), were both chartered in 1759 in response to the French and Indian War. The establishment of towns on or near the frontier was designed to encourage the backcountry settlers to live together to protect their lives and property in the event of Indian attack. Only Peytonsburg enjoyed any degree of success as a town. Daltonsburgh did not become important until it was made the site of the Charlotte County courthouse in 1767 and, despite being the focus of several important roads, never developed into a town in the eighteenth century. Chatham, established in 1769 as an interior trading town, was located at the future site of the Pittsylvania County courthouse. It was rechartered as the town of Competition in 1807 and later reverted to its original name.

Peytonsburg's brief success was linked to its location at the courthouse and distance from Petersburg. Of the total of 210 one-half acre lots in the town, sixty-seven were sold by town developer James Roberts to five different mercantile firms, four of whom were based at fall-zone locations. How many, if any, of these companies constructed store buildings is not known. However, eventually a wheelwright occupied one lot, a carpenter was located on another, at least four lots were residences, at least one lot was occupied by a store, and three ordinaries were located in the area.[42] Peytonsburg declined because of the relocation of the Halifax County courthouse. Apparently, both trade and court functions were necessary to support a backcountry trading town. In 1767 Pittsylvania County was created from the central and western territory of Halifax County. In order to be more central to the population in the older and considerably reduced county, the courthouse was moved a few miles eastward. Since Peytonsburg was now located just inside the Pittsylvania line but not sufficiently central to the population in the new county, it could not be considered as a site for the courthouse.

Peytonsburg was revived briefly when the Continental Army established a supply depot there during the Revolutionary War. With blacksmith shops, wagon repair shops, a canteen factory, and with the food and supplies brought to the site from the surrounding areas for distribution to the army, the town was a center of activity for a short period. But the activity could not be sustained after the war and the town quickly passed into oblivion. By 1791, according to Congressman Smith, the town contained only "two or three old houses inhabited by some wretched old women."[43]

Towns were chartered in the post-Revolutionary period in anticipation of navigational improvements in the Appomattox and Roanoke drainage basins. The most important proposed projects involved construction of canals around the falls of those two major rivers. These projects would permit direct water linkages between the Southside and the ports of the fall-zone and Tidewater regions. Above the falls, additional projects such as removal of shoals and the construction of canals and sluices would permit navigation deep into the interior of the region. Below the falls of the Roanoke, river trade was linked to improvements in the North Carolina Tidewater section of the river and the construction of the Dismal Swamp Canal that would connect Albemarle Sound with Norfolk.

Local planters saw navigational improvements as their economic salvation and as the panacea for all the problems created by the old trading structure dominated by the external entrepôts, primarily Petersburg. In their own words, they would no longer "have to travel up to two weeks to and from fall-zone ports." They would no longer "have to trade slaves for horses to replace stock worn out by the demands of overland travel." They would no longer be "alarmed and distressed" by their "cramped situation," which seemed to "exclude them from a means of procuring the common conveniences of life."

The average cost of carrying tobacco to market, comprising one-third to one-half the market value of the staple, could now be reduced by one-half. Wheat, not a viable crop because shipping costs often exceeded market value, could now be a commercial alternative to the ruinous tobacco.[44]

The new trading structure created by the improvements in navigation was to be focused on several new Southside towns. These town locations were primarily long-standing ferry sites that had access both to navigable rivers and productive backcountry hinterlands. The trading position of proposed towns in the Roanoke system was further strengthened by the presence of extensive areas of adjoining North Carolina, also traditionally tied to the Petersburg market. Southside towns were envisioned as interior entrepôts connecting the distant backcountry with the new markets of Norfolk and Richmond, which would reduce Petersburg's long-standing dominance of Southside trade. As part of this function, tobacco inspection warehouses were legislated for seven of the nine river towns (Table 2-4 and Fig. 2-10). Town developers promoted town locations by noting the usual positive characteristics of high ground, good water, and healthy climate, but trade hinterlands commanded the greatest attention. The trustees of Saint Taminy (Tamany, Tammany) in Mecklenburg County boasted that their town was ideally situated not only for the immediate area,

Table 2-4. Southside Tobacco Inspections

Name of Inspection	Town or County	Date of Establishment	Site
Bookers	Halifax	1791	Ferry
Saint Taminy	Saint Taminy	1792	Ferry
Dunkirk	Halifax	1793	Ferry
Danville	Danville	1793	Ferry, falls
Dixs	Danville	1793	Ferry
Towns	Jamestown	1796	Anticipated town development
Clements	Clementstown	1796	Ferry
Andersons	Meadsville	1797	Falls
Fork	Mecklenburg	1797	Ferry
Randolph	Farmville	1797	Ferry, bridge

Source: Hening, *Statutes*, vols. 12, 13; Shepherd, *Statutes*, vols. 1, 2; legislative petitions.

but for the extensive territory bordering on the Roanoke River and its tributaries. Boats loaded with fourteen hogsheads of tobacco would come from places located at distances greater than 100 miles. If not for Saint Taminy, they continued, planters would have to dispose of their tobacco early at reduced rates or travel overland to Petersburg.[45]

The intensity of town fever was revealed in a 1797 petition to the state legislature. Eleven separate versions of the petition contained over 1,100 signatures from the Southside counties of Halifax, Pittsylvania, Henry, and Patrick, and from nearby Franklin County. The petition asked the legislature to establish a town called Meadsville and a tobacco inspection warehouse on the Halifax County land of Meads Anderson at the Great Falls of Banister River, a tributary of the Staunton River. The site was on or near the main road from Charleston, South Carolina, to Philadelphia and already supported both a flour mill and a sawmill. The petitioners envisioned navigational improvements that would permit a single boat to carry ten to fifteen hogsheads of tobacco to Edenton, North Carolina, where they would be transshiped to Norfolk. They also believed that new towns and tobacco inspections in the region would themselves encourage the completion of navigation improvements necessary to "open markets for many articles that will not bear a land carriage."[46]

Despite the rhetoric and optimism, town development was not successful during the few remaining years of the eighteenth century and well into the nineteenth century. The primary cause of this failure was simply the failure to complete the necessary navigational improvements. Four of the twelve towns, Cooksburg, Ligontown, Clementstown, and Little York (Nelson), did not progress beyond the paper plans of their developers. The trustees of Cooksburg appeared not to have even decided on a site for their town. The slow growth of towns was indicated by numerous appeals for additional time for investors to build the sixteen-foot square house with brick or stone chimney that was usually required within five or seven years after purchase of the lots. Lot owners in Danville were given three-year extensions in 1799 and again in 1802 and those in Farmville were given a five-year extension in 1803. Lot owners in Meadsville made three separate requests for extensions, in 1804, 1811, and 1817.[47]

The building of houses within a certain period of time to satisfy the obligations of the town charter was a critical problem since most investors were planters and planter-merchants, who were based firmly on their rural holdings. This factor severely limited the potential number of people and houses in the new towns. It is likely that no residences were erected in any of these towns between the date of their charter and the end of the century. And most of the town sites probably had no more clustering than when they were ferry sites.

The functional combination of ferry and tobacco inspection warehouse offered the greatest potential for the erection of structures and for growth. The activities of ferry and inspection should have encouraged the siting of an ordinary, or tavern, and a store. Saint Taminy had at least an ordinary and a warehouse, which inspected an average of 198 hogsheads, or 237,600 pounds, of tobacco annually between 1793 and 1802 (based on an average of 1,200 pounds per hogshead). Danville had at least one functioning tobacco inspection, one store, one tavern, and probably a grist mill in the area. The Danville warehouse inspected 196 hogsheads of tobacco in 1798. Because of its backcountry location, the flour inspection legislated for Danville was never operational. The Dunkirk Warehouse at South Boston inspected 110 hogsheads of tobacco in 1798, but any activity at this town, like the others above, appears to have been related to the ferry site rather than the town. The trustees of South Boston gave its location as Boyd's Ferry, "on which there are valuable buildings erected." By 1820 only two lots had been developed in the town and in 1835 a respected gazetteer did not identify the site as even a hamlet.[48]

Although ferries forced the channelization of trade, created the opportunity for break-in-bulk transfers, and attracted a large number of service activities, their sites did not guarantee town success. A town never developed at Clementstown because of its close proximity to Richmond and Petersburg. The failure of Little York (Nelson), the rapid decline of Saint Taminy, and the lack of progress in South Boston can be attributed to the large number of ferries near the junction of the Staunton, Dan, and Roanoke Rivers, where competition actually discouraged successful town development. Such a large number of ferries was necessary to handle the decentralized trade of the dispersed population.

Events of the nineteenth century also gave clues to the viability of these towns and the emerging urban network in the region. In addition to those examples already cited, the decline and suggestion of the eventual disappearance of Jamestown, in Prince Edward County, is shown in the records of its inspection warehouse. From 1800 to 1803, an average of 286 hogsheads of tobacco was inspected each year. From 1804 to 1810, only about fifty-five hogsheads were inspected annually.[49] Little York (Nelson) may have suffered the greatest indignity of all Southside towns. It was re-established in 1817 by the same developer at the same site and with the same result. Not one lot was ever developed. By 1835 only Danville and Farmville, with 1,000 and 800 persons respectively, had more than 500 inhabitants. The remaining towns that were chartered in the late eighteenth century contained fewer than 100 persons each or were indistinguishable from the countryside.[50]

The Courthouse Site

Because county courthouses have been generally and rightfully recognized as the most important gathering places in the backcountry South, their function as focal points in a decentralized society and their potential as town sites merit special attention. Courts usually met each month for three or four consecutive days to process a variety of suits and to take care of the business of the county. Merchants and planters also met there to make business deals, and the court was used at additional times as the polling place for the selection of county representatives to the House of Burgesses. Stores, ordinaries, and taverns were located at or near the site to service the periodic and small population increase. These periodic and short sessions were also ideal for the trading regimen of itinerant merchants, who may have been as important as stores at these sites. To ensure greater viability, the meetings of adjacent county courts were held at different times of the month in order to attract the greatest number of people. This was especially helpful for externally based mercantile managers and other merchants who, because of the extensive trading network, had to bring suit in several counties to collect unpaid accounts. For example, an apprentice for one Southside merchant attended forty separate court sessions during a one-year period.[51]

Despite the obvious importance of their prescriptive functions, the Southside experience suggests that courthouses were not as important as foci of economic activity as ferries, were less likely to stimulate open-country neighborhood clustering, and exhibited little potential as places for town development. Only two of the twelve towns chartered in the post-Revolutionary period were located at courthouse sites. Both of these, Martinsville in Henry County and Taylorsville in Patrick County, were related more to the late establishment of each county and the arbitrary "town" designation of the county seat than to any size or functional significance.

In addition to the short and periodic sessions, courthouse sites were also highly artificial. To ensure that the population had equal access to these seats, courthouses were located as close to the center of the counties as possible. Each time that a new county was formed from an older county, a new courthouse site was selected to serve the new

county and the courthouse in the now-smaller parent county was re-
located at a place more central to the population of that much-re-
duced territory. With the number of counties reaching eleven by 1791,
this practice destroyed any advantage that the original courthouses
may have had and strongly curtailed their potential growth as trading
towns. More importantly, the potential town-building combination of
courthouse and ferry site never materialized because of the concern
for the centrality of the former and the location of large rivers off-
center and on county boundaries.

The paradox of the courthouse site, primarily its place inconsis-
tency, is revealed in numerous instances. For example, on July 17,
1765, an unusually large group of as many as 800 persons converged
on the Halifax County courthouse to elect the county's two representatives to the House of Burgesses.[52] Two years later, with the creation
of Pittsylvania County from the western territory of Halifax, this court
site was abandoned in favor of a more central location. In 1792 a
merchant who traveled extensively in the western Southside suggested
the level of visibility on the cultural landscape of one courthouse site
of twenty-eight years. "I set out for Mecklenburg Court, cross at Bibby
Ferry and 8 or 10 miles along small paths in the direction in which I
suppose the courthouse to be."[53]

Reacting to the creation of Nottoway County from the southern
half of Amelia County in 1789, the Amelia justices typically decided
to meet at the house of a prominent citizen rather than to continue
convening at the old courthouse. The old courthouse was still located
in the county but very near the Nottoway border and no longer central to Amelia's population. A further display of weak place association was evidenced by the location of the clerk's office four miles
from the new courthouse (Fig. 2-8).[54] Dissatisfaction with courthouse
sites was also the catalyst for numerous citizen petitions during the
late eighteenth century and continuing into the nineteenth century.
Some went as far as to suggest the creation of additional counties to
better serve those populations that were more distant from the courts.[55]

Hierarchy of Settlements

The final phase of settlement organization is the development of a
hierarchy of settlements that is the climax of settlement structure.
This hierarchy develops from the interplay among the temporal aspects of settlement organization that results in population growth over
time. But Southside settlement structure possessed only an abbreviated range of places concentrated in the lower end of the traditional

hierarchy of town, village, hamlet, and plantation/farm. Because the plantation was the focus of service activities in the region, the hierarchy was derived primarily from a division of the bottom levels. The range of settlements from least clustered to most clustered was composed of country places, country clusters, and hamlets. This hierarchy identifies no settlements as towns or villages.

A country place, the lowest level of the settlement hierarchy, was a single, separate activity—country store, tavern, ordinary, or mill—that was found on a plantation or farm, at a crossroads, or at other solitary locations. The country cluster took two forms, the more intense clustering of activities—combinations of store, tavern, ordinary, or mill—on a single plantation and the more open-country neighborhood pattern, where a variety of activities were located on adjacent plantations near ferries and courthouses. The hamlet designation is not based on any specific number of activities or any minimum resident population, nor is there any list of places that qualify as hamlets. The primary assumption of the hamlet designation is that some important long-developed ferry and courthouse sites may have reached a level of centrality beyond the plantation-dominated country clustering that could not be confirmed by primary and secondary source materials, especially the determination of the nonagricultural resident population that is a prerequisite for such designation. Only a few places would be likely choices for possible hamlet designation.

The key unit in this abbreviated and lower-rung-dominated settlement hierarchy was the plantation site. Plantations were the dominant sites for service activities, decision making, and political and economic power in the region. The plantation was the primary operative of decentralized trade. It was the dominant component of both the country place and the country cluster. Further, on these plantations were large slave populations that, it has been argued, were partially responsible for the incomplete settlement hierarchy by severely limiting regional demand for manufactured goods and reducing opportunity for the development of a middle-level wealth group of independent farmers among the white population.

The large and expanding slave population, of course, did not represent merely a group of people. Their presence as the primary component of the labor force in the Southside indicated that the plantation was also the dominant production unit in the region. As both the dominant settlement and production unit, the plantation provided the critical linkage between the failure of an urban network to develop and the economic cause of that failure, that being the dominance of the primary staple, tobacco.

Notes

1. For a sampling of contemporary views on the influence of rivers, estuaries, and bays on early Virginia, and additionally a criticism of these environmental factors, see O'Mara, *An Historical Geography of Urban System Development*, 114–23. I do not share O'Mara's criticism of environmental views expressed by early Virginians.

2. Kevin P. Kelly, "'In dispers'd Country Plantations': Settlement Patterns in Seventeenth-Century Surry County, Virginia," in *The Chesapeake in the Seventeenth-Century*, Thad W. Tate and David L. Ammerman, eds. (New York, 1979), 149–50.

3. The geographic focus of this study is on the modern territories of the counties of Amelia, Brunswick, Lunenburg, Halifax, Prince Edward, Mecklenburg, Charlotte, Pittsylvania, Henry, Patrick, and Nottoway. This territory comprises over 6,000 square miles. Because Bedford County and Franklin County were formerly part of the original Brunswick County, organized in 1732, and later Lunenburg county, established in 1746, they are included in general discussions of early settlement but not in more detailed analyses of settlement and economic development. Their inclusion in the region increased the territory to over 8,000 square miles.

4. Robert W. Ramsey, *Carolina Cradle: Settlement of the Northwest Carolina Frontier, 1747–1762* (Chapel Hill, N.C., 1964), 18; Nicholls, "Origins of the Virginia Southside," 85.

5. Carl Bridenbaugh, *Myths and Realities, Societies of the Colonial South* (New York, 1973; originally 1952), 125.

6. For contemporary comments on Southside soil, see Byrd, "History of the Dividing Line," in *Prose Works*, 232, 236, 240, 251, 289–90, 294; idem, "A Journey to the Land of Eden," in ibid., 384–85, 388–89, 394, 396, 402, 404, 406, 408; Roger Atkinson to Samuel Pleasants, September 27, 1772, Roger Atkinson Letterbook, University of Virginia, Charlottesville. On the influence of agricultural practices, see Arthur R. Hall, "Soil Erosion and Agriculture in the Southern Piedmont: A History," (unpublished Ph.D. thesis, Duke University, 1948), 5, 50, 68–69; Stanley W. Trimble, *Man-Induced Erosion of the Southern Piedmont, 1700–1970* (Washington, D.C., 1974), 22, 25, 27.

7. Smyth, *A Tour in the United States of America* 2: 123–40.

8. Clarence W. Alvord and Lee Bidgood, *The First Explorations of the Trans-Allegheny Region by the Virginians, 1650–1674* (Cleveland, 1912), 109–30.

9. Byrd, "History of the Dividing Line," 226–27, 231, 233–35, 239–40, 244, 268–69, 289–91, 305; idem, "Journey to the Land of Eden," 384–85, 396, 401, 403.

10. Frederick F. Siegel, *The Roots of Southern Distinctiveness: Tobacco and Society in Danville, Virginia, 1780–1865* (Chapel Hill, N.C., 1987), 68–74, 166.

11. Ibid., 69.

12.   Alan V. Briceland, *Westward From Virginia: The Exploration of the Virginia-Carolina Frontier, 1650–1710* (Charlottesville, Va., 1987), 3.

13.   Byrd, "History of the Dividing Line," 257–58. Byrd also noted that the Saura Indians abandoned some of the best land in the North Carolina Piedmont because of their fear of the Senecas. See "A Journey to the Land of Eden," 398.

14.   George Washington, *The Writings of George Washington From the Original Manuscript Sources, 1745–1799*, John C. Fitzpatrick, ed. (Washington, D.C., 1931), 477–491.

15.   Halifax County Pleas 2:104.

16.   Smyth, *A Tour in the United States of America*, 280. For Smyth's encounter with the Indian party, see 271–79.

17.   William W. Hening, ed., *The Statutes at Large: Being a Collection of All the Laws of Virginia from the First Session of the Legislature in the Year 1619* (Richmond, 1819–23) 7:306–7.

18.   Mitchell, *Commercialism and Frontier*, 144–45.

19.   For materials relating to the origins of Southside settlers, see Nicholls, "Origins of Southside Virginia," 46–49; Joseph D. Eggleston, "The Buffaloe Settlement and Its Makers," *Virginia Magazine of History and Biography* 49 (1941), 234–43; Herbert C. Bradshaw, "The Settlement of Prince Edward County," ibid. 62 (1954), 448–71; Maud Carter Clement, *The History of Pittsylvania County, Virginia* (Baltimore, 1981; originally 1929), 32–56.

20.   Earle, *The Evolution of a Tidewater Settlement System*, 47, 50–54, 203–14; Kulikoff, *Tobacco and Slaves*, 148–57; Darrett B. Rutman and Anita H. Rutman, *A Place in Time: Middlesex County, Virginia, 1650–1750* (New York, 1984), 236–40.

21.   Ramsey, *Carolina Cradle*, 18; Nicholls, "Origins of the Virginia Southside," 85. See also Merrens, *Colonial North Carolina*, 53–66.

22.   Nicholls, "Origins of the Virginia Southside," 46–48.

23.   Everett B. Green and Virginia D. Harrington, *American Population Before the Federal Census of 1790* (Gloucester, Mass., 1966; originally 1932), 149–50.

24.   Byrd, "History of the Dividing Line," 182–84, 187–88, 192–93, 195–96, 202–7.

25.   Nicholls, "Origins of the Virginia Southside," 35–37.

26.   Beeman, *The Evolution of the Southern Backcountry*, 25–26.

27.   Nicholls, "Origins of the Virginia Southside," 84.

28.   Ibid., 81.

29.   Beeman, *The Evolution of the Southern Backcountry*, 14–96.

30.   William P. Palmer, ed., *Calendar of Virginia State Papers and Other Manuscripts . . . Preserved . . . at Richmond* (Richmond, 1875–93) 1:223; "Letters of William Byrd II," *Virginia Magazine of History and Biography* 36 (1928), 353–54, 359, 360–61.

31.   There are no population figures before the census of 1790. To construct a population data base, the number of taxables (tithables) for each

county is multiplied by four. The usual procedure is to multiply white tithables by four and black slave tithables by two. Multiplication by a factor of four appears to be more appropriate for the Southside for several reasons. There were more whites than blacks for most counties in the precensus period. There was likely an undercounting of taxables in this frontier region where territory was extensive and county courts often appeared to be unstructured. Except for two counties, this procedure also provides an appropriate transition from the list of taxables to the Census of 1790. In Amelia and Prince Edward counties, where slaves outnumbered whites as early as 1755, taxables are multipled by a factor of three for 1760 through 1780.

32.　Beeman, "Patterns of Community in the Southern Backcountry: An Ethnohistorical View of Lunenburg County, Virginia," Paper Presented at Conference in Early American History, 1981, 15.

33.　John Dorman, comp., "British Mercantile Claims," *Virginia Genealogist* 13 (1969); 15–16 (1971–72); 18–21 (1974–77); 24–25 (1980–81). Population instability continued well into the nineteenth century. For example, between 1840 and 1850, more than half of the white male household heads in Prince Edward County moved elsewhere. See William G. Shade, "Society and Politics in Antebellum Virginia Southside," *Journal of Southern History* 53 (1987), 167.

34.　For Cunninghame, see Richard E. McMurran, "The Virginia Claims of William Cunninghame and Company, 1784–1811" (M.A. thesis, University of Alabama, 1965), 33; for Donald, see *Virginia Gazette*, Dixon, March 25, 1775.

35.　"Journal of William Loughton Smith," 69.

36.　Richard R. Beeman, "Robert Munford and the Political Culture of Frontier Virginia," *Journal of American Studies* 12 (1978), 169–83.

37.　Charlotte County Court Cases (Judgments), March–July 1767.

38.　The extent of Marable's business and agricultural holdings is found in *Virginia Gazette*, Rind, July 22, 1773; Mecklenburg Will Book 2:169–73. Yet another side of Marable, the strong sense of duty to family, is revealed in his will. He provided generously for his wife and five of his children. A sixth child, Matthew, apparently possessing more than just his father's name, was written out of the will because "he carried away with him which I believe was to the amount of one thousand pounds."

39.　All examples of functional arrangements on plantations are derived from Mutual Assurance Society, 1801–05, Virginia State Library.

40.　For Taylor's Ferry, see *Virginia Genealogist* 16 (1972), 104; for Booker's Ferry, see James Murdoch Ledger, 1770–71, Ragsdale Papers, University of Virginia Library, Charlottesville. Although Murdoch is not identified with the ledger, based on the identical operations and customers in the Murdoch Daybook, 1774–75, located in the Manuscripts Division of the Library of Congress, it is the same Scottish store.

41.　Legislative Petitions, Mecklenburg County, 1803–16.

42.　For land transactions relating to Peytonsburg, see Halifax County Deed Books 2–6; also see Charles K. Sparrow, Jr., "Historical Research on

Peytonsburg and the First Courthouse of Halifax County, Virginia," unpublished paper, Historical Archaeology, College of William and Mary, 1977, 21–27. Roger Atkinson and John Wimbish each later owned all or most of the town.

43.   "Journal of William Loughton Smith," 71.

44.   The expressions of hope by Southside planters are from the legislative petitions of Halifax County and Mecklenburg County.

45.   Legislative Petitions, Mecklenburg County, October 9, 1792.

46.   Legislative Petitions, Halifax County, December 6, 1797.

47.   For Danville, see Samuel Shepherd, ed., *The Statutes at Large of Virginia* (Richmond, 1835) 2:213, 442. For Farmville, see ibid., 3:55. Requests for extensions in Meadsville are found in Legislative Petitions, Halifax County, December 24, 1804, December 3, 1817.

48.   For Saint Taminy, see Auditor of Public Accounts, Virginia State Library; for Danville, see Pittsylvania County Deed Book 11:361. Data on Dunkirk Warehouse is found in Auditor of Public Accounts. Description of Boyd's Ferry is found in Shepherd, *Statutes* 2:48; 1835 description is found in Joseph Martin, *A New and Comprehensive Gazetteer of Virginia and the District of Columbia* (Charlottesville, Va., 1835), 186.

49.   Auditor of Public Accounts (Towns Warehouse).

50.   Martin, *Gazetteer*, 261, 268, and under appropriate county sections.

51.   Venable Diary.

52.   The possible number of people at the courthouse site is calculated by dividing the total number of votes cast (1345) by two and adding the usual nonvoting population that often attended these festive occasions. The results of this election are found in Halifax County Deed Book 3:392–401.

53.   Venable Diary.

54.   Details of the decision to move the courthouse to a temporary site are found in Amelia County Order Book 19:152–55.

55.   Legislative Petitions, Halifax County, January 12, 1784, November 6, 1787, October 12, 1814; ibid., Prince Edward County, December 8, 1830; ibid., Mecklenburg County, November 2, 1793, November 19, 1796, December 5, 1809, December 11, 1811.

3

Regional Economy

The regional economy of developing frontier regions of early America evolved over time from more pioneer economies, in which household production units consumed most of the bounty of their efforts, to more commercial economies, where production was primarily directed to the increased commercialism of the market place. The pioneer economy, with its emphasis on natural products such as skins, furs, and venison, and subsistence agriculture based on corn and livestock, eventually gave way to the commercial cultivation of tobacco, wheat, or other grains. This change occurred because of improved transportation that overcame the marketing restrictions imposed by distance, emerging complementarily with other regions, and perhaps technological innovation at one or all of the levels that included agricultural production, transport, and manufacturing.

Regional economic development was also the primary factor in the evolution of the regional settlement system. Because the pioneer economy normally produced few surplus products, widely scattered country stores took care of the regional trade that was based on the bartering of small quantities of furs, skins, leather, and salted meat for basic manufactured goods such as lead, flint, powder, bar iron, salt, sugar, rum, and cheap cloth. The well-developed commercial economy, with its demands for more collection, distribution, and manufacturing, and its enhancement of wealth that led to increases in consumer demand, gave rise to a settlement hierarchy composed of a dominant regional town, additional smaller towns, other centralized service centers and, for the more isolated areas, decentralized country stores.

The formulation of settlement theory is also based on the linkages between the progressing regional economy and the developing regional settlement system. Christaller's central-place theory was based on a closed economic system dominated by middle-level commercial farms. Lösch's modifications of the original central-place theory were based in part on the emergence of surplus products that supported a farm-based trading system that eventually progressed to a full-fledged urban network. Vance's mercantile model emphasized the distant markets of the early regional economy as the basis for the development of the regionally directed trading structure of the central-place system. And even more critical to economic and settlement development in Southside Virginia, Earle and Hoffman's interpretation of the staple thesis divided the commercial economy into two sections: a wheat economy that produced the expected evolution to a fully developed regional settlement hierarchy and a tobacco economy that did not so readily give rise to centralized places, thus maintaining much of the formative settlement system that was present in the pioneer economy.

Using a conventional three fold structure of economic types—primary (agriculture), secondary (processing), and tertiary (service)—Chapter 3 charts the development of the Southside economy and its influence on the development of the settlement system. The primary concern of this investigation is, in the context of Earle and Hoffman's model, to determine how tobacco production contributed to the failure of an urban network to develop in the region.

Primary Economic Activity

Primary production dominated the Southside economy throughout the eighteenth century. Whether the collection of natural products from a crude house in a forest clearing or the more specialized production of tobacco on large plantations, trade in primary products was focused primarily on distant markets. Except for wheat, the primary economy did not generate any significant local processing. But ironically, wheat, or flour, could not break out of the confinement of its local mold to become the export product that would in turn increase the level of regional secondary and tertiary activity sufficient to produce a regional settlement hierarchy. Secondary and tertiary economic activities were not only tightly linked to the primary economy; they were, with their locations primarily on plantation sites or controlled by local planters, also part of the primary economy.

Hunting and Trapping

The initial economic development of the Southside came from hunting and trapping, which were responsible for the penetration of the region between the mid-1640s and the 1670s. From bases of operations at the fall zone—Fort Charles on the James River and Fort Henry on the Appomattox River—traders spread out across the region in search of skins and furs. The two primary entrepreneurs, William Byrd I on the James and Abraham Wood on the Appomattox, promoted the locational apprenticeships of these two sites that became the dominant entrepôts for the Southside and led to the eventual establishment of Richmond and Petersburg. Since the Indians did most of the actual hunting and trapping, a few backcountry Indian villages served as focal points where European manufactured goods and wampum were exchanged for the valuable resources.

After the fall of Occaneechi Island in 1676, the most important and perhaps the only trading site in the Southside, Catawba Indian villages along the North and South Carolina border became the principal exchange points for the Virginia traders. At the peak of this trade to Carolina, caravans from the fall zone crossed the Southside with as many as 100 horses and fifteen to sixteen men. With their horses carrying 150 to 200 pounds each of trading goods, the traders might spend from four months to three years on a single trading expedition.[1] The Virginia traders did not expand their extractive operations beyond the Carolina Piedmont to the Appalachian Mountains. Traders from Charleston, South Carolina, later penetrated this region to capture this trade with the Cherokee Indians.

Hunting and trapping, after the early, more organized efforts, was carried on by less-structured smaller groups or by single individuals. Hunters and trappers working out of temporary camps immediately preceded permanent settlement in much of the region.[2] The first settlers also hunted and trapped both for subsistence and commercial purposes. The wild animals provided supplemental food and clothing for the family and their skins and pelts could be bartered for additional necessities at the country stores or from other settlers. The bounties paid on wolves was also an important component of this early exchange.

Despite the early exploitation that greatly reduced the numbers of wildlife in the region, the trade in animals continued to be an important component of the local economy in the area west of the Staunton River until well after the commencement of commercial agriculture. According to John Smyth, trade in skins and furs was still thriving in the Smith River valley during the mid-1770s. A cured deerskin sold for 15s.; a raccoon skin went for just over 4d. per pound; and an otter skin was valued as high as 4s.[3] Over a fifteen-month period in 1770–71, a Pittsylvania County planter was credited with twenty-six individual deerskins and an additional 169½ pounds of that item; twelve hogsheads of tobacco completed the transactions in this mixed commercial economy. Joshua Barton's account with the nearby Bedford County store of the Scottish firm of Robert Donald and Company suggested the variety of animals still present in the western areas in 1769. Barton was given £50 19s. worth of store credit in exchange for 131 raw deerskins, thirty-six bearskins, one panther skin, and one elk skin.[4] Settlers also purchased large quantities of powder, lead, shot, flints, and an occasional rifle and rifle parts from local stores during the period preceding the Revolutionary War.

Livestock

Livestock were more important to the early frontier and endured for a longer period of time than hunting and trapping. They provided a great deal of versatility by supplying a variety of products for both home consumption and local and long-distance markets. In addition to cattle and hog drives to distant markets, salted beef and pork, hides and leather, butter, cheese, tallow, soap, and lard were shipped to fall-zone ports and were bartered at local country stores.

The early Southside provided an ideal environment for the raising of cattle and hogs. Settlement was sparse, the land was little altered by agriculture, natural food was abundant, and the animal breeds were generally hardy. These factors, joined with similar practices inherited from the Virginia Tidewater and the relatively small amounts of capital available to early settlers, gave rise to an open range where cattle and hogs were simply turned loose to roam the nearby countryside in search of food. Naturally occurring or humanly produced grassy areas, wild peas, and cane fields in the floodplains were available as food for cattle, and the abundant mast on the forest floor and wild fruits and berries were sufficient to sustain large numbers of hogs for a considerable portion of the year. But the products of nature were not the sole source of livestock feed. Even in the more western areas of the region, corn was an important part of the diet of hogs as early as the 1770s. Corn, in part, was thought to firm the meat made soft by the consumption of mast.[5] The importance of the early livestock industry can be seen in the frequent occurrence of cattle and hogs in Southside estate inventories. During the 1740s, 83 percent of sixty inventories in Brunswick County listed cattle and 73 percent had hogs. For that same period, 69 percent of Amelia County's forty-eight inventories counted cattle and 65 percent had hogs. The average herd size for cattle was nineteen in Brunswick and fourteen in Amelia.

Average holdings for hogs were forty for Brunswick and twenty-six for Amelia.

Because livestock roamed freely about the countryside, some means of identification of ownership was necessary. Cattle and hogs were generally not branded, that being the primary means of identifying horses, but were identified by various marks on their ears, which were recorded at county courts. Usually cattle and hogs belonging to the same individual were identified by the same mark. For example, in 1735 George Marchbanks of Amelia County identified all of his stock by a crop and slit in the right ear and a half crop on the underside of the left ear. Less frequently, cattle and hogs carried different marks of identification. Another Amelia County resident marked his hogs with a crop in the left ear and cut their tails; his cattle received a crop in the left ear.[6] Over time, by necessity, the marks became more elaborate.

Greater attention to animals and a more intensive form of livestock economy gradually evolved during the eighteenth century, although the open range probably still prevailed in much of the region at the end of the century, especially west of the Staunton River. Over time, with increased density of population, acceleration of agricultural development, increased economic means to construct animal pens, and more rigid interpretation of property lines, there was a trend toward a reduction in the territorial range of stock and thus more dependence on the developed plantation. The increased presence of fodder in estate inventories in the post-Revolutionary period—listed in 21 percent of Amelia's, 19 percent of Brunswick's, and 14 percent of Mecklenburg's—and the presence of hay in the market economy suggested greater attention to the care of cattle.[7] Another indication of the trend away from the open range was increased emphasis on milk cows. In the 1790s a quarter of the Amelia and Pittsylvania inventories listed milk and butter containers or churns. Herd sizes also suggested changes toward a more intensive pattern of livestock economy. During the 1790s the counties of Amelia, Brunswick, and Mecklenburg—those counties with higher population densities and a stronger orientation to a plantation economy—had larger herd sizes than the western counties of Halifax and Pittsylvania. In these counties the plantations with the greatest number of slaves usually had the largest number of livestock. For example, in Amelia County Stephen Cocke owned 112 head of cattle, at least 177 hogs, and 103 slaves. In Brunswick County Owen Myrick's plantation contained 124 head of cattle, at least 388 hogs, and sixty-three slaves.[8] Final evidence of the shrinking of stock range was the sharp reduction in the number of stock marks registered after the 1750s. Any stronger statements concerning modifications in the livestock economy must be somewhat restrained considering the great importance attached to the fact that thirteen of William Walker's thirty-six hogs were actually housed in pens on his Brunswick County plantation and the reminder from Congressman Smith that the region had large areas that remained relatively undeveloped.[9]

Sheep were found in the Southside from the earliest settlement, but never rivaled the domination of hogs and cattle. Since sheep could not fend for themselves as well as other stock and were more vulnerable to attacks from dogs, wolves, and other predators, they were not abundant in the early settlement period. During the 1740s sheep were present in 11 percent and 42 percent respectively of Amelia and Brunswick inventories. After the 1760s sheep were usually found in over half of the inventories throughout the region. Hog-sheep ratios declined from 9:1 during the 1730s to 3:1 in the post-Revolutionary period. Cattle-sheep ratios followed a similar trend, with the ratio reduced to 2:1 by the 1790s. Sheep, like cattle and hogs, were used for both subsistence and commercial purposes and produced a variety of products. Wool was apparently more important than mutton in both commercial and subsistence uses, but neither appeared often in estate inventories and store accounts. The household use of wool was more in evidence as revealed by the frequent occurrences of wool cards in store purchases.

Horses played a different role in the economy of the Southside. With riders, packs, or pulling wagons or carts, they were the primary means of transportation in this region that was so heavily dependent on distant fall-zone entrepôts for final and intermediate market points. In addition, some of the more highly pedigreed animals provided a great deal of prestige for their owners and entertainment for the other local planters through horse racing. Southside planters frequently placed advertisements for stud services in the *Virginia Gazette*; the virtues of the horse and the cost per "jump" were usually included. Horse racing was a common vice among the population, and numerous "racepaths" were both the focus of this activity and one of the more important locational references in the region. Much of the socializing at local ordinaries, taverns, and stores was centered on the relative attributes of local horses. Whether because of problems in maintaining the supply of horses diminished by the demands of long-distance trade or from greater use of plows in cultivation, oxen and work steers became more common in the post-Revolutionary period. During the 1790, 43 percent of Amelia County inventories listed at least one of these bovine workers; in Mecklenburg County they were found in 30 percent of inventories.

A variety of additional, smaller livestock—geese, bees, chickens, "dunghill fowl," turkeys, ducks, and goats—was found on Southside plantations and farms. Although primarily for household consumption, any of these animals might be bartered at country stores. The most common commercial product that came from this group was beeswax. There were also special uses for some of the smaller livestock. Cockfighting was so popular that there was organized competition, with heavy wagering, among rival counties.[10]

In frontier areas with great distances to markets and with poorly developed road networks, cattle and hogs were reliable and versatile market commodities because they could be driven to market. According to John Smyth, hog drives were more common than cattle drives, and drives of as many as 500 hogs were made from the backcountry to the fall zone. Smyth observed that hogs sold for 25 shillings per hundred weight at the fall zone, an increase of 10s. over the price in the deep backcountry at the time.[11] Although there is no record of Southside sheep being driven to distant markets, that practice existed in some areas of Virginia. In the summer of 1776, a flock numbering several hundred was driven from the Tidewater county of Nansemond to Petersburg.[12]

Although most livestock drives were destined for the Virginia fall zone, drives to more distant markets also took place. In 1768 Richard White and George Astin (Austin), both of Pittsylvania County, drove eighty-seven head of cattle to the Philadelphia area. They paid £194 2s. to thirty-one local individuals for the cattle and then followed the Great Valley through Virginia and Maryland and into Pennsylvania to some point beyond "Shippey's Town" (Shippensburg), where they turned east to their destination at Abingdon. Only one other full-time drover, a white servant of a Pittsylvania County planter who was hired for £6, made the trip. Additional help was hired along the route whenever the need arose.[13] This was the only occurrence of trade between the Southside and Philadelphia in the extant records. The trading connection between Philadelphia and the Shenandoah Valley, however, was well developed.

Both contemporary observers and secondary studies have emphasized the importance of long-distance cattle drives from the southern backcountry to both southern and northern entrepôts. Although it is beyond the scope of this study to challenge the importance of stock drives from the Southside, the great quantity and variety of Southside primary sources indicate that there was little evidence of the large-scale movement of surplus animals. Based on the sizes of individual herds and the indications that cattle numbers were well below those of hog holdings, any such movement would have involved, like the effort of White and Astin, the holdings of several plantations. There is abundant evidence, however, that casks of salted beef were important exports from the region.

The Lesser Commercial Crops: Corn, Flax, Hemp, and Cotton

In a situation where a region is strongly identified with a particular commercial crop and where a potential heir waits for ascendancy, other important crops are often ignored or placed far in the wings of the evolutionary agricultural plot. Although tobacco dominated the economy and was the major influence on life in the Southside, corn and flax were more ubiquitous, reliable, and versatile. Like wheat, hemp and cotton could not overcome obstacles that would improve their positions in the regional economy.

Corn was the most common and versatile crop in the Southside economy. Perhaps no other area of European settlement in North America adopted this native crop so readily as the southern frontier. Locally, it was consumed by slaves, by both wealthy and poor whites, was fed to animals, and was even bartered at country stores. As the classic example of the indirect external marketing of a crop, corn left the region as livestock, whisky, and cured meat products.[14] Corn could be grown on the most rudimentary land and with the simplest of technology. It was easily preserved and could remain in the field until late autumn, thus making few harvest demands on the settlers during the busy summer and early fall seasons. Table 3-1 suggests the versatility of corn, with its presence solid in both early pioneer and later, more developed economies.

Flax, like corn, was an ideal crop for the pioneer economy. In this context it was most likely used to make linsey-woolsey, a durable clothing material ideal for the hard conditions of the frontier. It would appear from the increasing availability of inexpensive cloth in the country stores that flax production would not increase beyond the period of early settlement. But beginning in the late 1760s, flax production increased, and continued to do so until the end of the century. For example, in Brunswick County the percentage of inventories with flax or flax-related equipment—wheels, brakes, hatchets, and combs—increased from 2 percent during the 1760s to 46 percent during the 1790s. In Mecklenburg County the increase was from 7 percent to 51 percent (Table 3-1).

Table 3-1.
Percent of Inventories with Selected Crops, 1732–1799

Crop	Brunswick		Counties Amelia		Mecklenburg		Pittsylvania	
	%	Total No.	%	Total No.	%	Total No.	%	Total No.
Tobacco								
1732–39	7	27	0	9	-	-	-	-
1740–49	13	60	17	48	-	-	-	-
1750–59	13	85	26	66	, -	-	-	-
1760–69	32	82	23	95	7	15	-	-
1770–79	21	104	23	133	16	63	8	49
1780–89	21	75	17	147	17	87	16	70
1790–99	23	135	21	106	16	134	22	109
Corn								
1732–39	27	27	11	9	-	-	-	-
1740–49	18	60	19	48	-	-	-	-
1750–59	13	85	26	66	-	-	-	-
1760–69	51	82	33	95	7	15	-	-
1770–79	45	104	35	133	25	63	20	49
1780–89	45	75	30	147	24	87	16	70
1790–99	57	135	32	106	25	134	22	109
Wheat								
1732–39	11	27	0	9	-	-	-	-
1740–49	7	60	10	48	-	-	-	-
1750–59	11	85	9	66	-	-	-	-
1760–69	20	82	20	95	0	15	-	-
1770–79	22	104	18	133	14	63	2	49
1780–89	12	75	18	147	9	87	9	70
1790–99	21	135	22	106	16	134	9	109
Flax[1]								
1732–39	7	27	0	9	-	-	-	-
1740–49	0	60	10	48	-	-	-	-
1750–59	5	85	5	66	-	-	-	-
1760–69	2	82	18	95	7	15	-	-
1770–79	19	104	28	133	43	63	33	49
1780–89	32	75	30	147	48	87	44	70
1790–99	46	135	22	106	51	134	49	109
Cotton								
1732–39	11	27	0	9	-	-	-	-
1740–49	0	60	0	48	-	-	-	-
1750–59	5	85	0	66	-	-	-	-
1760–69	16	82	5	95	7	15	-	-
1770–79	15	104	8	133	8	63	4	49
1780–89	27	75	10	147	10	87	6	70
1790–99	33	135	6	106	9	134	6	109

Source: County will books.

[1.] Flax percentages include flax implements.

Increased flax production may have been related to the bounties established in 1764 and 1771, and the continued growth in the post-Revolutionary period may have been more related to real or expected shortages of imported cloth that had been formerly supplied by Scottish mercantile firms, but probably the most important factor was the continuing need for inexpensive materials for clothing. The post-Revolutionary growth appears not to be related to the expansion of linseed mills that occurred in other areas of Virginia. The uses for flax in the Southside during the latter period are revealed in Tench Coxe's enumeration of manufacturing in 1810. Coxe's data indicated that flax processing was a home industry, "flaxen goods in families," of some significance. Patrick, Halifax, Mecklenburg, Amelia, and Lunenburg ranked first, third, fourth, eighth, and tenth respectively in county production in the state.[15] The level of market orientation and the location of any potential market are not known.

Hemp was grown primarily in the western counties of Pittsylvania and Halifax, but production lacked both geographic and temporal continuity. The sporadic cultivation of the crop was tied to the dominance of tobacco and government efforts to diversify local economies or to increase the supply of naval stores. When tobacco prices were low, planters tended to diversify their commercial farm production, but with the return to higher prices, they ignored hemp and returned to the more familiar tobacco. The greater labor demands of hemp, especially the rotting and separating procedures, also placed the product in a less favorable position. It would appear unlikely that tobacco and hemp, both demanding in their need for labor, could be grown simultaneously in the same region. On growing hemp, William Byrd commented that "It thrives very well in this Climate, but Labour being much dearer than in Muscovy, as well as the Freight, we can make no Earnings of it."[16] Hemp was marketed through the same mercantile trading system as tobacco but, in addition to the fall-zone entrepôts, Norfolk was also an important market.

Most hemp production in the Southside occurred during the late 1760s and primarily in response to the colonial bounty of 4s. per hundred pounds.[17] Based on the records of the counties of Halifax, Pittsylvania, and Mecklenburg, fewer than thirty planters could be associated with hemp production. Among those who received bounties, production ranged from 1,895 to 5,769 pounds. Hemp was also sporadically produced after the Revolutionary War.

Cotton was produced primarily in the southern and eastern sections of the Southside, especially in Brunswick County. The distribution was most influenced by the longer growing season created by lower elevations, southern location, and slight maritime influence. A few of the early Brunswick settlers grew cotton, but its cultivation only began to increase during the 1760s. By the 1790s one-third of all Brunswick inventories listed cotton, but usually in small amounts (Table 3-1). The largest amount recorded in an individual inventory was 400 pounds. A few planters also had cotton gins.[18]

Prior to the 1790s, with the small amount of cotton and the lack of technology to process large quantities of the crop, most of the production was probably for household use. Cotton cards were common items in both inventories and store accounts. But in the 1790s, with the invention of the cotton gin, commercial production increased dramatically. In 1791, the entire United States produced approximately 4,000 bales of cotton. In 1801, the area that included Brunswick County and the adjacent Tidewater region alone produced 10,000 bales.[19] Presumptive thoughts on the subject of the expansion of cotton production in the region are quite inconclusive. Any gains in production from the delayed opening of the cotton expansion to the south and west would appear to be modest considering the destructive aspects of cotton cultivation on both old and new land. Yet, the destructive tobacco continued to expand along the southern borders of the region. The consideration of possible competition between the two staples is at the very least an intriguing proposition.

Tobacco

Tobacco, specifically the "Oronoko" (Orinoco) variety, was brought to the Southside by the early immigrants from the Virginia Tidewater.[20] The settlement of the region was strongly correlated with the need to expand tobacco production because of declining yields and reduction in quality of the Tidewater product. However, with the immediate need for clearing land, planting subsistence crops, and developing holdings in cattle and hogs, and with the distance from markets, tobacco was not a mainstay of the economy before the 1750s in Amelia and Brunswick counties and before the 1760s in Halifax County.

Many early settlers, nevertheless, came to the region with the requisite capital, skills, and labor to produce tobacco immediately. In the 1740s, 13 percent of Brunswick County's estate inventories and 17 percent of Amelia County's inventories listed tobacco (Table 3-1). Further, Amelia residents spent considerable time and effort in 1743 to build a bridge across the Appomattox River to aid in the transportation of tobacco to the inspection warehouses at the falls of the James

River and a year later generated three separate petitions for the establishment of new inspections at that same location.[21] Early tobacco production also took place in the western counties as well. In early 1754 the newly established frontier county of Halifax petitioned for an inspection warehouse across the Staunton River in Lunenburg County.[22]

By the 1760s the Southside had become one of the leading tobacco-producing regions in the colony. It is not possible to determine actual tobacco production in the region because it was part of the production of the Upper James River District. This district also included the important tobacco-producing county of Bedford and the counties between the James and Appomattox. By 1770 this district, one of six tobacco-producing regions of Virginia, accounted for 37 percent of all tobacco exported from the colony.[23]

The best indicator of the Southside's share of the colony's tobacco production was the amount of tobacco received at the Petersburg inspection warehouses, the primary but not the only market for the region's tobacco. A Petersburg merchant noted that the inspections at that location received 19,000 hogsheads of tobacco in a twelve-month period ending in August of 1772. With each hogshead containing approximately 1,000 pounds of tobacco, for a total of 19,000,000 pounds, the Petersburg inspections accounted for 27 percent of the 70,632,300 pounds of tobacco exported from Virginia in 1772.[24] With additional inspections available in Chesterfield County for Southside producers—Manchester, Osbornes, and Warwick—and non-Southside counties in the district traditionally linked to the Richmond inspections, the region south of the Appomattox was emerging as Virginia's leading tobacco producer. Even considering that both Petersburg and Chesterfield warehouses also inspected small amounts of tobacco from counties on the margins of the Southside, the region may have produced one-third of Virginia's total exports by the end of the colonial period. The Southside was producing more than half of the state's total production by the end of the century.[25]

Another indication of the increased production of tobacco in the Southside was the increased presence of Scottish chain stores. Prior to the expansion of tobacco, they had served the Southside from fall-zone locations or from a small number of stores scattered over the backcountry. During the 1760s they constructed or rented numerous stores and sent their factors and storekeepers into the region to purchase tobacco in exchange for store goods. Based primarily on this mercantile expansion into the backcountry, tobacco comprised 80 percent of all Scottish imports from North America by 1772. William

Cunninghame and Company proposed that at least 300 hogsheads of tobacco per year were necessary to support one store in the back-country. This business strategy was typical, but the anticipated volume was much higher than for most Scottish stores.[26]

Within the regional mercantile structure, the increasing importance of tobacco may be seen in the methods of paying debts to country stores. According to the court judgments of the counties of Charlotte, Halifax, and Pittsylvania, tobacco comprised 38 percent by value of remittances to accounts during the 1760s, 48 percent during the 1770s, and 65 percent in the latter two counties during the 1780s.

The most important indication of the increased importance of tobacco in the regional economy was the increasing presence of slaves to fulfill the labor-intensive cultivation of that staple. The crop required constant attention and often hard labor for much of the year. The preparation of seedbeds commenced during the winter and the preparation, packing, and transport to market continued into the next winter. In between were planting, hoeing to control weeds, topping and suckering to increase the weight of the leaves, cutting of the stalks, curing and stripping the leaves, and possibly stemming and grading. Slaves, it will be recalled, comprised almost 60 percent of taxables in Amelia County by 1755, more than 60 percent of the population of Amelia and more than 50 percent of the population in five other counties by 1790 (Table 2-2). By the decade of the 1770s, slaves made up over 70 percent of the total value of personal property in estate inventories in Amelia County. By the 1790s, slaves comprised over 60 percent of the value of personal property listed in the inventories of Brunswick, Mecklenburg, and Pittsylvania.

The increases both in the slave population and in the percentage of the value of personal property attributed to slaves suggest important backward linkages as Southside planters put profits back into the production of tobacco. Although these figures conform to suggestions made by Earle and Hoffman and by Baldwin regarding the influence of staple production on economy and society, the situation in the Southside was much more complex. Large tobacco operations with great numbers of slaves did not dominate the Southside nor did the region possess the degree of specialization of tobacco production found in the Tidewater. In 1790 the average number of slaves held by planters in the counties of Amelia, Lunenburg, and Halifax was 7.5, 4.5, and 3.7 respectively. In that same year, the percentage of plantations with only one or two slaves was 47 percent in Halifax, 42 percent in Lunenburg, and 32 percent in Amelia.[27]

As indicated by the slaveholdings, most Southside tobacco was produced by small-scale operators, with only one or two hogsheads, or just over 2,000 pounds, usually being the entire crop for the season. Tobacco production per planter never approached the output of the large Tidewater planters, who annually marketed more than sixty hogsheads. The largest Southside producers marketed twenty to thirty hogsheads per year. Of 240 estate inventories for the 1770s, 1780s, and 1790s, 116, or 48 percent, listed the equivalent of one to three hogsheads, or roughly 700 to 3600 pounds of tobacco. This can be considered only very general evidence because of the time of the year that the inventories were taken. Some inventories with ten to twenty slaves, for example, listed no tobacco because the crop had already been marketed.

The transactions of the Halifax County store of the Scottish mercantile firm of James Murdoch and Company provided better support for the dominance of small scale production. Between November 1770 and August 17, 1771, the store accepted 141 hogsheads of tobacco from seventy-one different planters. Of these seventy-one planters, thirty-five marketed just one hogshead and only one planter traded more than six hogsheads, that being eight hogsheads, or 8,573 pounds. Some of these planters may have produced more tobacco since almost three months of the year were not accounted for and planters also often dealt with more than one store. But the evidence from both merchant account books and court judgments indicates that other merchants accepted similar individual quantities of tobacco for payments of store debts.

Small producers may have dominated in terms of both numbers and volume of production, but there were many planters who produced large quantities of tobacco and had the potential to practice conspicuous consumption. During the period 1770–1800, 28 percent of 240 inventories indicated a specific quantity or value of tobacco greater than three hogsheads. The earliest instance of producing more than 10,000 pounds of tobacco in a single year occurred in 1753 in Amelia County. Among the many planters who produced large quantities of tobacco were John Smith of Pocket Plantation in Pittsylvania County, the ever-present Matthew Marable of Mecklenburg County, and Owen Myrick of Brunswick County. Smith shipped over 17,000 pounds of tobacco to the fall zone during a seven-month period in 1766 and over 26,000 pounds during a twelve-month period in 1772–73. Marable may have produced in excess of 40,000 pounds of tobacco on his four plantations in 1773, if his calculations may be believed. Myrick had 22,320 pounds of tobacco "on hand" in 1796.[28]

If the more extensive land use suggested by the relative abundance of land and the suspicious work ethic of planters implied by contemporary Southside observers was correct, then tobacco production per worker should not have been impressive. Previous estimates of tobacco production per worker in Virginia during the latter half of the eighteenth century ranged from 1,000 pounds to 2,700 pounds.[29] Such information was available for only two Southside plantations. If they were representative of the region, then production per hand usually fell into the low-average category for the period. On the Mecklenburg County plantation of Thomas Murry, each worker produced 1,386 pounds in 1780, 751 pounds in 1781, 811 pounds in 1782, 1,520 pounds in 1783, and 1,229 pounds in 1784.[30] On Matthew Marable's Finny Wood plantation, located along the county border of Charlotte and Mecklenburg, twenty-eight workers were expected to produce 30,000 pounds of tobacco in 1773 on land that "has ever distinguished itself as being remarkably fine."[31] These figures ranged from slightly higher to slightly lower than similar production efforts in the Maryland Tidewater during the same period.[32]

Primary staple prices were notoriously variable and mainly responsible for the endemic economic instability in such economies. Since Southside tobacco was produced exclusively for export, the primary variables determining prices for the local product were external in location. These variables that were often interrelated were financial crises or wars involving Britain or other market countries, fluctuating exchange rates, the institution of government regulations, and shifts in the marketing structure. Among the external factors that caused depression in the Virginia tobacco market were the French and Indian War, financial crises in Britain in 1761 and 1772, and the currency crisis and high exchange rates during the mid-1760s.[33] One of the most important external factors that kept the tobacco economy healthy in the 1730s and 1740s was the Tobacco Inspection Act of 1730, which improved the quality of tobacco by eliminating inferior quality tobacco from the market. It also forced marginal producers out of the market and toward wheat cultivation. The Scottish system of direct buying also resulted in higher prices for Southside producers. The Scots could give higher prices because of their profits on the store goods they exchanged for tobacco and the additional financial support from a variety of other economic activities both at home and abroad. Observation of such prices led one Tidewater planter to comment that the Scots "have some secrets in the Tobo. Trade, that you & I are unacquainted with, or they could not give such prices here & carry all before as they do."[34]

Local influences on tobacco prices were usually overproduction and weather. Overproduction, brought on by good weather and planter confidence, resulted in a glut on the market that resulted in sharply reduced prices. Overproduction in 1752 resulted in reduced prices and a credit crisis. An extended period of dry weather during the growing season during the late 1760s created a shortage of tobacco and forced up prices. Severe drought could also result in such poor quality that prices were lowered to a point detrimental to the economy. A spring drought in 1758 destroyed most of the young seedlings and resulted in one planter in the central Piedmont county of Louisa making not a single pound of tobacco on a plantation where he usually would expect to harvest 25,000 pounds. During the late 1750s and early 1760s, heavy late summer rains created mold and rot that destroyed part of the crop.[35]

Whether tobacco was purchased for cash or exchanged for store goods also influenced the price of the crop at the local level. Tobacco brought a higher price if exchanged for store goods. For example, in 1773 a Bedford County merchant paid 18s. Virginia currency per hundredweight to satisfy store debts but only 16s. 8d. Virginia currency for an outright cash purchase.[36] In 1789 tobacco sold for 17s. and 18s. for cash and 19s. and 20s. for store goods.[37] The merchant might also lower the price offered for tobacco if the planter wished to dispose of additional commodities such as furs, skins, beef, or pork.

Appendix B summarizes the boom-and-bust character of tobacco production in the Southside. Tobacco prices before 1750 are probably not very reliable because of the small sample. Tobacco prices during the 1730s and 1740s were generally high, probably because of the influence of the Inspection Act, the relatively low exchange rates, and the freedom from overproduction in the developing region. Prices from 1750 to the Revolutionary War were highly erratic in response to a variety of influences. Prices were generally low from 1750 to the late 1760s because of a combination of overproduction, the French and Indian War, the financial crisis of 1761, the currency crisis of the early and mid-1760s, high exchange rates, and some unfavorable weather conditions. Prices bottomed out at under one pence sterling per pound from 1763 to 1765. The exchange rate averaged 60 percent during this period. Prices began to increase in 1766 and reached a high average of 2.18 pence sterling per pound in 1769. These increases were primarily in response to the great reduction in the exchange rate and several dry years that created short crops and increased demand. Prices were generally stable until 1773, when the bank crisis of Britain forced prices downward. This financial crisis awakened Scottish merchants to the huge debts owed to them from years of granting easy credit. Their response was to call in the debts and tighten additional credit to planters.[38] Merchants were not likely to pay high prices for tobacco under these circumstances. Prices increased in 1775 in response to the impending political break between colony and mother country that would create severe shortages in the tobacco supply and to the lowering of the exchange rate.

Prices after 1775 are not as reliable as in previous periods because of the fluctuating values of local paper currency and the lack of equivalent sterling values. Tobacco prices did, of course, continue to fluctuate. Inflation during the Revolutionary War that reached 1,000 percent in December of 1781 drove tobacco prices to unprecedented high levels. Following the war, tobacco prices declined but remained relatively high and stable until the early 1790s. The low prices during the early 1790s drove some Halifax County planters to petition the legislature that they were "burdened & discouraged by the present reduced price of that commodity [tobacco]."[39] Prices then increased through the mid-1790s, averaging a peak of 6.5 pence per pound in 1798. Lewis Gray attributed these high prices to a decline in tobacco production brought on by increased wheat cultivation. Prices in 1800, however, dropped precipitously to an average of 2.6 pence per pound.

Wheat

When considering agriculture in eighteenth-century Virginia, wheat cultivation must always be approached in the context of tobacco production. Wheat was always being suggested as the appropriate crop to replace tobacco and end the destruction of soil and the uncertainty of prices in the foreign-controlled marketing system of the dominant crop. Several factors were responsible for the changeover to wheat that was ongoing throughout the eighteenth century. Wheat could be grown on worn-out tobacco land, needed less labor, could be grown in conjunction with tobacco, was stimulated by crop failures in southern Europe during midcentury, and prices kept rising at a rate that made it more profitable than tobacco. From 1742 to 1772, the average annual value of tobacco to grain exports in Virginia declined from a ratio of 14:1 to 4:1.[40] Wheat challenged or replaced tobacco as the dominant crop by following the same Tidewater to Piedmont pattern of the original expansion of tobacco; that is, with the exception of Southside Virginia. With wheat positioned as the leading commercial crop in most of the state, the region's share of the state's tobacco production continued to increase, reaching 62 percent by 1840.[41]

Although wheat was not a commercial rival to tobacco in the Southside, it was nevertheless cultivated throughout the region. It was grown during the period of early settlement and expanded in production over time. During the 1730s and 1750s, wheat was listed in 11 percent of Brunswick County inventories (Table 3-1). Grist mills were also common on the Southside landscape, if county court proceedings are any measure. Any individual who considered erecting a mill had to have the permission of the court since that construction, especially the damming of streams, was likely to affect other residents and activities in the area. By the 1790s wheat had increased to a level that found it present in 21 percent of Brunswick's inventories, 22 percent of Amelia's, and 16 percent of Mecklenburg's.

The expansion in the more eastern counties was also indicated by one traveler's observations in 1791. Congressman Smith was especially impressed with the abundance of wheat fields in the counties of Amelia, Prince Edward, and northeastern Charlotte. Whether his many laudatory remarks on wheat fields and his lack of comment on tobacco suggested that wheat had replaced tobacco or that he simply had a negative bias toward the dominant staple and simply dismissed it is not known.[42]

Wheat cultivation west of the Staunton River lagged well behind the more eastern counties (Table 3-1). Based on accounts in Halifax and Pittsylvania County court judgments, wheat comprised less than 1 percent of payments to country-store accounts from the 1750s through the 1770s. Individual store accounts document a similar picture. During two separate years, 1770–71 and 1774–75, the Scottish firm of James Murdoch and Company recorded no remittances of wheat nor did they purchase any of that staple at their store in northeastern Halifax County. But there was also evidence of change. Wheat comprised 12 percent, or a value of £129 4s., of total payments to one Pittsylvania County store in 1799–1800.[43] The legislation of flour inspections at Meadsville and Danville during the 1790s also suggests increased wheat production, although neither apparently ever functioned.

Wheat was a component of the plantation economy in Southside Virginia. The increases in wheat production were not associated with any increase in the number of yeomen farmers but rather with continuation in existing practices in plantation operations. Unlike most other areas of Virginia, there was no change in crop dominance. Wheat "coexisted" subserviently with tobacco, and slaves were still the primary labor force.[44] For example, the estate inventory of Amelia County planter Benjamin Crawley listed 265 bushels of wheat along with sixty slaves and almost 10,000 pounds of tobacco in 1794. Richard Eggleston's inventory listed 700 bushels of wheat and forty-five slaves on his plantation in the same county in 1796. The Brunswick County plantation of Benjamin Haskins held over 200 bushels of wheat, at least 10,000 pounds of tobacco, and fifty-three slaves.[45] West of the Staunton River, the inventory of William Watkins contained 111 bushels of wheat and twenty-one slaves in 1794.[46]

If Southside Virginia was increasing its wheat production and tobacco was destroying the land, or as Roger Atkinson noted, "tobacco does not grow as kindly as formerly it used to do,"[47] then why did wheat not challenge the hegemony of tobacco production? Atkinson suggested some kind of regional inertia. He observed that tobacco producers stated they would grow wheat if the price reached 2s. 6d. per bushel. However, when the price reached 5s. per bushel, according to Atkinson, planters still grew tobacco. That inertia came from a marketing system that diluted innovation by taking care of all the needs of the planters—easy credit, store goods, transportation, and a variety of financial services. If the dominance of local and long-distance merchants created economic rebellion, especially if the constant debt became overwhelming, the reformer then came into conflict with his landlocked position, his economic control by Petersburg and foreign markets, and his inadequate infrastructure that could only support tobacco. Efforts at developing other sectors of the economy, such as secondary and tertiary activities, were always challenged by the strong inertial character of the dominant tobacco.

Secondary Economic Activity

The dominance of the primary staple, tobacco, created a domino effect on the rest of the Southside economy. Because tobacco was shipped from the region without any processing and was exchanged for European manufactured goods, there was little necessity or opportunity for local processing. The potential regional manufacturers— those individuals with the most economic and political power, those with the greatest access to venture capital, and those with lifelong experience at everyday decision making—were the tobacco planters who committed themselves to the continuation of the tobacco economy. Potential investors in manufacturing from external locations, whether based at the fall zone or in Great Britain, traced their financial success to the maintenance of the tobacco trade. Manufacturing in the Southside, because it always took place within the large shadow of the primary staple economy, was poorly developed. Most processing actually took place on the plantation, although numerous decentralized, low-level activities were scattered throughout the region.

Tench Coxe's manufacturing census of 1810 provides a general summary of the weakness of the secondary economy of the Southside at the end of the eighteenth century. The region ranked high only in those types of manufacturing that could be undertaken on plantations. Several Southside counties ranked high in the production of "flaxen goods in families," "cotton goods in families," distilleries, and in the number of looms and spinning wheels. Pittsylvania ranked fifth among Virginia counties in number of pairs of shoes produced; Patrick County was rated third in number of tanneries; Prince Edward was second in quantity of soap and candles produced. However, there were no tobacco manufacturers, no flaxseed oil mills, no forges, few fulling mills and sawmills, and most importantly, only one county, Amelia, had commercially significant flour mills.

Secondary economic activity was focused on the plantation because it contained or had access to the requisite investment capital necessary to finance manufacturing development and held the labor necessary to produce manufactured goods. This locational dominance may be best seen in milling activities. Contrary to Coxe's data, the most common type of processing in the Southside was the manufacture of wheat into flour. Because of the need to own or have access to appropriate stream sites, to provide capital for mill and millrace construction, and to be able to afford or own the necessary labor, most mill owners had to possess substantial wealth. In the primary staple economy of the Southside, this meant that milling activities were located primarily on plantations. Of 135 mill owners who left records, 84 percent could be identified with at least 200 acres of land and at least three slaves. Only three mill owners did not own land and only eleven did not own at least one slave. The median size of landholdings was just over 500 acres. Of the forty-seven mill operators who left estate inventories, one-half were valued over £1,000; almost 70 percent were valued over £500.

Although mills were plentiful in all areas of the Southside, Coxe listed only Amelia County as a commercial producer of flour. Both Amelia's production (3,895 barrels of flour) and value of production (over $31,000) ranked twenty-ninth among the state's counties. Petitions against proposed navigational improvements on the Appomattox River also suggest the importance of the county's mills. One 1787 petition summarized the prevailing sentiment: "We trust your honors that you will never indulge so chimerical a business, at the expense of our best and first of convenience, the River mills."[48]

Secondary economic activities were also concentrated on the plantation as a function of the orientation toward the self-sufficiency of the region's dominant focal point. Containing the greatest regional concentrations of both labor and market, and requiring relatively few specialized manufactured products, the plantation housed much of the region's processing activities. Because of the rudimentary character of secondary activities and considering that larger plantations also had slaves who performed more specialized jobs, much of the blacksmith, cooper, wheelwright, and cobbler work, carpentry, carding and spinning of wool and cotton, spinning of flax, and construction of clothes was performed on the plantations.

Despite the strong concentration of secondary activities on plantations and the fewer manufacturing demands that tobacco placed on the region, there were nevertheless numerous individuals engaged exclusively in some form of processing. The relatively large number of these manufacturing specialists, usually located on their small landholdings or on small portions of large landholdings through lease arrangements, were dependent on work tasks provided by large planters. Although these small manufacturers existed as appendages of the dominant tobacco economy, they provided, by virtue of their local orientation, a departure from the linkages of the primary staple economy with distant suppliers of manufactured goods. These craftsmen were usually carpenters and blacksmiths, with tailors, coopers, wheelwrights, cobblers, saddlers, and hatters also represented. Carpenters did a variety of small building tasks and repair work, but also frequently built entire plantations, from plantation house and furniture to slave quarters and other outbuildings. For example, Bryant Ferguson of Charlotte County built a dwelling house, barn, spring house, milk house, corn crib, slave quarters, chest, and table, and sawed 500 feet of white oak plank in 1765 for Nathaniel Barrett for £87 3s. 9d. He had previously, in 1764, constructed a smoke house, kitchen, corn crib, hen house, and spring-house facilities for Baker DeGraffenreid.[49] Blacksmiths made hoes, axes, hatchets, chisels, nails, horseshoes, and other items, although most of their work was in mending old plantation implements and shoeing horses. Over the period 1763–64, Henry Caldwell made an ax and bell, and repaired hoes and both the wood and metal parts of a great plow for Thomas Pollet at a cost of £1 19s. 5d.[50]

Although occasionally paid cash for their efforts, craftsmen were more likely to be paid in goods from the store where the planter for whom they had provided their skilled labor had an account, or in tobacco or cash from third parties indebted to their customer. This type of third-party debt permitted the non-tobacco-producer to function in this plantation-dominated economy. As indicated in Jean Russo's study of Maryland's Eastern Shore, these skilled workers fitted very neatly into the barter system characteristic of formative periods of development and in areas with primary staple production.

Although there were a variety of manufacturing activities in the Southside, they produced strictly for consumption within the region. Not only was the trade in these goods intraregional, the exchange system was primarily localized within sections of counties. Because manufacturing was heavily dependent on tobacco production, it only functioned in a supportive capacity. The plantation was the focus of manufacturing activity because it had access to capital for investment, especially in costly ventures such as mills, because it had access to avenues of credit to support independent craftsmen, such as carpenters and blacksmiths, and because it possessed a large labor force that could be used for processing activities, primarily cooper work to supply the hogsheads for tobacco shipment, carpentry, and blacksmithing. The most ironic aspect of the Southside's secondary economy, and most illuminating when considering Earle and Hoffman's staple thesis, was the importance of wheat processing in the region. But only in Amelia County was this processing linked to interregional trade; only in Amelia County did milling activities bring money into the region. This situation paralleled the subservient role of wheat to tobacco discussed in the previous section on agriculture.

Tertiary Economic Activity

The majority of tertiary activities were associated with the marketing of the primary staple tobacco. There were three components of this long-distance trade—the plantation, the entrepôt, and the country store. The dominant movement was the transfer of tobacco from the backcountry plantation where it was produced to an entrepôt where it was inspected and exported. Although tobacco physically rarely passed through the country store in this system, the store was the organizational focus of the tertiary economy at the local level. Based on the purchase price of the tobacco, which was transferred to the credit side of the planter's account, the country store made available easy credit for consumer goods; provided cash loans; and made payments of cash, goods, and services to satisfy debts to third parties.

Tobacco Marketing System

The expansion of tobacco into the Virginia backcountry created a new marketing system. Because of its interior location, the backcountry was both distant from the focus of the marketing system in the Tidewater region and inaccessible from that region by continuous water transportation. Scottish mercantile companies, through their backcountry store systems, quickly filled this trading breach. The focus of their shipping and wholesaling activities was the fall zone, the link between water and land transportation. With inspection warehouses for backcountry tobacco also positioned at these locations, fall-zone towns began their dominance of backcountry trade that would, through the continuation of long-distance trade, lead to their preemption of town functions in the Southside.

Prior to the expansion of tobacco into the backcountry, most of the product was marketed through the consignment system. This marketing system was designed more for the larger and wealthier Tidewater producers, who had greater access to navigable waterways. Under the consignment system the local planter assumed responsibility for all shipping costs. An agent, usually in London, sold the tobacco for the planter and with the proceeds paid the various costs associated with shipping and storing the product, extracted his fee for services rendered, and used the balance to purchase goods for the planter. Because Southside planters were small producers and were located too distant from points of continuous ocean communication, little effort was made by the English-dominated consignment traders to tap this new source of tobacco. However, the trade may have continued through the efforts of a very few wealthier Southside planters. Peyton Skipwith, of Prestwould Plantation in Mecklenburg County, shipped eighty-seven hogsheads of tobacco directly to London between 1773 and 1775. Mecklenburg planter-playwright, Robert Munford, shipped thirty-seven hogsheads to England in 1773.[51]

Southside tobacco was marketed through a direct purchasing system in which local country-store merchants with trading connections at the fall-zone entrepôts exchanged manufactured goods and services for the tobacco of the primarily small backcountry producers. These stores were operated either by local planter-merchants or Scottish merchants in the employ of Glasgow trading companies. The overall operations of Scottish stores were supervised by factors, or managers, located at the fall zone. Lesser factors supervised the operations of one or more stores in the backcountry. Two or more storekeepers for each store completed the complement of mercantile personnel in the backcountry. But even local independent merchants usually had to deal with Scottish buyers and wholesalers before, during, and after the Revolutionary War. If the Union between Scotland and England in 1707 initiated legal trade with North America, it was the expansion of tobacco into the Piedmont of Virginia that shredded the linkages with the old consignment system and brought Scotland into trading prominence.

The Scots filled the backcountry trading void so successfully because of several business advantages. Their mercantile firms were able to expand because of early infusions of capital from wealthy landowners, banks, and merchants in Scotland. They could offer higher prices for tobacco and extend more credit in Virginia because of their connections and even incorporations with manufacturing and shipbuilding concerns that enabled them to cut costs on manufactured goods and Atlantic transport. Their trading system in Virginia was more competitive because of a better business organization, especially the factor system that had tobacco warehoused and ready for export when ships arrived, and a solid work ethic that permitted a greater volume of business that, combined with as much as a week's advantage in shipping time compared to southern English ports, resulted in a faster turnaround time from unloading goods to sailing with tobacco. The final link in the system was the profitable reexporting of Virginia tobacco from Scotland to the primary market in France.[52]

Based on their landlocked position, geographic proximity, and trading precedents established by the deerskin trade, the fall-zone areas of the Appomattox and James Rivers were the "natural" trading outlets for Southside Virginia. This most favorable geographic and historical status was further strengthened in 1730 with the creation of a tobacco inspection system. The Tobacco Act of 1730 not only regulated the quality of tobacco by requiring every hogshead to be opened and inspected before export, but also assigned producers in particular landlocked counties to specific fall-zone inspection warehouses. In addition, the use of tobacco notes, also created by the Tobacco Act, was structured geographically with circulation in counties contiguous to the location of the inspection granting the notes. Precedent for this was established in 1735 when notes from Shockoes, at the site of Richmond, were permitted circulation in Amelia County; and in 1742, when notes from Lawrences, in the Tidewater county of Nansemond, were allowed to circulate in Brunswick County.[53]

As new Southside counties were carved from the original two counties, they were assigned to specific inspection warehouses. Most of the Southside counties were required to market their tobacco in Petersburg and at sites in nearby Chesterfield County (Figs. 3-1 and 3-2). In 1776, for example, the inspection points, all high-volume warehouses, were Bollings Point, Bollingbroke, Cedar Point, Boyds, Davis, and Blandford at or near Petersburg; and Carys, Warwick, Osbornes, and Manchester (Rocky Ridge) in Chesterfield County. Counties that

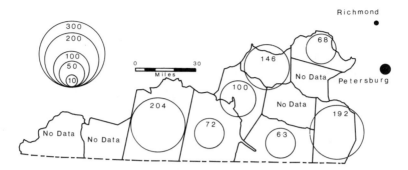

Figure 3-1. Tobacco trade with Petersburg, 1750–1800 (number of hogs-heads). *Source*: County court judgments and will books; account books; personal papers.

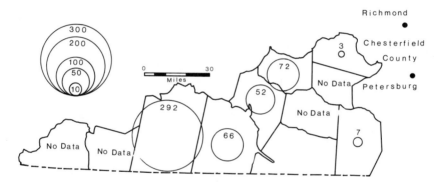

Figure 3-2. Tobacco trade with Chesterfield County, 1750–1800 (number of hogsheads). *Source*: County court judgments and will books; account books; personal papers.

did not conform entirely to the dominant pattern were Brunswick, located farther eastward, and Prince Edward, with a more northern location. In addition to marketing tobacco in Petersburg, Brunswick producers could also ship their product to the Tidewater counties of Surry and Nansemond. Brunswick was thus shut out of both the Chesterfield County and Richmond warehouses (Figs. 3-2 and 3-3). Prince Edward County, in addition to Petersburg and Chesterfield, could also market tobacco at the Richmond warehouses, primarily the Byrd's and Shockoe inspections. Figures 3-1, 3-2, and 3-3 show the dominance of Petersburg, the strong position of Chesterfield County, and the lower standing of Richmond.

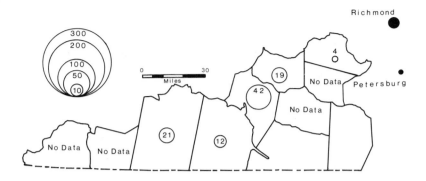

Figure 3-3. Tobacco trade with Richmond, 1750–1800 (number of hogsheads). *Source:* County court judgments and will books; account books; personal papers.

The legislation of eight inspections in the Southside during the 1790s had little influence on the dominant long-distance marketing system as long as tobacco continued to be exported. Southside-inspected tobacco still had to pass through the fall-zone entrepôts for export and by law could be reinspected at these sites. During the same period, when five Southside warehouses each were inspecting from 144,000 to 240,000 pounds of tobacco annually, Petersburg was inspecting over 30 million pounds and tobacco was piling up in the streets for lack of inspection and storage space. Southside planters, although desiring more local control over the marketing system, had to give in to the old trading structure, as is indicated by a petition from Mecklenburg County pleading for more warehouses in Petersburg.[54]

The marketing structure was reinforced by the location of British merchants. Wholesale merchants who traded with the Southside located factors, stores, and warehouses in Petersburg and Chesterfield County. Merchants with an interest in the central Piedmont were more likely to locate in Richmond. Because of this concentration of inspection warehouses and wholesale merchants, other trade followed the dominant long-distance market flow. Cattle and hog drives and the marketing of other Southside agricultural products were more likely to be shipped to Petersburg and Chesterfield than to Richmond. Based on this traditional, prescriptive, and layered trading structure, Norfolk was rarely involved in trade with the Southside.

Transport System

One of the critical points of the staple thesis is that the marketing of a primary staple made few demands on the regional transportation system. This was certainly the case with tobacco carriage in Southside Virginia. Indeed, the system had difficulty even servicing this less-demanding staple. In addition to the reticent character of tobacco, distance, physical environment, and the lack of revenue and organization to build or improve roads made the marketing procedure even more difficult. Although tobacco may not have made heavy demands on the transport system, that is not to say that this relationship was not complex.

The transport of tobacco to market was a five-step operation. The making of hogsheads, the bringing in order of the tobacco, and the packing, or prizing, of the product took place on the plantation. The carriage of tobacco between the backcountry plantation and the fall-zone warehouses, and the reception of tobacco at the latter sites, completed the marketing operations. Hogsheads, or large barrels, were the containers in which tobacco was stored and transported. If of acceptable quality and properly packed, the tobacco would remain in the same container from the plantation until it was removed for manufacturing in Europe. Because specialized coopers appear to have been rare at any time in the region, the hogsheads were usually constructed on the plantation premises by the planter, slaves, or part-time help. In 1730, with the initiation of the tobacco inspection system, hogsheads had to contain at least 800 pounds of tobacco. In the Southside hogsheads averaged over 1,000 pounds of tobacco from the middle 1760s, and by the end of the century averaged just over 1,100 pounds. Although the dimensions of the container varied as much as the weight of the tobacco, most hogsheads were close to 48 inches in length and 30 inches in diameter at the head.[55]

In order to be packaged in the hogshead for travel, the tobacco had to be in order, or in a condition to permit handling. This was a softening of the tobacco from its more brittle condition after curing. This new condition was accomplished by increasing humidity and decreasing temperature either from natural circumstances or from placing the tobacco in a covered pit or basement. Prizing of the tobacco was simply the packaging of the staple in the hogshead. By this process the tobacco was pressed into the hogshead by a screw or lever device to reduce the area of the tobacco and enable more of the product to be packaged, and to make the hogshead less vulnerable to accidents because of poor balance. This was not a simple matter, for it was common for hogsheads to be damaged or not approved at inspections because of poor prizing.

Southsiders had three methods of transporting tobacco to market—

rolling, wagoning, and boating. The majority of Southside tobacco was transported in wagons, rolling ranked second, and the use of rivers was a distant third. The rolling of hogsheads was the simplest method of transporting tobacco. In its simplest form, shafts were affixed to each end of the hogshead and it was rolled on its hoops by a person or pulled by a draft animal. An improvement on this technique removed the direct connection between the hogshead and the surface of the road by attaching wheels to the hogshead. The persistence of rolling into the early nineteenth century suggests the enduring primitive character of the transport system. More efficient and more common were carts and wagons. Wagons usually carried two hogsheads each and were either owned by the planter or a professional wagoner. Several small planters might also share a common wagon for this duty.

The means of water transport were either two canoes that were attached at their sides or flat-bottom boats known as *batteaux*. The canoes held from five to ten hogsheads, while the latter conveyance could carry five to eight hogsheads.[56] But water could not be an important means of transport in a region where the largest drainage system, the Roanoke, flowed away from Petersburg into North Carolina. The planters of Amelia and Prince Edward, however, used the Appomattox, and a few Pittsylvania County planters who dealt with mercantile companies having stores in Lynchburg, and previously at Lynch's Ferry, shipped via the James River.

There were many perils between plantation and inspection warehouse that defied the simple linear pattern of the trading system. Most common were the problems associated with the clay roadbeds that could become quagmires and cripple all movement. Although spring was the obvious season associated with transport problems, heavy rains could occur at any time. Travelers, local planters, and early agricultural reformers were particularly aware of the inadequacies of the region's overland transport system. In 1791 Congressman Smith speculated that the roads of Amelia County, dry at that time, were probably impassable in periods of more inclement weather. Smith described a section of the main road in Halifax County as consisting "of stumps, roots, stones, gullies, steep hills, and everything which can compose an execrable road." A letter from Mecklenburg County written in 1811 expressed concern that a proposed new road should be constructed (if possible) on gray, gravelly, and sandy land and should "shun all that mountainous [hilly] red land about the forks of Meherrin and Nottoway Rivers." Concerning existing conditions, the writer stated that "The old road is too well known for me to undertake a description of it to any person living in this section of the country, indeed it may be said that there is no road."[57] A Mecklenburg planter stated perhaps the region's most common expression in regard to the shipping of tobacco: "As soon as roads are in order, shall send more tobacco."[58]

It was not only the combination of water, clay, and topography that made travel difficult. Frozen winter roads, an important condition of travel in order to avoid the spring quagmires, could literally tear wagons and hogsheads apart. Human error in conjunction with severe natural conditions often created a great adventure out of the trek to market. Poorly made hogsheads fell apart, exposing the tobacco to the elements; poorly prized tobacco did not usually pass inspection and had to be reinspected at the producer's expense; and tobacco was packed too high in order and fermented or it was not packed in proper order and did not hold up under the rigors of freighting. At the fall zone, inspection warehouses also closed periodically for workers to give attention to their own crops and at other times were so crowded that it was difficult to get tobacco inspected.[59]

The experiences of one Southside planter suggest the difficulty and frustration experienced in moving tobacco from the distant backcountry to the fall zone. John Smith, owner of Pocket Plantation in northern Pittsylvania County, dealt directly with two different Scottish mercantile firms at Manchester in Chesterfield County, across the James from Richmond. He used plantation slaves and local wagoners to carry tobacco to fall-zone inspections and to bring backloads of store goods to the plantation. In April of 1768 none of Smith's six hogsheads of tobacco made it past inspection. Three were left behind on the road and the remainder were rejected for being poorly prized. In November of that year, an additional two hogsheads did not pass inspection because of improper prizing. Other tobacco passed inspection but the price was below expectation because of "mismanagement in prizing." At another time Smith paid an additional £8 12s. to hang and dry eight hogsheads of tobacco damaged by water. Even his trusted factor could be a problem. On one occasion he advised Smith to wagon all his tobacco because it arrived in better shape. Later he said that rolling was preferable. Did Smith finally find the best means of transport, when in July of 1771, twenty-five of twenty-six hogsheads shipped on the James arrived without damage, or was that success merely the law of averages in operation?[60]

Transportation Costs

Transportation costs included the freight rates or the actual costs of transporting the particular commodity; food and supplies for wagoners, rollers, and horses; and tolls for ferries. Freight rates were dependent on several variables—distance of the trip, whether tobacco was rolled or wagoned, the weight of the hogshead, and whether it was the movement of an agricultural commodity to the fall zone or the transport of goods to the backcountry. Because distance from the fall zone was the most critical cost factor, the more interior counties, especially those west of the Staunton River, were at a decided disadvantage in the marketplace. William Tatham stated that the cost of carrying one hogshead of tobacco 100 miles was £2 Virginia currency in the latter part of the century.[61] Although additional factors of a local and individual nature could create variations in these rates, Tatham's rate provides a sound working figure for carriage costs. During the early 1760s the cost of wagoning one hogshead from the more distant Halifax County to Petersburg was £1 5s.; from Amelia County the rate was only 10s.[62] In 1785 the rate for rolling one hogshead from Mecklenburg County to Petersburg was £1 4s., while the rate from more distant Pittsylvania County to Petersburg was as high as £3 3s. 9d. in the same year.

It cost more to transport one hogshead by wagon than by rolling even though the former method carried two hogsheads. In 1750 the rate for rolling a hogshead from Brunswick County to Petersburg was 5s. while the rate for wagoning one hogshead was 10s. In Pittsylvania County the rate was £1 15s. to wagon one hogshead in 1766 and 12s. 6d. to roll one hogshead in 1769. In 1792 the rate for wagoning was £2 5s. and in 1793, £1 16s. for rolling in that same county. However, this differential did not exist at other times. In Pittsylvania in 1785, rolling ranged from £3 3s. 7d. to £3 13s. 9d. per hogshead, and in 1787 the rate for wagoning was £3 15s. per hogshead. Rates for wagoning sharply escalated in the late 1790s, rising to £6 1s. 6d. per hogshead in Pittsylvania. No information was available for rolling rates during that period.

Because of the infrequent marketing of wheat at distant fall-zone sites, freight rates were available for only one Southside transaction during the eighteenth century. A Pittsylvania merchant paid 5s. per hundredweight, or just over £14, to ship 93½ bushels (or 5,610 pounds) of wheat in 1799. In 1800 the same merchant paid 4s. per hundred, or £6 17s. 9d., to transport 3,440 pounds.[63] Based on prices ranging from 6s. to 8s. 3d. per bushel, freight rates alone absorbed over half of the market value of the staple. This relatively good profit may have been the explanation for its market entry. Wheat normally did not perform that well against the costs of transport. As late as 1820s, wheat was not a viable commercial crop because shipping costs often exceeded the market value.[64] Earlier, Petersburg merchant David Ross advised against the cultivation of wheat because it was a commodity of small value that was subject to damage over long hauls, and its bulk made carriage and storage expensive. He further suggested that wheat production should take place at locations convenient to the fall zone.[65] These observations support Earle and Hoffman's calculations of the maximum distance from the fall zone that commercial wheat could be profitably grown.[66] That distance extended only to the central sections of Lunenburg and Prince Edward counties during the period preceding the Revolutionary War. Beyond this distance were Mecklenburg, Charlotte, and all the counties west of the Staunton River.

Additional expenses associated with carrying backcountry commodities to the fall-zone markets, usually food for wagoners and horses, could increase transport costs as much as 25 percent. A southern Pittsylvania County planter had additional expenses of £1 11s. 3d., £3 4s. 3d., and £3 10s. 9d. on three separate livestock drives to Petersburg in the mid-1780s and early 1790s. On another occasion, the same planter allocated 86 pounds of beef for the use of the wagoners.[67] The total costs of transporting one hogshead of tobacco from the Lynchburg area to Richmond in 1799 were £5 0s. 7d., comprising £4 0s. 8d. for freighting a 1,195-pound hogshead, 11s. 6d. for 10 pounds of bacon and meal, 4s. 8d. for warehouse costs, and 3s. 9d. for ferriages.[68] Presumably, from the lack of information on the feeding and care of animals, actual additional costs were even greater.

Wagoners and Keepers of Ordinaries and Taverns

Because of the dominance of long-distance trade, wagoners were critical to the economy of the Southside and were in great demand despite the relatively reduced demands of the dominant primary staple. Wagons carried tobacco, wheat, corn, salted meat products, hemp, and other commercial products to fall-zone markets. Wagons were also the primary means of carrying European goods from the fall zone to country stores and plantations in the backcountry.

Wagoners were a varied lot. Many conformed to the traditional characterization of crude, nomadic, and strongly individualistic types with few material possessions. Certainly the Southside had an ample supply of such characters. Wagoners engaged by John Smith of Pocket Plantation precariously packed goods, overturned wagons, left hogsheads of tobacco along the roads, and were generally unreliable. But other wagoners evidenced a high degree of stability, owning land and slaves, living in the community for long periods of time, and in some instances operating other businesses such as stores and ferries. Some wagoners were planters who, because of ownership of a wagon, provided hauling services for other planters. Many planters had the potential to do this because wagons and carts were common items in estate inventories. For example, during the 1770s, 44 percent of Amelia County's estate inventories listed a wagon or cart. The availability of wagons in other counties ranged from 37 to 18 percent during that period; for the 1790s, the range was 56 to 32 percent for five counties.

The strong community ties of some wagoners and their drive for personal financial improvement are revealed in the region's land records. Thirty-four percent of those forty-four wagoners (out of 104 recognized wagoners) who could be identified with land records in the period 1765 to 1800 owned over 1,000 acres, and only 2 percent owned no land. Of the twenty-six wagoners who could be identified with slave records, twenty owned slaves. Both the number of wagoners and their level of wealth would rise dramatically if more than "wagoner" status were used. With his command of wagons and wagoners, John Smith, planter, was also in the transport business.

The business arrangements between wagoner and employer showed great variation. Some wagoners hired themselves out to anyone, while others worked primarily for one person. The Scottish firm of James Murdoch and Company employed at least eleven wagoners during the 1770–71 business year at their store in Halifax County. John Smith employed at least nineteen wagoners between 1766 and 1773 and in addition, like other large planters, had at least two slaves who drove wagons to the fall zone. Conversely, one wagoner did almost all the carriage work for Edward Dromgoole's Sligo store in Brunswick County during 1791–92.

As traveler John Smyth noted in 1784, there was little or no distinction among inns, taverns, ordinaries, and public houses in Virginia.[69] In the Southside the most common designation for places that provided overnight accommodations for travelers and food and shelter for their animals was the "ordinary." Although the term "tavern" was rarely used before the post-Revolutionary period, this designation became virtually interchangeable with the "ordinary" in the postwar period. On his trip across the Southside in 1791, Congressman Smith used the term "tavern" to refer to the numerous places he stopped for food, drink, socializing, and overnight accommodations. Although Smyth suggested that three-fourths of the ordinaries and taverns were little better than shelters, and other travelers may have been less generous in their appraisal, the most interesting descriptions came from that thorough observer of the Southside landscape, Congressman Smith. Commenting on his place of retirement one evening,

> I put up this night at one Pridie's, a sorry tavern; I had for company an idiot, the landlord's brother, who was himself but one remove from it, and I was waited on by an ugly broken backed old negro woman. My fare was indifferent, and as I was kept awake a great part of the night by bugs and fleas, and the united groaning and grunting of the hogs under the window, and my man Ben in the chamber with me; all this agreeable music was enlivened by; perpetual peals of thunder and the rattling of heavy rain on the shingles over my head, which continued nearly the whole night, and began just as I entered the tavern.[70]

What does not appear in Smith's commentaries is the additional function of an evening gathering place for locals. At certain ordinary-taverns, local planters spent evenings drinking, gambling, and entertaining. The Virginia legislature even had to legislate the distance between these establishments and regular dwellings because of raucous behavior. Ordinary-taverns also sold convenience goods such as rum, salt, sugar, and common types of cloth.[71]

Ordinary- and tavern-keepers came from a broad spectrum of Southside society. Almost destitute families opened their homes to travelers without understanding any of the amenities that they should have provided. Wealthy planters operated such establishments in part because of their command of property on major roads, at crossroads, and near ferries and courthouses. Planters also often rented these properties to other more narrowly oriented entrepreneurs. Planter-merchants and even Scottish merchants kept an ordinary either on the store premises or at a nearby location. These latter places seemed oriented more toward local entertainment and the creation of a higher level of clustering to increase the competitive level of the place for store goods than with overnight accommodations. While in North Carolina, traveler Smyth suggested a strong correlation between the occupation of innkeeper and military and political careers.

> Because by that public, but inferior station, their principles and persons became more generally known; and by the mixture and variety of company they conversed with, in the way of their business, their ideas and their ambitious views were more excited and extended than the generality of the honest and respectable planters, who remained in peace at their homes.[72]

This association did not appear to be that widespread in the Southside, but the idea may perhaps be an additional factor in wealthier planters' involvement in a variety of business activities. Numerous planter-merchants, who also operated ordinaries and other commercial activities, served as county justices and sheriffs, and even as representatives to the House of Burgesses. The Southside debt network suggests that individuals who wished to disseminate their views generally did this by increasing their mobility—that is, by visiting numerous ordinaries in the region—not by remaining sedentary.

Wealth Distribution

The economic organization of the Southside, which was based on the commercial production of tobacco, suggests that the region had distinctive wealth groups and important differences among levels of wealth. Most of the wealth differential was created by the ownership of numerous slaves by the larger tobacco producers. And because the region's economic organization was based on the development of successive western frontiers that placed a pioneer economy and a commercial agricultural economy within the same region, there were also significant subregional differences in the pattern of wealth distribution.[73]

The early Southside was characterized by the accumulation of little wealth by individuals. The process of settling and developing the land did not permit the rapid accumulation of property. For those destined for economic success, the purchase of substantial household items, luxury goods, and additional slaves and the diversification of business interests that would provide greater wealth took many years to accomplish. Capital was provided by selling land to new settlers; marketing natural and livestock products and tobacco; and perhaps operating a store, ordinary or grist mill or providing carriage services. The great majority of people had the bare necessities—shelter, cooking and eating utensils, clothes, a gun, a horse, and a few cattle and hogs. Others, both the destitute and the more affluent, continued the adjustment process by moving westward. This fluid character not only delayed the settling process, but also dictated against the accumulation of unnecessary, burdensome personal property.

The wealth structure for Brunswick and Amelia in the 1740s and 1750s reflected the continuing process of settlement and economic adjustment. For the 1740s, inventories for the two counties were valued very low, with three of four inventories valued at £100 or less and only five of the total of 104 valued greater than £500. During the 1750s, almost six of ten inventories were valued at £100 or less. But during this early period, there was still evidence of wealth accumulation. Amelia County had five inventories valued over £1,000 during the 1750s (Table 3-2).

Table 3-2.
Value of Southside Inventories (Personal Property) 1740–69

Virginia							
	Number of Inventories						
	1740-49		1750-59		1760-69		
£s	Brunswick	Amelia	Brunswick	Amelia	Brunswick	Amelia	Halifax
over 1,000	0	0	1	5	2	11	1
901–1,000	0	1	0	0	1	1	0
801–900	0	0	0	2	0	4	0
701–800	1	1	0	0	0	1	0
601–700	0	0	2	1	2	3	0
501–600	1	1	1	0	4	4	3
401–500	0	0	3	1	4	9	1
301–400	2	4	5	3	11	1	4
201–300	2	3	8	4	8	8	2
101–200	5	5	14	10	9	14	9
51–100	11	13	8	7	8	7	6
25–50	8	12	17	0	15	14	19
0.1–24	15	19	21	19	15	7	17
Total	45	59	80	52	79	84	62

Source: County will books.

Later decades continued the same trend of previous years. The older counties of Brunswick and Amelia continued to show an increase in individual wealth and the later settled, more interior counties possessed wealth characteristics similar to the older counties in previous decades. By the 1790s, 47 percent of Brunswick and Amelia inventories were valued higher than £500, 21 percent were higher than £1,000, and only 20 percent were valued at £100 or less. In the later settled counties, 35 percent of Halifax inventories and 40 percent of Pittsylvania inventories were valued at £100 or less, while the figures for inventories over £500 were 31 percent and 25 percent respectively (Table 3-4).

The wealth structure for the earlier decades was very similar to that of another eighteenth-century Virginia frontier region, the Shenandoah Valley.[74] But a strong trend developed that separated the two regions in later years. Southsiders accumulated wealth more quickly than did Valley settlers. A much greater number of Southside inventories were valued over £500 and over £1,000, and fewer Southside inventories were valued in the lower ranges (those valued at less than £50). The greater accumulation of wealth was most present in the three counties of Brunswick, Amelia, and Mecklenburg, where the percentage of inventories valued over £500 were 28, 26, and 32 respectively in the 1770s (Table 3-3). During the same period, the corresponding figures for three Shenandoah Valley counties—Augusta, Frederick, and Shenandoah—were 8 percent, 22 percent, and 6 percent. Augusta, Frederick, and Shenandoah had 46 percent, 41 percent, and 50 percent respectively of their inventories valued under £100, but Brunswick, Amelia, and Mecklenburg had only 25, 25, and 27 percent respectively for that category.

A second trend in the comparative wealth of individuals in the Southside and the Shenandoah Valley was the emergence in the 1780s and 1790s of the two interior Southside counties, Halifax and Pittsylvania, to surpass all the Shenandoah Valley counties in individual wealth. Through the 1770s, Halifax and Pittsylvania had been at parity with or below the Shenandoah counties in percentage of inventories over £1,000 and level with or above the Valley counties in inventories under £100. In the 1790s the percentage of inventories valued above £500 were 32 for Halifax and 25 for Pittsylvania. The corresponding percentages for four Valley counties were 19, 29, 11, and 6. The percentages of inventories valued under £100 for those two decades were lower in Halifax and Pittsylvania than in the Valley counties. During the 1790s the median value of Halifax inventories was over £200, greater than the highest Valley county, and Pittsylvania was higher than the middle-ranking Valley counties. All these were easily surpassed by the medians for Amelia, over £400, and for Brunswick, over £300.

Because the Southside was a more commercially oriented agricultural region and depended more on slave labor than the Shenandoah Valley, it should have had a greater range of wealth, with a greater percentage of wealthy, a greater percentage of poor, and a smaller middle-wealth group. This, however, was not entirely correct. It was true that the Southside had more of the very wealthy, but that was where the expected wealth characteristics ended. The Southside also had a considerably smaller percentage of its population in the

Table 3-3.
Value of Southside Inventories (Personal Property), 1770–79

Virginia £s	Number of Inventories				
	Brunswick	Amelia	Halifax	Mecklenburg	Pittsylvania
over 1,000	11	10	4	6	4
901–1,000	6	3	0	0	1
801–900	3	3	1	6	0
701–800	3	2	0	1	1
601–700	1	5	2	4	0
501–600	5	5	3	3	3
401–500	2	10	2	3	1
301–400	11	9	4	1	0
201–300	7	7	7	3	1
101–200	14	13	7	9	9
51–100	14	15	19	10	3
25–50	7	12	16	10	10
0.1-24	19	15	25	7	8
Total	103	109	90	63	41

Source: County will books.

Table 3-4.
Value of Southside Inventories (Personal Property), 1790–99

Virginia £s	Number of Inventories				
	Brunswick	Amelia	Halifax	Mecklenburg	Pittsylvania
over 3,000	4	7	0	3	1
2,001–3,000	3	6	4	2	3
1,001–2,000	18	14	17	18	10
901–1,000	2	5	4	2	0
801–900	4	5	4	6	2
701–800	6	3	0	6	3
601–700	8	7	3	10	3
501–600	7	7	11	5	7
401–500	13	5	10	9	4
301–400	10	8	7	10	11
201–300	9	5	10	11	7
101–200	24	16	20	13	17
51–100	11	12	15	15	21
25–50	12	4	16	16	16
0.1-24	7	4	15	5	9
Total	138	108	136	131	114

Source: County will books.

lower-wealth categories. For the 1790s, all five Southside counties had fewer inventories valued below £100 than the four Valley counties of Frederick, Augusta, Shenandoah, and Rockbridge. It was generally true that the Valley had more inventories in the £100 to £500 range, but Brunswick had more middle-wealth inventories than either Frederick or Augusta, and all Southside counties had more middle-wealth inventories than Frederick.

If the Southside had fewer people in the middle-level wealth categories of £100 to £500, and that was true for some areas, it was because the region had far more of its inventories in the higher-wealth categories. For example, during the 1790s, one-half of Amelia's inventories were valued over £500. Frederick, the Valley county that most closely paralleled the Southside, with a greater concentration of tobacco and slaves than the other areas of the Valley, had far fewer inventories in the upper-wealth levels (29 percent), far fewer people in the middle-wealth levels (26 percent), and far more in the lower-wealth categories (45 percent) than the Southside as a whole.

The explanation for the greater individual wealth in the Southside was obviously the greater investment in slave labor. Slaves were easily the most valuable property of the region. For example, for the decade of the 1790s, slaves comprised 70 percent of the total value of Southside inventories. In 1790 slaves as a percentage of the value of inventories ranged from a high of 80 percent in Brunswick to a low of 59 percent in Halifax. The Southside rapidly adopted tobacco cultivation with slave labor and continued a strong allegiance to that staple over time, while the Shenandoah Valley as a whole remained more of a diversified agricultural economy with relatively few slaves. These contrasting wealth characteristics do not suggest that the Southside was a more prosperous region nor do they imply a higher quality of life. Rather, the large slave population reflected the opaque wealth that was characteristic of a primary staple economy. The value of the large slave population that was responsible for the high level of wealth in the region indicated concentrated investment in sustaining a narrowly focused commercial economy that was geared to the greater support of external regions, not directed to the spread effects of developing a diversified economy that would provide greater support for the local region.

It is apparent that this discussion is directed more toward the further elaboration of the influence of tobacco on a regional economy rather than with concern for the actual general wealth characteristics of the region. Probate records are obviously biased in favor of wealthier groups. Other contemporary records must be used in conjunction with probate records in order to present a more accurate assessment of general regional wealth. For example, county tax lists contrasted with estate inventories by representing a larger sample of the population and by including landholdings. Initially, tax lists were comprised of all white males over the age of sixteen and all black slaves over that age; beginning in 1782, all black slaves over the age of twelve were listed. The tax lists revealed that a greater number of Southsiders were considered poor than was suggested in the inventories. In 1767 the tax list of Raleigh Parish of Amelia County, the territory of present-day Amelia, indicated that 38 percent of the white taxables owned no land or slaves. In that same year 67 percent of the white taxables in Pittsylvania County owned no land or slaves.[75] In 1800 that category increased to 39 percent in Amelia, but had decreased to 54 percent in Pittsylvania. By contrast, only 7 percent of Amelia's inventories and 21 percent of Pittsylvania inventories were valued below £50 during the 1790s.

The British mercantile claims that were based on debts incurred just prior to the Revolutionary War also suggest that a large number of poor, landless people lived in the Southside. These records, a sampling of Southsiders who owed debts to British merchants, offer a closer look at the wealth status of a few selected individuals. The majority of these individuals appeared to have been quite poor. Statements such as "unable to pay his debts," "insolvent," "indigent," "not in good circumstances," "never was solvent," "extremely poor," and "no property except a horse" were common entries beside the names of debtors. These records also indicate the lack of vertical mobility and the fall from economic grace of some individuals.

Economy and Settlement Evolution

Settlement evolution is based on the linkages between the primary economy and the secondary and tertiary economies. In Southside Virginia the dominance of tobacco production so severely weakened those linkages that the settlement system remained in a decentralized state. Without centralization of economic activities, the focus of both secondary and tertiary activities was the same location as the primary production, the plantation. Wheat production, with its strong linkages with the centralization of processing and service activities, was merely a subservient component of the dominant tobacco economy and therefore not a factor in settlement evolution.

However, because tobacco was not processed in the region and required only minimal input from manufacturing specialists, primarily coopers, blacksmiths, carpenters, and wheelwrights, the milling of wheat ironically was the leading processing activity in the region. But the mills were located on plantations and generally produced only small volumes of flour, primarily for personal and local consumption. Although most manufacturing took place on the plantation, with more-skilled slaves and indentured servants providing the labor, much of the regional processing was performed by small, independent artisans. But because their work was primarily with planters on plantation sites, they also were dispersed or were likely to be itinerant.

If the dominant crop was the basis of settlement evolution in Earle and Hoffman's staple thesis, the tertiary sector of the economy was the catalyst for that process. In the Southside service activities were surpassed only by agricultural production. Numerous wagoners and rollers transported great quantities of tobacco to the fall zone, and drovers and haulers of other plantation products followed in their tracks. Ordinary- and tavern-keepers and blacksmiths serviced this trade at numerous intermediate locations. And beginning during the 1790s, tobacco inspection warehouses were established within the region. But the tobacco trade remained linear in structure, moving from plantation to port as quickly as the quality of roads and the work habits of the teamsters would permit. The few Southside inspections, with their low volumes and their requirement to transport the product to the fall zone for export and likely reinspection, caused no changes in the dominant trade pattern.

Despite its generation of tertiary activity, tobacco made little impress on settlement evolution in the region. The fact that such a variety of methods and people were involved in the tobacco transport business indicates that it required little from the regional infrastructure. Road quality was probably the most common complaint heard in the region, but a high-quality road system was not necessary for such a transport-amenable product. Earl and Hoffman suggest that wheat production, because of its greater demands on the regional infrastructure, would not have been a viable commercial crop west of Lunenburg County in the period before the Revolutionary War. With the tolerance of poor roads by the tobacco trade and additionally the poor natural conditions for road building, it is quite evident that commercial wheat production had little chance to develop in the region. The service support for the tobacco trade—the taverns, ordinaries, and blacksmiths—were likely to be located on plantation sites as part of the backward linkages of the primary staple. Tobacco cast a powerful shadow over the Southside. Secondary and tertiary economies, with activities that were the cornerstone of settlement evolution to an urban system, were held hostage by the tobacco economy.

In the absence of towns, the country store was the focus of local trade. Established to serve the scattered population of the pioneer economy, it persisted in its domination of local trade because of the hegemony of tobacco. But the country store did not merely fill a trading void created by the failure of the tobacco trade to create town development in the region. The country store was an integral part of that tobacco trade. Its primary location was on the plantation and its continued mercantile dominance was dependent on the reduced consumerism created by the large slave populations.

Notes

1. Byrd, "History of the Dividing Line," 308.
2. Drury Stith's Survey Book, 1737–1770, 10, 54, 55, 62, 69, 71, 124, Virginia State Library.
3. Smyth, *A Tour in the United States of America* 1:289–90. Smyth, in the same reference, indicated that another important component of this pioneer economy, ginseng, which grew in great abundance on the rocky and thin soil, sold for 15d. per pound.
4. See respectively Pittsylvania County Judgments, March 1774; ibid., June 1772.
5. Smyth, *A Tour in the United States of America* 1:292.
6. Amelia County Order Book 1:2.
7. In December of 1784, a Prince Edward planter sold four loads of hay for £20. In 1785–87 the same planter sold twenty-one loads of hay for £105. See Francis Watkins Account Book, 54, 55, 128, Manuscripts, Hampden-Sydney College.
8. The Cocke inventory is in Amelia County Will Book 5:321–24; Myrick's holdings are listed in Brunswick County Will Book 6:17–26.
9. Brunswick County Will Book 5: 269–70.
10. For the competition between Brunswick and Sussex County, see *Virginia Gazette*, Purdie and Dixon, March 17, 1768; Lunenburg County v. Dinwiddie County is discussed in Beeman, *The Evolution of the Southern Backcountry*, 85–86.
11. Smyth, *A Tour in the United States of America* 1:291.
12. *Virginia Gazette*, Purdie, July 5, 1776.
13. Details of the drive are found in Pittsylvania Judgments, June 1772.
14. Stills were found in only 6 percent of the total eighteenth–century Southside estate inventories. Southsiders appeared to prefer local brandy and cider over whisky. The overwhelming choice of drink, of course, was the ubiquitous New England rum.

15. Tench Coxe, *A Statement of the Arts and Manufactures of the United States of America for the Year 1810* (Philadelphia, 1814), 88.

16. Quoted in Lewis C. Gray, *History of Agriculture in the Southern United States to 1860* (Gloucester, Mass., 1958; originally 1932) 1:181.

17. Ibid., 180; Hening, *Statutes*, 8:363.

18. Brunswick County Will Book 5:151-53, 270-75.

19. *Atlas of American Agriculture*, Part V, Section A, United States Department of Agriculture (Washington, D.C., 1918), 16.

20. "Oronoko" (Orinoco), named for the South American river valley of its presumed origin, was the more common variety of tobacco in Virginia and Maryland and was the only variety produced in the backcountry. The sweet-scented variety was grown only in a few selected areas of the Virginia Tidewater, primarily York County.

21. Amelia County Order Book 1:247, 251, 283, 285, 302.

22. Halifax County Pleas 1:320.

23. Calculated from letter of Roger Atkinson to Lyonel and Samuel Lyde, November 17, 1770, Roger Atkinson Letterbook, University of Virginia.

24. Ibid., Letter of August 25, 1772; *Historical Statistics of the United States, Colonial Times to 1970*, United States Bureau of the Census (Washington, D.C., 1975), 1191.

25. Post-Revolutionary tobacco production is from Beeman, *The Evolution of the Southern Backcountry*, 167, 170.

26. Letter of James Robinson to John Turner, October 6, 1777, William Cunninghame and Co. Letterbook, Colonial Williamsburg Research Center, Williamsburg.

27. Personal Property Taxes, 1790.

28. For Amelia, see Will Book 1: 85–86. Smith's production is found in Pocket Plantation Papers, Boxes 1 and 2, University of Virginia. For Marable, see *Virginia Gazette*, Rind, July 22, 1773. For Myrick, see Brunswick County Will Book 6:17–26.

29. Gray, *History of Agriculture* 1:219.

30. Mecklenburg County Loose Papers, 1787.

31. *Virginia Gazette*, Rind, July 22, 1773.

32. Earle and Hoffman, "Urban Development in the Eighteenth-Century South," 69.

33. Coulter, "The Virginia Merchant," 136–249.

34. Quoted in T. H. Breen, *Tobacco Culture: The Mentality of the Great Tidewater Planters on the Eve of Revolution* (Princeton, N.J., 1985), 74n.

35. Coulter, "The Virginia Merchant," 137, 143.

36. Letter of David Ross to John Hook, August 14, 1773, John Hook Papers, Manuscipts, Duke University.

37. Charles T. Nall, ed., "A Letter From Petersburg, Virginia, January 10, 1789," *Virginia Magazine of History and Biography* 82 (1974), 145–49.

38. Richard B. Sheridan, "The British Credit Crisis of 1772 and the American Colonies," *Journal of Economic History* 22 (1962), 161–86.

39. Legislative Petitions, Halifax County, September 24, 1792.

40. David Klingaman, "The Significance of Grain in the Development of the Tobacco Colonies," *Journal of Economic History* 29 (1969), 268–78; Paul G. E. Clemens, *The Atlantic Economy and Colonial Maryland's Eastern Shore: From Tobacco to Grain* (Ithaca, N.Y., 1980); Thomas M. Preisser, "Alexandria and the Evolution of the Northern Virginia Economy, 1746–1776," *Virginia Magazine of History and Biography* 89 (1981), 282–93.

41. Beeman, *The Evolution of the Southern Backcountry*, 170.

42. "Journal of William Loughton Smith," 69–70.

43. Philip Grasty and Samuel Pannill Ledger Book, 1799–1800, Mt. Airy Store, Manuscripts, Duke University.

44. Slave labor was often more common in wheat cultivation than in tobacco production in the northern and central Piedmont of Virginia during the antebellum period. See, for example, James R. Irwin, "Tobacco, Wheat, and Slaves in the Virginia Piedmont, 1850–1860," paper presented at the Conference on Cultivation and Culture, University of Maryland at College Park, April 1989.

45. For Crawley and Eggleston, see Amelia County Will Book 5:225–28, 318–20. Haskins is found in Brunswick County Will Book 6:248–52. Schumacher, *The Northern Farmer and His Markets*, 43, states that the average farmer in the middle colonies produced no more than 131 bushels of wheat annually. The Southside figures presumably represent exceptionally high totals.

46. Halifax County Will Book 3:148–49.

47. Letter of Atkinson to Lyonel and Samuel Lyde, August 25, 1772, Roger Atkinson Letterbook.

48. Legislative Petitions, Amelia County, October 20, 1787. See also petitions of October 29, 1787, and November 6, 1787.

49. Charlotte County Court Cases, September–October 1765; July–September 1766.

50. Ibid., March–July 1767.

51. Robert P. Thompson, "The Tobacco Exports of the Upper James River Naval District, 1773–1775," *William and Mary Quarterly* 3d Ser. 18 (1961), 406–7.

52. For details of Scottish ascendancy, see Price, "The Rise of Glasgow in the Chesapeake Tobacco Trade," and *France and the Chesapeake: A History of the French Tobacco Monopoly, 1674–1791, and of Its Relationship to the British and American Tobacco Trades,* 2 vols. (Ann Arbor, Mich., 1973); Devine, *The Tobacco Lords*; Soltow, "Scottish Traders in Virginia."

53. The inspection act is found in Hening, *Statutes* 4:247–71. Reiteration and modification of the act are found in ibid., vols. 5, 6, 8, 10, 11. For Amelia and Brunswick see, respectively, ibid., 4:387, 480; 5:136.

54. Legislative Petitions, Mecklenburg County, 1776–91.

55. William Tatham, *An Historical and Practical Essay on the Culture and Commerce of Tobacco* (London, 1800), 55–64; Gray, *History of Agriculture* 1:219–23.

56. Tatham, *An Historical and Practical Essay*, 55–64.

57. For Smith, see "Journal," 67, 71. For Mecklenburg letter, see Legislative Petitions, Mecklenburg County, October 1, 1811.

58. Mecklenburg County Loose Papers, 1793.

59. Letter of Alexander Banks to John Smith, December 3, 1772, Pocket Plantation Papers.

60. For these and additional problems associated with transporting tobacco and for the details of other marketing matters, see the correspondence between Smith and his factors, Alexander Stewart and Alexander Banks, Boxes 1–2 of Pocket Plantation Papers.

61. Tatham, *An Historical and Practical Essay*, 57.

62. Transport costs are derived from county court judgments, will books, and merchant account books.

63. Grasty and Pannill Account Book, Stony Hill Store, Manuscripts, Duke University.

64. "To the People of Charlotte, Prince Edward and Halifax," 3.

65. Letter from Ross to Hook, June 4, 1774, John Hook Papers.

66. "Urban Development in the Eighteenth-Century South," 74–78.

67. Wilson and Hairston Papers, Southern Historical Collection, University of North Carolina, Chapel Hill, vols. 63, 64, 71.

68. Pittsylvania County Judgments, May, June, August, 1800.

69. Smyth, *A Tour in the United States of America* 1:49.

70. Smith, "Journal" 71.

71. The focus of Thorp's "Doing Business in the Backcountry" was a tavern that also sold store goods.

72. Smyth, *A Tour in the United States of America* 1:114–15.

73. The primary bases for discussion of the wealth structure of the Southside are the estate inventories of county probate records and the county tax lists. The inventories have already been used extensively in this chapter to evaluate the regional economy. The use of these records to interpret wealth structure must be considered in the context of several limitations. Because they do not include landholdings, they tend to underestimate the wealth of individuals, especially those in an agricultural economy. The inventories also represent only a small sample of the total population and generally are more representative of middle- and upper-class wealth. There is additionally an obvious age bias to the probate records. Wartime values also had to be adjusted to reduce the influence of rampant inflation. Despite these problems, the estate inventories remain the best method of evaluating individual wealth in Virginia before 1782 and for comparing the wealth distribution of regions within its borders.

74. All wealth characteristics for the Shanandoah Valley, and also the design of the "wealth" tables, are from Mitchell, *Frontier and Commercialism*, 109–21.

75. "Tithables of Pittsylvania County, 1767," *Virginia Magazine of History and Biography* 23:79–80, 371–80; 24:180–92, 271–74.

4

Temporal Patterns of Country Trade: Merchants, Locations, and Structures

---

Change over time was the primary dynamic component of the American frontier. With an economy that evolved from pioneer to well-developed primary staple production and with a settlement history characterized by steady growth and expansion, Southside Virginia generally followed that temporal precept. But the region, because of the dominance of tobacco production, did not conform to the expected spatial change from dispersed to centralized settlement that characterized temporal change in frontier trade. Although country trade still prevailed, there were nevertheless both dramatic and subtle changes in the regional mercantile structure.

Several broad mercantile patterns were discernible in Southside Virginia during the eighteenth century. These patterns are structured into four loosely discrete time periods: (1) the formative period, 1732 to 1760, (2) the period of Scottish dominance, 1760 to 1776, (3) the Revolutionary War period, 1776 to 1783, and (4) the period of planter-merchant dominance in the post-War period.

The Formative Period, 1732–60

The formative period, which began with the organization of the first county, was a period of less-structured mercantile activity as merchants adjusted to the advance of the Southside frontier. This early period was a combination of continuing old and accepted mercantile practices and the devising of new strategies for overcoming the problems of distance as settlement continued to expand into the more interior parts of the region. Five general types of merchants participated in the trade of the Southside during this period: English at the fall zone; Virginians at the fall zone; local merchants, including the dominant planter-merchants; Scots at both fall-zone and interior locations; and a variety of itinerant merchants.

The variety of merchants operating in the region during this period is revealed in the Halifax County court judgments during the 1750s. Of eighty-one mercantile firms that could be identified, forty-three were local backcountry (Halifax and surrounding counties); nineteen were Scottish, with operations both in the backcountry and at the fall zone; and nineteen were either Virginia or English companies based at the fall zone. Although this is an accurate view of general mercantile patterns in the region at the time, the large number of firms represented was a function of the many nonresident consumers who sought refuge in the Southside to avoid payment of their debts in other parts of Virginia.

English merchants were primarily associated with two older business practices: the consignment system and the concentration of trading activity at the more populated edge of the newly settled territory. English merchants had relied primarily on the consignment system in Tidewater Virginia, where plantations were larger and navigable waterways more readily available. Under this system, the Tidewater planters assumed all responsibility for shipping tobacco to the English market. When the tobacco arrived in England, an agent provided for the sale of the crop, collected his fee, paid the various shipping and port charges, and purchased goods to be sent back to the planter in Virginia. Most English merchants who practiced this type of trade arrangement were not structured to handle the risks of trade with customers located great distances from navigable waterways and where individual tobacco production and consumer needs were on a smaller scale. During this early mercantile period, however, a few Southside planters may have participated in the consignment system because of proximity to the fall zone and previous experiences with the system before migrating from the Tidewater region. Several London merchants, including Humphrey Bell, Christopher Smith, Richard Oswald, and John Hornbury, brought suit against debtors in Brunswick and Amelia counties during this period.

The English firms that attracted the largest volume of Southside business bought tobacco directly from Southside planters and assumed the risks of shipping and marketing. They were located primarily at the fall-zone ports of Petersburg, Blandford, Warwick, and Osbornes, with Richmond as a secondary fall-zone focus and distant Norfolk as only a rare host. Southside customers were drawn to these sites by the relatively short distances and the tobacco inspection warehouses located at or near these places. The firms of Neill Buchanan and Samuel and Lionel Lyde were two of the more active companies. The Buchanan firm appeared to have at least one store in the Southside, but it is not clear if the Lyde firm followed that business strategy. Roger Atkinson, chief factor for the Lyde firm, brought numerous suits against debtors in several Southside counties, especially Halifax, both for his employers and for his own company of Atkinson and William Newsum. He also had extensive landholdings in the region and later, in 1766, purchased most of the Halifax County town of Peytonsburg.[1] It is also possible that the numerous suits simply reflected his Petersburg location, the traditional focus of Southside trade.

More active than the English merchants were the many Virginia merchants based at or near the fall zone. Some of these merchants may have been former factors for English or Scottish companies, while others emerged from a colonial, agrarian base. Among the more active Virginia traders were Alexander Spaulding and John Lidderdale of Williamsburg, Samuel Gordon of Blandford, Theophilus Field and Robert Bolling of Prince George County, Benjamin Harrison of Surry County, and Patrick Coutts of Curles Neck. Field also operated an additional store in Brunswick County.

The largest group of merchants were locally based. The majority of these local merchants were generally unstructured and part-time in their business ventures. They were either planters, herders, wagoners, or trapper-hunters who were sufficiently successful in their initial occupations, and who had control of or access to strategic locations, to branch out into trading on a part-time basis.[2] Many of the early merchants were planters who sold only a portion of their own supplies in response to the demand created by newly arrived settlers in the area. The volume of their business often depended upon their own individual wealth. For example, Littleton Tazewell of Brunswick County, whose wealth was valued over £2,000 in 1754 and included twenty-three slaves, a carriage, and 142 bushels of wheat that suggested a mill, was capable of providing a substantial quantity of goods from his plantation storeroom.[3] Potential sale items could be drawn from the more than 20,000 nails, the £30 worth of cloth, the 345 pounds of sugar, and the 100 panes of window glass. The estate of Joseph Parks of Brunswick County, which was valued at £138 in 1749, offered only the 1,500 eightpenny nails and the pair of money scales as evidence of merchant activity—and the more than £105 worth of debts owed by forty separate individuals.[4] The three slaves, forty cattle, twenty-four hogs, nine sheep, and six hives of bees in combination with five horses, a bell, and a cart suggest that Parks was in transition between peddling and a more stationary mercantile business.

The most structured merchants were planters who operated stores as part of their broad entrepreneurial pursuits that included land speculation, money lending, and manufacturing and who occupied the most favorable commercial locations along major roads and trails, at crossroads, and near ferries. These varied business ventures, often aided by local political and family linkages and external mercantile contacts, were typical of the aggressive commercial-minded behavior of selective individuals on the American frontier. Among the more prominent local merchants were Thomas Tabb, a planter and justice of the Amelia County court who operated two stores in the county, and Edward Booker, also a planter and justice in the same county. In 1752 Booker's personal property, spread over two plantations, was valued at over £2,000 and contained twenty slaves and over 15,000 pounds of tobacco. Amelia resident William Thornton Smith's £208 worth of store goods, of a total estate of £711, was probably typical of the inventory of larger-volume Southside merchants.[5]

Various itinerant merchants, primarily peddlers and wagon merchants, filled important niches in this evolving trading structure that local and fall-zone stores could not satisfy. Although peddlers were usually outsiders based at the fall zone or other distant locations, they often had local contacts that provided regular lodging and even held money in order to allay thievery along isolated roads and trails.[6] Because most peddlers were not local and avoided the required county license, little information is available on their numbers and behavior except in tragic instances involving robbery, sickness, or death. However, two local peddlers, William McDaniel and John Hickey of Halifax County, parlayed their itinerant businesses into permanent store locations. McDaniel later became a wealthy planter and a justice of the county court.

Wagon merchants were enterprising wagoners who purchased goods as backloads after transporting tobacco to fall-zone warehouses. Although all independent wagoners were potential itinerant merchants, apparently, either through lack of inclination, shortage of investment capital, or lack of wholesale contacts, very few actually pursued the business. Robert Wade and John Boyd, both located near the same Halifax County ferry site, were two wagon merchants who later achieved success at fixed-mercantile locations.

The incompleteness and changing character of the human landscape provided little stimulus for the structured location of country stores. Neither infrastructure, population density, nor level of economic development gave any great significance to specific store locations. Although a local merchant might seek a location made more accessible by the presence of a road, ferry, or courthouse site, his plantation site in an area of relatively dense population might produce more significant activity for his low-volume business. In most areas roads were only trails, ferry sites were so abundant and traffic was so light that they provided little utility for the concentration of commercial activity, and courthouses remained too distant from most of the population. Travelers passing through the Southside during this period were so overwhelmed by the great distance between settlers that the existence of stores and other services on this landscape seemed almost implausible.

Two store locations in western Halifax County (modern Henry County) during the mid-1750s suggest the range of store locations. James Roberts operated a store in a more densely settled and accessible area, employed a full-time storekeeper, and had sufficient goods to attract three thieves bent on stocking their own itinerant businesses. Only part of the store's stock resulted in contraband that required the services of five pack horses. At the opposite end of the locational spectrum, John Hickey's store was sited at such a remote location that a group of Moravian travelers, who expressed disbelief at commerce practiced in such isolation, had to be guided to the establishment.[7] Hickey's store, in a section of his house, was undoubtedly the rustic affair with deerskin-clad customers portrayed by popular culture's interpretation of the early American frontier.

Despite the prevailing locational pattern that was in accordance with the region's population and infrastructure, there were significant aberrations in the more developed eastern areas that were harbingers of future patterns. Drury Stith's plantation, for example, with store, ordinary, and grist mill, and with a location near a bridge site on a major road near the junction of the courthouse road, was an early example of the country clustering that would dominate the spatial character of Southside trade during the remainder of the eighteenth century.

The Scots, who were eventually to dominate wholesale, retail, and tobacco trade in the Southside, expanded from their fall-zone operations during the 1750s. From these bases they sent out itinerant merchants and factors to test the region's trading potential and to select sites for permanent stores. By 1755 Archibald Buchanan and Company had established a store at Prince Edward Courthouse, and Andrew Buchanan and Robert Hastie had set up a business, probably in the southern part of that county or in adjoining Lunenburg County.[8] Before 1758 the firm of James Murdoch and Thomas Yuille had established a store in northeastern Halifax County at Booker's Ferry that operated until 1775.[9] Whether from locations at the fall zone, or from temporary or permanent locations in the Southside, the Scots made impressive advances in the region as attested by their increased appearances as plaintiffs in county court dockets.

It was during this period of expansion into the backcountry that some of the individuals who were to become the eventual heads of the largest and wealthiest mercantile companies in Glasgow served apprenticeships in the backcountry trade. Alexander Speirs purchased a plantation in Amelia County in 1742 and William Cunninghame spent fourteen to sixteen years in Virginia supervising his company's operations. The heads or factors of lesser companies also practiced this business regimen. James Murdoch owned land and probably lived in Halifax County for a period of time. Thomas Yuille settled in the same county where he supervised the company's backcountry operations and, in addition, became a prominent local planter and was sheriff of the county for a brief period. Robert Hastie owned a plantation and possibly lived in Prince Edward County during the 1750s.[10]

The Period of Scottish Dominance, 1760–76

The rapid expansion of the Scottish chain stores to mercantile dominance was in response to the rapid expansion of tobacco production in the region. Scottish firms clearly controlled wholesaling and tobacco marketing from their fall-zone bases of operation and dominated local retail and service activities from their dispersed backcountry stores. Although local planter-merchants continued to operate, their mercantile activities were greatly reduced in the face of the virtual Scottish monopoly.

The Scottish mercantile firms operating in the Southside located their flagship stores and wholesale warehouses near tobacco inspections at Petersburg and Blandford on the Appomattox River and at Warwick, Osbornes, and Manchester on the James River in Chesterfield County, and then established country stores in those areas of the Southside where the volume of tobacco production was high or rapidly expanding. The three largest Glasgow merchant houses—the firms of Alexander Speirs, William Cunninghame, and John Glassford—were prominently active in the region. The Speirs company concentrated more of its activities in the Southside, while the region was only one of several in which Cunninghame and Glassford traded. Speirs had stores in the counties of Prince Edward, Halifax, Mecklenburg, Lunenburg, and Charlotte, and also in adjacent Bedford County. Cunninghame and Company operated stores in Halifax, Mecklenburg, and Brunswick counties. The Glassford firm, with a more complex internal structure, had several subsidiary companies operated by different combinations of shareholders. Henderson and McCall operated a store in Pittsylvania County, and the Alexander Donald store in Mecklenburg County also may have had some association with Glassford.

Among the smaller Scottish operations, although one of the more active traders in the Southside, was the firm of Andrew Buchanan and Robert Hastie and Company, who operated single stores in Prince Edward, Charlotte, and Halifax, and two stores in Lunenburg. James and Robert Donald, with stores in Brunswick, Prince Edward, and Mecklenburg; Robert Dinwiddie and Thomas Crawford, with two stores in Mecklenburg and an additional store in Brunswick; James Murdoch, with stores in Halifax and Pittsylvania; Robert Watters, with a business in Charlotte County; and John McCall and Company, with a store in Brunswick County where one of the partners, Allen Love, was the factor, were other important firms in the Southside trade. Andrew Cochrane and Company probably operated at least one store in the region. James and William Donald operated a store in nearby Bedford County that attracted numerous patrons from neighboring Southside counties.

There were undoubtedly other Scottish stores in the region at various times during this period. From the large number of storekeepers present in Pittsylvania County in 1775, it would appear that there were additional Scottish firms operating in that county. Because of the tobacco marketing system, several additional Scottish firms, operating strictly from the fall zone, also did business with the region. Among these were George Kippen, Alexander Shaw, John Baird, James Lyle, Archibald Ritchie, Alexander Mackie, Robert Bogle, and Colin Dunlop.

The high point of Scottish mercantile activity occurred between 1769 and 1770, when tobacco imports comprised more than half of the total tobacco imports to Great Britain. Earlier, in 1758, Glasgow (through its ports of Greenock and Port Glasgow) had surpassed London as the leading British tobacco port. The importance of the tobacco trade may be seen in export and import figures for 1766–69. During that period, almost 88 percent of Scottish imports from

America came from Virginia and Maryland, and 81 percent of Scottish exports to America went to those two colonies.[11] Although their share of the overall tobacco trade declined slightly after 1770, the Scots continued to expand their operations in the Southside.

The sites of the Scottish stores generally corresponded to five primary locational considerations: tobacco production, ferry and bridge sites, main roads, courthouses, and plantations. Tobacco production was the single most important locational factor. Because the purchasing of tobacco and the reselling of that staple in Europe, primarily to France, was the primary trade of the mercantile firms, proximity to producers, who were also the most important consumers of store goods, was paramount to the Scots. The many stores located in the general vicinity of the confluence of the Dan, Staunton, and Roanoke Rivers attested to that area's tobacco production in the 1760s and 1770s. As previously indicated, many of these stores were located on plantations situated in the midst of their customers. Figure 4-1 reveals that Scottish stores were more numerous in the central part of the region, where tobacco production was expanding. The more eastern counties had fewer stores in part because of proximity to the fall zone, but primarily because of the relative decline of tobacco in that area that had actually forced the closing of some stores. The Cunninghame store at Brunswick Courthouse had only £1,642 in debts to be claimed at the end of the Revolutionary War, but the company's stores in Halifax and Mecklenburg counted debts of more than £6,101 and £4,514 respectively.[12]

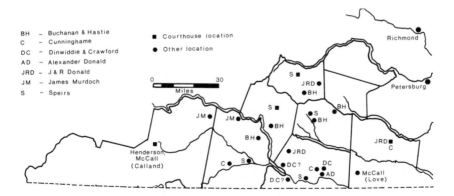

Figure 4-1. Scottish store locations, 1768–75. *Source*: County order books, deed books, and judgments; McMurran, "The War Claims of William Cunninghame," 33; "British Mercantile Claims."

Ferry sites were the single most important specific site for the location of Scottish stores. The advantage of a ferry location was in the reduction of the geographic separation created by a river and in the forced channelization of trade into a more restricted area. During the seven-year period prior to the Revolutionary War, as many as ten stores were located adjacent to ferry sites. Furthermore, at least two stores were located at bridge sites on smaller streams, sites that previously may have contained ferries. To insure trade with both sides of the Roanoke River, and additionally to tap the North Carolina trade, Alexander Speirs and Company paid the owner of a ferry £12 per year to permit free passage to customers of their store.[13]

Roads, whether in association with ferries or in a singular context, were also important factors in the location of stores. Although Southside roads were not of high quality and were often impassable, they nevertheless tied the region together and linked it to the fall-zone entrepôts. Among the stores that were located on major roads, but were not associated with ferry sites, were two Pittsylvania County stores. The operations of James Murdoch and Company and Henderson, McCall and Company were located on Hickey's Road, a pioneer road that connected much of the distant southwestern portion of the Southside with the Staunton River. The Halifax County store of Buchanan and Hastie, under the supervision of Thomas Hope, was located at a place with obvious locational clout called the "Crossroads."

Courthouse sites were chosen for store locations because they were usually the focus of several roads and because of their attraction to people each month for the meeting of the county courts. Courthouses, however, lagged well behind ferry sites as choice locations for Scottish stores because of aggressively and artificially induced centrality that usually defied the reality of population concentration and economic expansion. The earliest Speirs store in the backcountry was located at Prince Edward Courthouse, but other companies did not follow this lead. Speirs likely had a store at Charlotte Courthouse because of the meeting of several important roads at that site.

The closing of the Brunswick Courthouse store of James and Robert Donald in 1768, and the low volume of trade of the Cunninghame store at the same site, indicated the court function alone had difficulty sustaining trade. This is also suggested by the location of the Henderson, McCall store at the Pittsylvania Court. The store's location had greater significance because of Hickey's Road and expanding tobacco production. The best example of the importance of the courthouse site may be seen in neighboring Bedford County, where at least two Scottish and two local merchants had thriving operations in New London.

The majority of Scottish stores were located on landholdings of 150 to 400 acres in size that were purchased by the company. Several operations, as seen in Chapter 2, were on functioning plantations, where stores were part of the more intense country clustering. In 1771, the James and Robert Donald store in Mecklenburg County, for example, was located among a group of buildings that included a smokehouse, a lumber house, and a separate counting room. That company's operations in Brunswick County, at Smokey Ordinary, contained a house, storehouse, counting room, and lumber house on 355 acres of land. A Scottish-store complex in Prince Edward County contained a storehouse, counting house, lodging room, warehouse, tailor's shop, smith's shop, house for an ordinary, and other buildings on 150 acres of land.[14] The size of only one Scottish store could be determined. The Alexander Donald store in Mecklenburg County contained 1,408 square feet, the largest store in the region, as revealed by extant records.[15] Presumably, the Cunninghame and Speirs structures were larger.

The open-country neighborhood pattern of clustering was especially prominent near ferry sites. A Scottish storekeeper's own words best described the pattern of mercantile activities along the Roanoke River in Mecklenburg County. "The many stores in this neighbourhood which of consequence causes a rivalship oblidge me to keep a better assortment both of European and W. Indian goods than what I would else do."[16]

It is likely that Scottish companies, because of the rapid expansion of tobacco and their generally business-only presence in the region, also rented or leased store property. However, there is only one instance of that type of transaction in the Southside records. The firm of Robert Dinwiddie and Thomas Crawford leased five acres of land from David Dortch in 1772 for the site of one of their Mecklenburg County stores. William Park, the factor for the firm, paid £500 for a twenty-one-year lease. For this, they received the land and the right to cut the timber to construct buildings and barrels, and to burn for firewood. Dortch supplied only the land; the company built the store and all additional buildings.[17]

There were several local planter-merchants with sufficiently broad entrepreneurial bases to compete in this intensely competitive market. Matthew Marable, with stores in both the counties of Charlotte and Mecklenburg, appeared to be most active against the better-armed Scottish competition. William McDaniel, William Stokes, Edward Booker, and Hampton and Robert Wade in Halifax; James Henderson and John Tabb in Amelia; Alexander Boyd in Mecklenburg; and James Calloway in nearby Bedford were other active local planter-merchants. Part of their success may have come from close association with fall-zone companies that possibly provided easy credit, less expensive wholesale goods, and other services from these more centralized focal points of commercial activity. For example, William Stokes had some business arrangement with Petersburg merchant John Baird. Edward Booker of Halifax County may have had a similar relationship with John Esdale. John Hook of Bedford County, former storekeeper for the Scottish firm of James and William Donald, had a partnership with Petersburg-based David Ross. Matthew Marable, by virtue of his small tobacco-export operations in Petersburg, would appear to have had close ties with wholesalers in that port.

For local planter-merchants who were able to compete with the Scottish firms, prime locations near ferries and along major roads were critical. The large number of stores near the many ferry sites along the Roanoke River in Mecklenburg County also suggests the presence of local planter-merchants. Most local merchants also had other activities clustered on their plantations to attract customers. For example, in Halifax County, Robert Wooding and William McDaniel each operated a store, mill, and ordinary on their plantations, and William Stokes had a store and a mill on his property. Matthew Marable, the most successful of the local planter-merchants during this period, had store, tavern, and mill on his primary plantation business site. And of course, he had that distinctive business acumen that was enhanced by his supreme confidence, aggressive operative style, and previous success.

The Revolutionary War Period, 1776–83

Merchant activity was sharply curtailed during the war years. Most British merchants were expelled from the colony and most manufactured goods were scarce because of the disruption of the normal trade patterns between Great Britain and the colonies. At the beginning of the war, all citizens of Great Britain had to pledge their loyalty to the cause of the revolution or depart the colony. Despite this requirement, several representatives of Scottish companies stationed in the Southside chose to remain in Virginia. At the time of the commencement of hostilities, twenty-three of the forty-four Scottish merchants who were active in the seven counties of Brunswick, Mecklenburg, Halifax, Pittsylvania, Charlotte, Prince Edward, and Lunenburg, and in nearby Bedford County, were still living in Virginia (Table 4-1). Of the twenty-three merchants who remained, the ratio of continued backcountry residence to fall-zone migration was approximately 2:1.

Considering the general patriotic tenor in the Southside and the fact that these merchants were closely associated with local planter indebtedness, this was an extraordinarily large number of individuals who chose to remain among their "adversaries" in a region with strong anti-Scot feeling.[18] Those Scots who remained in the Southside were not loyal to the independence movement, but were willing to sign the loyalty oath in order to keep their acquired backcountry wealth that had been gained over relatively long tenures in the region and to ensure their opportunity to add to that wealth in the future. Both John Fisher, factor for Buchanan and Hastie, and Ebenezer McHarg, storekeeper for Alexander Donald and Company, took the oath of allegiance only when confiscation of their property was imminent.[19] Allen Love and Samuel Calland were heavily involved in Southside investment. By 1788 Love's personal property was valued over £2,600 and included forty-six slaves and a cotton gin. Calland eventually owned over 3,000 acres that were valued in excess of £7,000. His personal property, worth almost £6,800, included seventy-four slaves, twenty-four horses, and a "road wagon" with a value in excess of £17.[20]

John Hook of neighboring Bedford County managed to keep his holdings despite his criticism of the patriot cause, a potentially dangerous act considering that Charles Lynch, who provided the origins for the terms "lynch," "lynching," and "lynch law" for his supposed actions against Tories, lived in the same county. Hook later moved to nearby Franklin County, where he continued to operate his successful mercantile firm and, additionally, became sheriff of the county. Perhaps the 1768 letter of William Jameson (Jamieson), factor for Buchanan and Hastie in Charlotte County, to his brother-in-law, Isaac Read, best reveals the Scottish merchants understanding of the means to wealth in the region.

> I have an intention of erecting a mill near the upper Bridge on Little Roanok. If you would mention it to the court and get me an order for it as I do not understand The method of application myself. I will pay you a lawers fee & besides acknowledge the favors done to your very humble servt.[21]

As indicated by Jameson's experience, marriage was an additional but not always reliable way to remain in the backcountry. For Jameson, marriage into one of the most respected families in the Southside seemed to protect him from the county committees that were in charge

Table 4-1.

Responses of Scottish Merchants to the American Revolution

Name	Company	County	Decision
William Buchanan	Unknown	Brunswick	Remained
John Drummond	Independent		Remained
James Gilmore	Unknown		Remained
Allen Love	John McCall		Remained
Simon Pollance	Dinwiddie, Crawford		Departed
James Ross (Rose)	Unknown		Remained
Alexander Scheiviz	Unknown		Departed
Alex Burt	Buchanan, Hastie	Charlotte	Departed
William Jameson	Buchanan, Hastie		Remained
John Calder	Speirs	Halifax	Remained
James Calland	Unknown		Departed
John Fisher	Buchanan, Hastie		Remained
Thomas Hope	Independent		Remained
Hector McNeill	Speirs		Remained
Donald McNicholl	Murdoch		Remained
Walter Robertson	Independent		Remained
John Smith	Murdoch		Departed
James Stevens	Buchanan, Hastie		Remained
Thomas Yuille	Murdoch & Yuille		Remained
James Burns	Unknown	Lunenburg	Departed
John Gortam	Unknown		Remained
James Mercer	Buchanan, Hastie		Remained
John Patterson	Speirs		Departed
Thomas Banks	Speirs	Mecklenburg	Departed
Robert Burton	Dinwiddie, Crawford		Remained
John Brown	Unknown		Remained
William Duncan	Unknown		Departed
John Johnson	Unknown		Remained
William McClure	Unknown		Departed
Ebenezer McHarg	Alexander, Donald		Remained
Adam Newell	Unknown		Departed
William Turnbull	Dinwiddie, Crawford		Departed
Samuel Calland	Henderson, McCall Independent	Pittsylvania	Remained
Alex Cummins	Unknown		Departed
James Falconer	Calland		Departed
Lewis Gilliam (Gwillium)	Unknown		Unknown
George Murdock	Murdoch		Departed
Gideon Rucker	Unknown		Departed
John Salmon	Unknown		Remained
Archibald Smith	Unknown		Departed
James Crosse	Speirs	Prince Edward	Departed
John Brandary, Jr.	Unknown	Bedford	Departed
John Hook	Independent		Remained
James McMurry	Unknown		Departed

Source: County order books; will books; deed books; tax lists; court judgments; merchant account books.

of ferreting out local Tories. Perhaps the most pragmatic marriage was that of Samuel Calland. He married Elizabeth Smith, daughter of the late John Smith, former proprietor of Pocket Plantation, on December 14, 1776, exactly four days before the date for the final expulsion of British merchants from the colony. In February of 1777 the Pittsylvania court indicated that Calland refused to take the oath and still remained unfriendly to the country, but could remain because he had "intermarried with a national of this county."[22] Thomas Yuille also must have used his marriage to a local woman to protect him from the Halifax County patriots, for he did not sign the loyalty oath and apparently demonstrated little support for the revolutionary cause, even though he had resided in the county for almost twenty years.

The Scots who moved from the Southside to the fall zone—a group that included Thomas Hope, a factor for Buchanan and Hastie, and Hector McNeill, a storekeeper for Speirs and Company—joined a large contingent of fellow merchants who either signed loyalty oaths or managed to remain in the colony by other means. Several continued their mercantile activities from these sites during the war, if they were in good standing, while others bided their time until its termination. The presence of Scots in Richmond during the war led one traveler to comment, "with the exception of two or three families this little town is made up of Scottish factors who inhabit small tenements scattered here and there from the river to the hill."[23] Among the more prominent Scottish merchants based at the fall zone were James Buchanan and John McKeand in Richmond, Robert Donald and Alexander Banks in Chesterfield County, and Christopher McConnico and Thomas Shore in Petersburg. Once the war was over, no matter who was the victor, the Scots at the fall zone would once again dominate trade, primarily because of the lack of a viable native merchant class.

Postwar Mercantile Patterns

With the termination of the war, Virginia continued its earlier trade patterns. This meant that, because of the state's strong agrarian bias and failure to encourage or assist Virginia merchants, Scottish or other British merchants continued their mercantile dominance from the fall-zone entrepôts.[24] For example, in 1789 a French visitor to Petersburg observed that

> In this little place there are sixty very rich English [British] storehouses, for the most part they belong to Scotsmen who barter goods for tobacco. They are well supplied and provide for every need of the planter.[25]

But there were also important variations from the prewar pattern. These fall-zone merchants operated smaller and more independent mercantile companies and had closer ties with Virginia. The primary traders of the prewar period—the firms of Alexander Speirs, William Cunninghame, John Glassford, Andrew Buchanan and Robert Hastie, and Robert Dinwiddie and Thomas Crawford—no longer participated in the Virginia trade. Because of their absence, mercantile change was more dramatic in the Southside. The chain-store operations of these companies were not revived and only the few stores run by their expatriated former factors and storekeepers provided any linkage with the prewar period. Most of their properties were seized and sold during the war. For example, the Speirs property in Prince Edward County that contained 400 acres had been given to the Presbyterian Church to serve as the site for Hampden-Sydney College.[26] In Mecklenburg County properties belonging to the larger Scottish firms had been auctioned for £29,000.[27]

The merchants who dominated local Southside trade during the postwar period were local planter-merchants, most of whom had not been active before the Revolution. Like earlier planter-merchants, they had expanded into mercantile enterprises from a local agricultural base. These local merchants filled the void created by the departure of the many Scottish firms and offered the same retailing and financial services as provided by the Scots and earlier planter-merchants. For example, the percentage of store business allocated to cash advances and payments to third-party creditors kept pace or surpassed the level of those functions during the Scottish era. Cash advances comprised 13 percent by value of store business in the period from 1784 to 1789 and 5 percent in the period from 1790 to 1800. That function had comprised 4 percent of the total value of business during the 1770–75 period. Payments to third parties were 17 percent by value of store business from 1784 to 1789 and 19 percent between 1790 and 1800, both comparable with the 21 percent of the 1770–75 period (Table 6-1).

The relatively rapid emergence of the new group could not have occurred without support from the fall-zone wholesalers. As John Hook observed in 1770, independent backcountry merchants needed a strong trade connection with merchants at fall-zone entrepôts.[28] This support was usually in the form of long-term credit for wholesale purchases, connections with British sources of capital and goods, and acceptance of Southside agricultural products as payment for goods.

A better relationship was an actual partnership with a fall-zone merchant, a partnership similar to the one that Hook had with David Ross of Petersburg in the prewar period. Robert Colquhoun of Petersburg and Brunswick County planter-merchant Allen Love, both formerly associated with Scottish firms, may have had such an arrangement after the Revolutionary war. The firm of Blow and Barksdale, plaintiffs in a number of suits in Halifax and Pittsylvania counties after the War, operated stores in Petersburg, Halifax County, and Northampton County in North Carolina. Richard Blow or Peter Barksdale probably ran the Petersburg operation while Beverly Barksdale managed the store in Halifax. The firm of Hector McNeill and James McCraw also operated in this manner. McNeill, the former storekeeper for Speirs and Company who moved to the fall zone during the war, managed the firm from Petersburg and McCraw operated the Halifax store. Additional members of the Barksdale family were involved in the firm of Brown and Barksdale. Five partners, William Barksdale, John Brown, James Brown, Randolph Barksdale, and James Strange, invested £1,750 to finance the firm that was to be based in Manchester and have an additional store in Halifax County.[29]

Wholesale connections were also extended beyond the backcountry and fall-zone linkage during this period. For example, Payne Harrison, a Bedford County merchant with Philadelphia connections, advertised to a market that included some Southside areas.[30] These connections, however, made little impact on the traditional Southside-fall-zone trading axis that was dictated by the tobacco inspection system.

Several planter-merchants overcame their initial shortage of capital by forming partnerships with other local planter-merchants. James Bruce of Halifax County, who became the leading Southside merchant during the early nineteenth century, had an early partnership with John Pannill in 1788 and with his brother, Charles Bruce, in 1796. David Pannill of Pittsylvania County operated stores at Chalk Level and Sandy River, but also had a one-half interest in a store with William Wimbish, a one-third interest with Grasty and Pannill, and a similar arrangement with Jessee Leftwich and Company. Philip Grasty and Samuel Pannill also had a partnership, at least from 1799 to 1801.

There were three primary characteristics of postwar planter-merchants. First, many of the later planters, like their prewar counterparts, were among the region's wealthiest individuals. In addition to their plantation holdings, their businesses included wagoning, the operation of ordinaries and taverns, and milling. Representative of the wealthier planter-merchants were Stephen Cocke of Amelia and John Wilson of Pittsylvania. Cocke owned 103 slaves and a large number of livestock in 1795. Wilson owned twenty-eight wagons, twenty horses, and forty-eight slaves and, in 1795–96, marketed forty-four hogsheads of tobacco.[31] Except for those planter-merchants with large numbers of slaves, store goods usually comprised the greatest value of personal property. But when land was included, the relative value of mercantile goods declined sharply to a clear minority position. Wilson owned over 7,000 acres and fellow Pittsylvania County planter-merchant George Adams's holdings were in excess of 6,000 acres. Planter-merchants generally employed some of their slaves in the store operations. William Keene of Halifax County designated two of his fourteen slaves as "company slaves." Some merchants designated a portion of their vast, discontiguous holdings as the "store tract." The landholdings of James Glenn of Halifax County contained a "river tract," with 641 acres, and a "store tract," with almost 636 acres.

Second, in contrast to pre-Revolutionary planter-merchants, there were a few emerging merchants whose trading activities did not appear to be extensions of agrarian and other economic interests, but rather functioned as their sole support. A few of these merchants were associated with the early clustering of activities in and around the fledgling towns, primarily Danville and Farmville in the early nineteenth century. Among this small group were Edmund Mitchell and Remenias Williams of Pittsylvania County, and George Backas of Prince Edward County. Little is known about other nonagrarian-based planters in the region. However, John Andrew Schwartz, a recent immigrant from Germany, devoted full attention to his store-tavern operations on 200 acres of land in Nottoway County. Phillip Jackson, who operated a store at the Amelia County courthouse, possessed no land or slaves. Jessee Leftwich of Pittsylvania County, who owned only a horse, was, as indicated earlier, a partner of prominent planter-merchant David Pannill.

Third, variations among individual merchant operations continued to exist between east and west. Similar to the prewar period, the larger and more diverse operators were located in the western section of the region. This pattern suggested the greater speculative opportunity in the less-developed western areas and indicated the locational advantages of distance from the fall-zone ports. In 1800 the median size of landholdings of thirteen merchants, of a total of seventeen in Pittsylvania County, was almost 2,300 acres. In Halifax County the median size was almost 700 acres for seventeen merchants, of a total of twenty. In Amelia County, the median size was just over 500 acres for twelve of seventeen merchants. Median size of slave holdings for those same merchants in the three counties were, respectively, eleven, seven, and eleven.

Store locations appeared to be more widely dispersed than during the period of Scottish dominance. Although ferry sites remained the most important location for country stores, the relative level of ag- glomeration at those places appeared to be greatly reduced compared to the period before the war, when high-volume stores competed from these points. Despite the beginnings of a trend away from the planta- tion location of stores, that site was still the most prevalent location for mercantile activities. For example, William Morton's store in Charlotte County was located in two rooms on the first floor of his plantation dwelling. David Pannill's primary store was sited only twenty feet from his plantation house. William Cassels sited his store behind his dwelling house and between the granary and the lumber house on his Amelia County plantation (see also Figs. 2-6 to 2-9).[32]

Amelia County in 1787 provides an indication of the distribution of country stores in the postwar period, although the locational fac- tors are biased by the absence of important ferry sites, the close prox- imity to the fall-zone ports of Petersburg and Richmond, and the high density of roads coalescing toward those two destinations. Of the fourteen Amelia merchants who purchased licenses in 1787, eight had operations in Raleigh Parish (modern-day Amelia County), the north- ern part of the county that comprised just over half of the county's territory; and six merchants located their stores in Nottoway Parish (present-day Nottoway County) (Fig. 4-2).

The stores were fairly evenly distributed throughout the county, with only the southwestern part of Nottoway parish and the areas along portions of the Appomattox River not having stores. Some trade ar- eas obviously overlapped, especially those of the Davis and Henderson stores located in close proximity in central Nottoway. Based on its more than £3,600 of store goods, the William Walthall store probably controlled a much larger trade area.[33] Only seven of the stores could be identified with a plantation location. The remaining store loca- tions were at sites adjacent to other rural functions, suggesting the development of low-level service centers. Robert Wilson's store was located at Williamson's Ordinary, known today as Jenning's Ordinary, on a well-traveled road leading to the counties of Prince Edward and Charlotte. Gresset and John Davis located their store at Pride's Church at the intersection of important north-south and east-west roads. This location had a store, mill, tavern, and church in 1820. The Phillip Jackson store was located at the courthouse, and the Joseph Scott store was located adjacent to a grist mill. John Andrew Schwartz and James Henderson, the latter from his plantation that had long dominated the area and would eventually become the site of the Nottoway County courthouse, located their stores at the union of several roads leading from the backcountry to the fall zone. In this long-settled county,

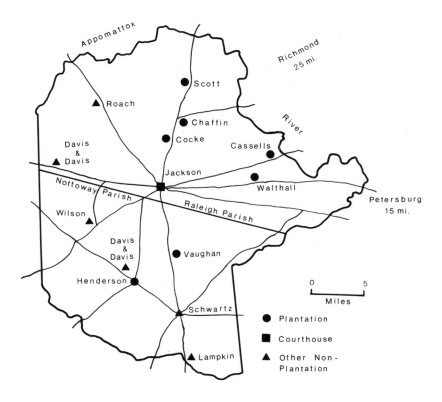

Figure 4-2. Store locations in Amelia County, 1787. *Source*: Amelia County Order Book 18:65, 72, 75, 76, 98; Amelia County deed books.

country-store clustering, in a few instances, appears to have evolved toward the formation of distinct hamlets.

Reflecting their lack of centrality, most stores in the post-Revolutionary period were small in size. The mean size of nineteen stores available for study between 1801 and 1805 was 603 square feet, or a structure approximately 25 feet by 24 feet (Table 4-2). The largest store, that of the former Scottish storekeeper Samuel Calland, measured over 1,000 square feet. The smallest store was only 324 square feet. However, some of the smaller stores actually may have been storerooms. Only two stores had more than one story (or floor), but several stores had additional sheds or wings that were added as the businesses expanded. Southside stores were considerably smaller than stores located in emerging towns in the backcountry north of the region. The store of George Rust, located in the Campbell County town of Rustburg, measured 1,760 square feet. Samuel White's store in New

London, now also in Campbell County, was 1,536 square feet in size. Based on the relatively small firm of Alexander Donald and Company, Scottish stores were considerably larger than those of local planter-merchants. Their Mecklenburg store, as previously indicated, contained over 1,408 square feet.

Table 4-2.
Size of Store Structures

Merchant	Year	Location	Size
Edward Dromgoole	1803	Brunswick	22 x 15
John Drummond	1802	Brunswick	10 x 15 (shed)
William Cassells	1805	Amelia	26 x 24
John Goodrich & Philip Thurmond	1803	Amelia	16 x 10
John Jeter	1805	Amelia	18 x 18
John Royall	1805	Amelia	32 x 18
Thomas Eldridge	1803	Prince Edward	16 x 16 (store)
			14 x 16 (room)
			12 x 10 (wing)
Curtis Haynes	1803	Prince Edward	32 x 30
Robert Venable	1801	Prince Edward	18 x 26
			8 x 26
George Backas	1805	Farmville	20 x 16 (2 story)
			16 x 16 (1 story)
William Baskerville	1805	Mecklenburg	40 x 16
Joseph Speed	1803	Mecklenburg	18 x 32
John Thomas	1803	Charlotte	36 x 16
William Watkins	1803	Charlotte	32 x 30
Samuel Calland	1805	Pittsylvania	38 x 18
			38 x 10 (shed)
Remenias Williams	1803	Pittsylvania	26 x 16 (2 story)
John Winbish, Jr.	1803	Pittsylvania	24 x 16
Edmund Mitchell	1805	Danville	18 x 28

Source: Mutual Assurance Society.

Although the dominant mercantile firms changed over time, there was little variation in the structure of mercantile activity. That structure was dictated by the fall-zone ports where tobacco was marketed and where wholesale activities were concentrated. The focus of Southside trade continued to be on country stores located primarily on plantation sites near ferries, crossroads, and courthouses. Planter-merchants from both the early settlement period and post-Revolutionary period, Scottish mercantile firms in the pre-Revolutionary period, and itinerant merchants with both distant and local origins all conformed to this dominant trading structure.

Notes

1. Halifax County Deed Book 2:294–97.

2. For entrepreneurial aspects of early settlers, see Mitchell, *Frontier and Commercialism*, 1–14, 59–92, 133–60; Rutman and Rutman, *A Place in Time*, 205–9; Charles S. Grant, *Democracy in the Frontier Town of Kent* (New York, 1970; originally 1961), 12–54.

3. Brunswick County Will Book 3:241–44, 300–01.

4. Brunswick County Will Book 2:171–72.

5. For Booker and Smith, see Amelia County Will Book 1:85–86, 61. Other planter-merchants in Amelia County were William Booker and Alex Erskine; additional planter-merchants in Brunswick County were Lewis Parham, Sterling Clack, Drury Stith, Hugh Miller, John Luke, and John Maclin. Parham and Stith had grist mills; Stith, Clack, and Luke operated ordinaries. Stith and Clack were active in public affairs; Stith was a county justice and Clack built the new county courthouse building.

6. Halifax County Pleas 2:102; Pittsylvania County Accounts Current 1:97–101.

7. For Roberts and Hickey, see respectively Halifax County Pleas 2: 103–5 and Hinkle and Kemper, "Moravian Diaries of Travel Through Virginia," 12:276.

8. Devine, *Tobacco Lords*, 58; Bradshaw, *History of Prince Edward County*, 93; Halifax County Judgments, 1757, inclusive.

9. Murdoch and Yuille as plaintiffs, Halifax County Judgments, February–March 1761. See also a petition for a new road in the county in ibid., April, June, August, 1772. Yuille was identified as the individual who opened the old road from Booker's Ferry to the courthouse during the 1750s.

10. Speirs's landholdings are found in Amelia County Deed Book 1: 386–88. For Cunninghame's tenure in Virginia, see McMurran, "The Virginia Claims of William Cunninghame and Company," 1–12. Hastie's ties to the Southside are indicated in a detailed lawsuit against Zacharia Leigh in Prince Edward County Court Papers, 1770.

11. Lewis C. Gray, *History of Agriculture in the Southern United States to 1860* 1:214; Coakley, "Virginia Commerce During the American Revolution," 13; Price, "The Rise of Glasgow in the Chesapeake Tobacco Trade," 187; Soltow, "Scottish Traders in Virginia," 85n.

12. McMurran, "The Virginia Claims of William Cunninghame and Company," 96.

13. "British Mercantile Claims," 16:104.

14. For Donald's Mecklenburg store, see Halifax County Judgments, May Court, 1772, A to D; Donald's Brunswick complex is found in *Virginia Gazette*, Purdie and Dixon, January 6, 1774, May 26, 1774; for the Prince Edward County store, see *Virginia Gazette*, Purdie and Dixon, November 2, 1769.

15. *Virginia Gazette*, Dixon and Hunter, March 11, 1775.

16. Letter of Ebenezer MacHarg to Neil Jamieson, June 13, 1770, The Papers of Neil Jamieson, Library of Congress, Manuscripts, Washington, D.C.

17. Mecklenburg County Deed Book 3:318–19.

18. See for example, Courtlandt Canby, ed., "Robert Munford's *The Patriots*," *William and Mary Quarterly* 3d ser. 6 (1949), 437–503.

19. S. Harrell, *Loyalism in Virginia* (New York, 1965; originally 1926), 91.

20. For Love, see Brunswick County Will Book 5:270–75; for Calland, see Pittsylvania County Accounts Current 4:188–98.

21. Charlotte County Court Judgments, August–September 1771 (Part 1) and August 1772.

22. For the marriage, see Catherine L. Knorr, comp., *Marriages of Pittsylvania County, Virginia, 1767–1805* (Pine Bluff, Ark., 1956), 15. For the report of the court, see *Virginia Genealogist* 16 (1972), 85.

23. "Letter of Elizabeth J. Ambler to Mrs. Dudley," *Virginia Magazine of History and Biography* 38 (1930), 167–69.

24. For merchant activity during the early period of independence, see Richard M. Harrington, Jr., "The Virginia Merchant Community: A Case of Arrested Development, 1783–1789" (M.A. thesis, University of Virginia, 1972).

25. Charles T. Nall, ed., "A Letter From Petersburg, Virginia, January 10, 1789," *Virginia Magazine of History and Biography* 82 (1974), 147.

26. Harrell, *Loyalism in Virginia*, 99–100.

27. Ibid., 95.

28. Letter from Hook, December 26, 1770. See also letters from David Ross to Hook, May 5, 1772, and May 23, 1772, John Hook Papers.

29. Barksdale Family Papers, 1787–1844 file, Manuscripts, University of Virginia.

30. Harrison's advertisement in the *Lynchburg and Farmer's Gazette* appeared in Pittsylvania County Judgments, June, July, August, 1795.

31. For Cocke, see Amelia Will Book 5:221–24; for Wilson, see Siegel, *The Roots of Southern Distinctiveness*, 28.

32. Mutual Assurance Society.

33. Amelia Will Book 4:332–36, 346–50.

5

Consumer Opportunity in a
Primary Staple Economy

To this point, the broader aspects of settlement, economy, and trade have been emphasized, with only a hint of the individual consumer who supported this decentralized exchange. In a system of central places, consumers are expected to shop at the nearest place that offers the desired good or service. In a system of central places, consumers travel greater distances to purchase higher-order goods that are not locally available. But what opportunities were available to the consumer in a primary staple economy, where decentralized places were the only shopping alternatives and where the next step in the trading hierarchy was composed of large and distant places that exerted an extraordinarily strong field of influence on the region? In comparison to opportunity in an urban network, were there fewer local and regional places to shop? Were consumers forced to travel greater distances for basic lower-order goods and services? Were local consumers more likely to patronize distant, externally located central places?

Discussion of the spatial aspects of country trade is structured around two separate approaches that vary in scale and complexity. A broad consumer-opportunity framework looks at the Southside consumer in the context of local, regional, and long-distance contexts. Decentralized trade area analysis, essentially the application of the general aspects of central-place theory to decentralized trade, provides a more detailed look at the locations and social and economic characteristics of the clientele of local country stores.

135

Consumer Opportunity at Local and Regional Levels

Because of the similarity of shopping places across a large geographic spectrum and the high level of mobility of Southsiders, no distinction is made between consumer opportunity at local and regional levels. The primary factors in consumer opportunity at both these levels, ranked in order of decreasing importance, were distance minimization, debt avoidance, presence of itinerant merchants, regional business travel, and the estate sale. An additional factor, tobacco prices, was a floating variable, ranking either near the middle or near the bottom of the consumer opportunity scale.

Although operating in a highly mobile society, Southside consumers nevertheless were most influenced by distance minimization. By primarily patronizing the more local stores, consumers were following the basic human impulse of least effort that is the basis of central-place theory. The notorious and periodically impassable roads of the region would also suggest the more favorable trading position of the local stores. William Cunninghame and Company expected to draw most of its customers from an area that extended twelve to fourteen miles from the store. At the Halifax County store of Scottish merchant James Murdoch and Company, 84 percent of the customers and 92 percent of store visits came from within ten miles of the retail establishment during the year 1774–75 (Fig. 5-1). During the year 1791–92, all but one of the customers of the Edward Dromgoole store in Brunswick County lived within ten miles of the store (Fig. 5-2).[1]

But distance was not equal. Unlike the assumptions of central-place theory that render the physical environment and other potential obstacles impotent, therefore guaranteeing equal access to goods and services to consumers located equal distances from the retail establishment, distance in a decentralized frontier region varied considerably. The availability of stores in a local area made the neighborhood store a highly variable part of consumer opportunity. In early periods of settlement and in continuing isolated or sparsely populated areas, the local store could be twenty miles or more from the consumer. If the consumers lived near a ferry site, they may have traveled only a mile or two. And the ferry location also expanded the local trade area of the store. The Murdoch store actually had almost as many customers originate from the five- to ten-mile distance as from the area within five miles of the store. The Dromgoole store, not located near a ferry, had a smaller local trade area, with 94 percent of the customers originating within five miles of the store. But with both stores, the key to distance minimization was the acceptance of individual mobility. If

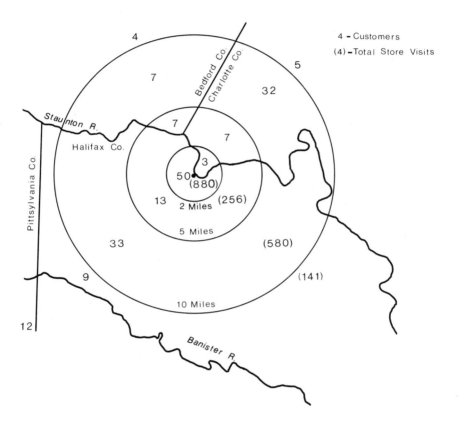

Figure 5-1. Murdoch store trade area, 1774–75.

two miles is invoked as the limit of the measure of distance minimization, then only 29 percent of Murdoch customers and 22 percent of Dromgoole customers would fit this category.

Country stores were not the only retail and service establishments available at the local level. Some ordinaries and taverns, in addition to the lodging, food, and drink for travelers and the drink and socializing for the local population, also sold store goods such as salt, sugar, and coarse cloth. With later hours and with functions that might alter regular purchasing patterns, ordinaries and taverns were early conve-

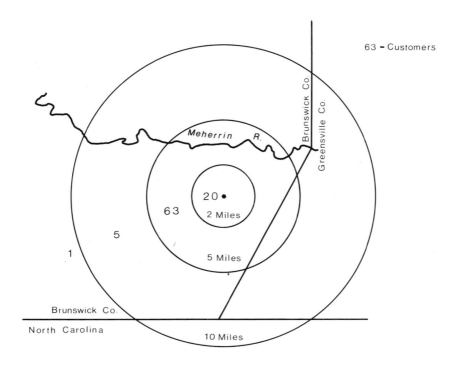

Figure 5-2. Dromgoole store trade area, 1791–92.

nience places for some consumers. In 1753 and 1754, Halifax County ordinary-keeper Robert Wooding sold a customer gunpowder, shot, small amounts of cloth, a knife, and six pounds of sugar in addition to rum, punch, and meals. In 1754, in the same county, John Owen sold John Scogins small amounts of cloth, salt, and the ubiquitous rum.[2] Prices were expectedly higher than at the country stores. Owen sold oznaburg cloth for 1s. 6d. per ell (39 inches) at the same time that two local store operators were getting 1s. 2d. and 1s. 3d. for that item. He sold Irish linen for 3s. 6d. per yard when the price at a local store was 2s. 9d.

Debt avoidance, the consumer's decision to seek out an additional store in order to evade debts made at a previous store, was endemic in the Southside, where credit was the expected method of transacting business and where communications between merchants was weak. Indeed, many of the inhabitants of the Southside had migrated to the region to avoid payment of debts in other areas of Virginia. Among the many examples of this practice, only a few illustrative spatial examples will be cited. In Halifax County, Parham Booker transacted £65 worth of business at James Murdoch's store in 1774–75 after Alexander Speirs and Company had brought suit against him in 1773 for debts in excess of £296 incurred at the firm's store in the same county. Epa White, who did £25 worth of business at Murdoch's store in 1774–75, previously had been sued by Robert Donald and Company for more than £112 worth of unpaid purchases at their nearby Charlotte County store. Tscharner DeGraffenreid, a resident of Lunenburg County, traded farther afield to avoid his debts. He patronized the Dreghorn, Murdoch store in Prince Edward County and the store of William Cunninghame in Mecklenburg County. Among the many individuals who patronized local stores, regional stores, and distant fall-zone establishments was the highly mobile Thomas Tunstall of Halifax County. Between 1773 and 1775 Tunstall purchased goods at Murdoch stores in Halifax and Pittsylvania, Field and Call and Buchanan and Hastie stores in Charlotte, Speirs stores in both Halifax and Charlotte, and William Cunninghame stores in Halifax and at Petersburg.[3]

Merchants, well aware of the general practice, obviously made up for these losses through manipulation of store and tobacco prices, and other services. The Scottish companies, with their control of the tobacco marketing system and with their multifunctional trading companies, were better able to make adjustments to counter the losses incurred by the practice of debt avoidance. Indeed, debts were just one of several components of Scottish investment practices in the tobacco trade, although the staggering number of small debts, the result of wide-scale debt avoidance, was a bookkeeping nightmare.[4] Illustrative of the function of debt in the tobacco trade, one Scottish storekeeper went so far as to dismiss a suit to collect a debt owed the store if the defendant would agree to purchase goods only at his store.[5] The storekeeper's primary motive was the acquisition of a monopoly on the planter's tobacco.

Itinerant merchants traded in the Southside throughout the eighteenth century. The conditions that permitted these merchants to be a continuing factor in the mercantile network were the same conditions that supported the country store trade: the dispersed population and the lack of towns. James Soltow has suggested that early Scottish mercantile efforts in the Virginia backcountry may have been as itinerant merchants.[6]

Peddlers, the primary itinerant traders, rarely appeared in the county records despite the requirement that they purchase a license, but obviously there were many more than these records would indicate. Wagon merchants, the other itinerant merchants, were less visible and more unstructured in their trading patterns. Unlike the externally based peddlers, wagon merchants were usually residents of the local area. For protection, company, or the complementarity of individual specialization in certain goods, peddlers usually traveled in groups. A peddler by the name of Buchanan, possibly an early representative of a Glasgow firm, was robbed of more than £10 in western Halifax County in 1756 by a roving band of men who preyed upon isolated travelers.[7]

Peddlers provided the Southside consumer with two different levels of shopping. They stopped by individual houses on a regular basis and also made the rounds of the county courthouses during court days. At his home the consumer had access to a single peddler or a group of two or more peddlers at one time, while at the courthouse he had the benefit of several groups who provided a greater variety of goods. Like sedentary merchants, peddlers provided both cash and credit sales. Credit sales were a necessity even for itinerant merchants in this cash-poor region, but presumably that type of transaction took place only after a period of familiarization of the territory by the seller.

The variety and value of goods that peddlers carried on their pack horses and in their carts may be seen in the inventory of Abel Tillison. Tillison was apparently on the road selling his wares when he died in 1801 at the home of Thomas Wilkinson in Pittsylvania County. Among the predominantly kitchen goods that were carried in a cart pulled by a single horse were fifty-six coffee pots, twenty-eight milk pails, and eighteen cotton handkerchiefs. Surprisingly, he carried no cloth, usually the most frequently purchased item at fixed-location retail establishments in the backcountry. In addition to the more than £27 worth of goods, Tillison also carried about £6 in cash.[8]

The only contemporary account of the itinerant trade is provided by the diary of an Irish peddler.[9] During the winter of 1807–08, the narrator and two other peddlers traveled the court circuit from Charlottesville in the north to Henry, Pittsylvania, Halifax, Charlotte, Prince Edward, Lunenburg, and Amelia counties in the Southside. Their encounters with other peddlers at courthouses suggest a large and regular itinerant trade available to Southsiders at that location. Although their strategy primarily was to focus on the potentially larger crowds that periodically gathered at the courthouses, they also sold goods by cash and credit to regular customers along the trek. On December 5, for example, the troupe stopped at the home of a Mr. Mason in Charlotte County, where one of the peddlers collected money and sold an additional £20 of goods. The trading in a specific and narrow line of goods was indicated by their traveling in groups. That business strategy also depended heavily on luck. As the narrator observed, "My friend Downing done the most being perfectly fixed besides having an assortment of Goods that suited."[10]

The narrator has presented more than just an account of business matters. The rich diversity of moods and conditions reveals an intriguing itinerant subculture. On good days they were rowdy, libidinous, jocular, good-natured, and playful, and were reminiscent of characters from an O. Henry story. They often moved along at a rate of over thirty miles per day and there were good friends and accommodations waiting as night approached. On other days, they fell prey to the cruelty of the weather and the regional infrastructure. Rain and snow created sickness for the exposed travelers and made the clay roadbeds slow and dangerous passages. Bad food and lodging also weakened the body and added to the frustration and misery of the road. And for this, the peddler had to purchase, in addition to the general fee required by the state, a separate license for the privilege of trading at each courthouse. It must be assumed that most peddlers were young in age and spirit to survive this punishment and possessed lots of "road smarts" to avoid thieves and county officials.

The wagon merchant was a wagoner who usually carried tobacco to the fall-zone inspection warehouses and returned with a load of European goods for a specific planter or planter-merchant. In addition the wagoner also purchased goods for himself and sold them on the trip back home or in the home county. Wagon merchants usually remained small and sporadic operators. Among several such itinerant and part-time merchants in Halifax County was Richard Dudgeon. During the 1750s, Dudgeon sold a customer £9 of goods that included two kinds of cloth, salt, two Dutch blankets, lead, powder, a scythe, rum, and sugar. Dudgeon apparently was not too successful with his carriage or merchant activities. In 1776 his estate was valued at only £52, with fifteen cattle, some hogs, two horses, and no slaves.[11] Although few became established merchants, two early Halifax County merchants, Joseph Mayes and John Boyd, probably began their mercantile activities as wagon merchants. Both men also operated ferries and hauling services after becoming fixed-location merchants.

Mobility and periodic travel over great distance were facts of life in regions dominated by primary staple economies. Although all Southsiders were involved in this high level of mobility, the more affluent planters were more likely to be participants in regional business travel to courthouses for monthly court sessions, militia musters, and visits to additional plantation quarters in both contiguous and distant counties. Sporting events, such as horse races and cockfights, and just socializing were also integral components of this "business" travel for the gregarious Southsiders. In the course of these business travels, they often frequented stores, ordinaries, and taverns located beyond their immediate local areas (especially at courthouse and ferry sites) and additional stores in a chain system during the period of Scottish mercantile dominance.

The monthly meeting of the county court gave the Southside consumers their most important periodic market. But there was serious competition to the act of purchasing goods and services. Although there were probably at least one or more stores and ordinaries in the general area, and peddlers regularly set up their wares here, the most important activities at the court were legal, higher-level business and, of course, entertainment. The business transacted by the merchants and customers at the courthouse was in a completely different context from their activities at the stores. Court was used to strike business deals, bring suit against debtors, give loans, collect from debtors, and exchange business and social information. With the travel and concentrated activity of a two- or three-day court session, there was little opportunity for those traveling to court to purchase goods at the seat.

The "Diary of a Peddler" portrays the paradoxical aspects of the courthouse as a place for shopping opportunity. The descending of several groups of peddlers upon the court site indicated its importance as a higher-order and periodic shopping place, but the existence of so many peddlers, who openly displayed their goods without serious local complaint, also suggests that the site itself was not an important place for fixed-location businesses unless the adjacent area were heavily populated. By contrast, in the more urban Shenandoah Valley, merchants with stores at county seats were openly hostile to peddlers and took measures to prohibit their activities.[12]

The linkage of death and debt created the estate sale, the periodic sale used to pay the numerous debts of Southside planters. Most of the sale items were slaves, stock animals, and plantation-associated products such as hoes, barrels, hogsheads, and transportation equipment, primarily carts and wagons. Store-type goods usually were not present in sufficient volume to offer any competition to the store. Slaves, when available, were the most important property for sale. Local planters could purchase slaves who had already conformed to local work patterns and did not require additional seasoning. Estate sales that featured slaves also attracted interested parties from outside the region. Of the forty-two slaves offered for sale from the estate of Mecklenburg County planter-playwright Robert Munford, twenty-nine were purchased by Southsiders, five by residents of the Tidewater county of Charles City, seven by North Carolinians, and one by an individual from the northern Virginia county of Spotsylvania. At the less pricey end of the estate-sale spectrum, at least thirty-two individuals purchased leather, livestock, small quantities of grain, hoes, nails, hats, linen, salt, shoes, a saddle, and a bedstead from the estate of a late Amelia County resident.[13]

Although tobacco prices were supposedly firmly set at the meetings of merchants in Williamsburg and from agreements among factors for the "tobacco lords," price variations existed between stores and between customers at individual stores (Appendix B). This discussion is only concerned with situations at the local level that may have slightly altered prices offered for tobacco. It is quite apparent that the "tobacco lords" and other externally based trading companies controlled tobacco prices. These price variations do not relate solely to whether the crop was purchased outright for a lower price or traded for store goods and services for higher prices. That practice was followed by all trading companies.

The mercantile accounts indicate the differences in tobacco prices, but do not reveal the explanation. Because tobacco was not normally viewed before purchasing, did price variations suggest that the product of certain plantations was accepted as being of higher quality because of perception by the merchant, reputation of the planter, or quality of the soil? Or was the viewing of tobacco in the field or during the postcuring and prepackaging stage more common than previously suggested? Or was there more vigorous competition between Scottish trading firms, despite their complex family linkages? Or did the variations in prices merely reflect the events of the moment or the time at which the tobacco was purchased, especially when the factor was trying to acquire the final hogsheads to complete his portion of the next shipload? The inability to answer these questions satisfactorily makes tobacco a highly variable factor in consumer behavior.

Although there may not be sufficient evidence to satisfy the above questions, it is quite clear that tobacco, as the basis of the Scottish trading system, had some impact on store competition. Certain large companies established territorial and volume thresholds in their quest for the valuable weed. The highest density of country stores, the greatest frequency of new store openings, and the highest-volume stores were located in areas of expanding tobacco production, primarily the central and western counties in the period preceding the Revolutionary War. If store competition was primarily based on the greater access to tobacco, did that competition support higher tobacco prices for planter-consumers? If those tobacco prices were established and manipulated primarily by the volume of store goods in this barter economy, tobacco prices may have been a factor in providing consumer opportunity at the local and regional levels. How this operated, whether by advertising, word of mouth, dissemination at meetings of the county court, or from agents scouring the countryside, is not clear. And most critical to consumer opportunity, were planter-consumers aware of price advantages created by store competition?

Consumer Opportunity at the Long-Distance Level

Central-place studies indicate that consumers travel to distant and larger places to purchase higher-order goods not available at the local level or to purchase a greater variety of goods in the multipurpose trip. By inference, larger purchases of a single item or a bulky product also occur during these less-frequent trips. Southside consumers used Petersburg, Manchester, Osbornes, Warwick, and Richmond at the fall zone to purchase more luxury goods and large quantities of other goods. This was especially true of wealthier backcountry planters, who often purchased large quantities of goods from fall-zone factors, who also tended to a variety of other planter needs and concerns. For these special and personal services, the planter marketed all of his tobacco crop through the mercantile company that the factor represented.

John Smith of Pocket Plantation, one of the largest tobacco producers in the Southside, ordered his goods primarily by letters sent through wagoner intermediaries who carried his tobacco to the inspection warehouse at Manchester. During an eight-month period in 1770, Thomas Pettus of Lunenburg County had an account of over

£80 at Crenshaw and Company of Petersburg that included £62 13s. 9d. in cash advances, £6 10s. 9d. in payments to third parties, and 14s. 5d. paid to satisfy tobacco inspection expenses. Pettus built his account through sixteen separate business contacts with the store. His credits to the account were provided primarily by the marketing of five hogsheads of tobacco through the store.[14] This consumer pattern of wealthier backcountry residents primarily patronizing distant and larger places was also true in Frederick County in the wheat and cattle economy of the Shenandoah Valley.[15]

Both James Vance's long-distance settlement model and Earle and Hoffman's staple theory of settlement and economic development ignore the existence of retail trade within the context of long-distance trade. In a spatial context, wholesaling and retailing functions were not mutually exclusive. Not only did a flourishing country-store trade take place within this long-distance trade, but the entrepôts were also components of the retail trade network of the Southside. The Crenshaw store had thirty-six customers from Lunenburg County, twenty-six from Amelia, seventeen from Brunswick, sixteen from Pittsylvania, eleven each from Halifax and Prince Edward, and nine from Mecklenburg.

In a primary staple economy, where markets were at distant locations and where there were no places between decentralized country clustering and large fall-zone entrepôts, long-distance trade was not the sole domain of the wealthy. Indeed, middle and lower wealth groups had greater access to long-distance-based retail and service activities. Wagoners and rollers made frequent and regular trips to the fall-zone entrepôts to deliver tobacco to inspection warehouses. Cattle and hog drives also brought additional consumers to these places. Residents of eastern Amelia and northern Brunswick also shopped at the fall zone because of its close proximity. Additional evidence of the more universal aspects of long-distance retail trade are revealed by accounts that showed no difference between the kinds of goods purchased at the fall zone and those purchased at the local country stores. Similar to purchases at the local stores, fall-zone purchases were primarily cloth, hardware, food and drink, and household items. Except for the relatively rare purchases of slaves or Madeira wine, even the wealthier planters purchased the same items from their factors as other Southsiders purchased from local stores.

Representative of the range of Southside customers shopping at the fall zone were several accounts at the Crenshaw store. In addition to Thomas Pettus's account of over £80, wagoner Peter Rogers had an account of £42 that was created by five separate visits over a period of eight months. Other customers had accounts that were less than

one pound. Adam Finch's purchases, totaling 15s. 2d., were made
during three separate visits. Asa Oliver had an account for only 9d.,
the price of a small quantity of nails.

Since there was no urban network in Southside Virginia, did consumers have reduced access to goods and services and were there
fewer shopping opportunities available to these consumers? Although
considered in the context of a lack of knowledge about consumer behavior in similar-sized regions with urban networks and a secondary
staple economy, Southside consumers did not have the same access
to goods and services that was present in regions such as southeastern Pennsylvania and the Shenandoah Valley. Given the high level of
consumer mobility, the scattering of stores across the region, the
concentration of stores at some ferry sites, the range of shopping
opportunity, and the variety of goods and services offered by local
country stores, Southside consumers had access to a variety of goods
and services. But any sort of parity with these two regions was ne-
gated by both the greater mobility that was necessary for Southsiders
to acquire a variety of decentralized goods within their region and to
gain access to a centralized variety and quantity of goods available
only at the distant fall zone, and the lack of opportunity for half of
the population to participate in the retail and service trade.

Store Trade Areas

The trade area of the Southside country store was generally large because of the dispersed population, the considerable mobility of the
population, and the high rate of debt avoidance. The James Murdoch
store in Halifax County and Edward Dromgoole's Sligo Store in
Brunswick County are used to determine the characteristic eighteenth-
century backcountry trade area. For the Murdoch store, 182 customers, or 45 percent of the total number of customers, were located. For
Sligo, eighty-nine customers, or one-third of the total number, were
located.

The Murdoch store, operated by a Glasgow-based firm, was located
adjacent to Booker's Ferry in northeastern Halifax County near the
confluence of Childress Creek and the Staunton River.[16] Customers
came primarily from the west and southwest along the side roads and
trails of Hickey's Road in Halifax County, from the northeast along
similar transport lines leading into Bookers Road in Charlotte County,
and from the northwest by several smaller ferries that crossed the
Staunton from Bedford County. Established before 1760, an unusu-

ally early date for a Scottish store to be permanently located this far
into the interior, the store was probably the dominant mercantile establishment in this section of the tricounty area. This is suggested by
its location, its relatively long history, the 407 customer accounts in
1774–75, and the listing of 610 credit customers in the ledger of 1770–
71.

Mapping the locations of Murdoch customers revealed two dominant spatial patterns. First, a large number of consumers lived near
the store; and second, the store attracted large numbers of patrons
from considerable distances (Fig. 5-1). The most active customers were
those who lived within two miles of the store. They had the greatest
number of total visits of any of the distance units. The fifty-three
customers who lived within this small inner-trade area visited the store
880 times during the year. Eight of these customers, including one
with seventy visits, averaged twenty-six or more shopping trips.
Twenty-seven customers, including one with sixty-one visits, lived
between two and five miles from the store and visited the store a
total of 256 times during the year. The largest number of customers
in this highly mobile society, seventy-two, lived five to ten miles from
the store.

The Dromgoole store, operated by a local planter-merchant, was
located three to four miles south of the Meherrin River in Brunswick
County at or near a place known as Randle's Ordinary, long a focus
of several roads. This store, the first in a five-chain operation, was
established on property purchased in 1787.[17] The Dromgoole trade area
was considerably smaller than the Murdoch store hinterland. Almost
all of the customers whose residences were located lived within five
miles of the store (Fig. 5-2). The shorter history of the Dromgoole
store and its nonferry location gave it a more limited area from which
to draw customers. This spatial pattern of consumers also suggests
greater population densities, decreased mobility, and more store competition.

Because of its trading function, the local country store was also a
community focus. In an area devoid of towns where services were
extensively arranged, the store was one of the few places that brought
a large number of people together on a frequent basis. As foci of
community, stores easily surpassed the few and relatively unpopular
Anglican churches and offered a greater availability than the more
periodic meetings of the county court and the rapidly increasing Bap-
tist and Methodist churches established in the latter part of the eighteenth century. At least 200 customers in 1774–75 had accounts at
the Murdoch store five years earlier. Many members of extended fami-

lies shopped at the two stores. Eleven Hunts, eight Bookers, seven Easts, and six individuals with Glass as a surname were customers at the Murdoch store. At the Dromgoole store, there were thirteen Waltons, eight Wessons, seven Williamses, six Woolseys, and a like number of Simses, Jacksons, and Harrises. A large number of customers at both stores shared one or more property boundaries, and later arrivals often purchased land from earlier settlers. Within the five- to ten-mile trade range, eleven Murdoch customers were concentrated on the upper branches of Bradley Creek in Halifax County. At least ten Dromgoole customers were located along the short Rocky Run east of the store, and perhaps as many as twenty-two customers were clustered along Rattlesnake Creek and its tributaries. Because Dromgoole was also the leading disseminator of the Methodist Church in the region, many of his customers may have had an additional community bond with the store.

Women as widows, as components of guardian accounts, and as independent consumers also had accounts at these two stores. Although comprising a distinct minority, seventeen women patronized the Murdoch store and sixteen women shopped at the Dromgoole store. By contrast, the Grasty and Pannill store in northeastern Pittsylvania County counted only one female customer during the year 1799–1800. Women's names were listed in the daybooks, but whether they actually paid a physical visit to the stores or whether intermediaries made their purchases is not known.

Wealth Characteristics of Store Customers

Analysis of the land and slave holdings of Murdoch and Dromgoole customers reveals their varied wealth characteristics and the "democratic" character of the store trade. Country stores served the wealthy and the poor, the land owners and the landless, slaveholders and laborers, and the locally prominent and the virtually unknown.

Although these two stores catered to a broad spectrum of the population, they served the lower- and middle-level groups much more frequently than the more affluent. If the middle level is defined as owning from 100 to 500 acres and having one to ten slaves, and if the lower level is defined as owning no land or less than 100 acres and having no slaves, then the majority of the customers of both stores fell into these two categories. Overall, just over 75 percent of the Murdoch customers were situated in these two wealth categories as compared to 90 percent of the Dromgoole clientele (Tables 5-1 and 5-2). Because only 44 percent of Murdoch's 407 customers and only

Table 5-1.
Land-Ownership Characteristics of Store Customers

Land (acres)	Murdoch Store		Dromgoole Store	
	No.	%	No.	%
no land	15	8	56	39
1–99	9	5	6	4
100–200	56	31	23	16
201–300	24	13	23	16
301–400	21	12	12	8
401–500	12	7.	10	7
501–600	10	5	5	3
601–700	9	5	0	0
701–800	4	2	1	<1
801–900	5	3	3	2
901–1,000	3	2	1	<1
1,001–1,500	8	4	1	<1
1,501–2,000	0	0	1	<1
over 2,000	5	3	3	2
Total	181		145	

Source: County deed books, will books, and land taxes.

Table 5-2.
Slave-Ownership Characteristics of Store Customers

Slaves	Murdoch Store		Dromgoole Store	
	No.	%	No.	%
no slaves	67	38	50	34
1	10	6	25	17
2–5	43	25	48	33
6–10	20	11	11	8
10–20	19	11	8	5
over 20	15	9	3	2
Total	174		145	

Source: County will books and personal property taxes.

55 percent of Dromgoole's 265 customers appeared in deed books and on land and personal tax lists, and therefore were available for classification, the proportion in the lower wealth group would presumably increase upon moving toward a more complete population.

Despite their greater opportunity to trade directly with fall-zone companies as a part of long-distance trade, the wealthy and powerful also shopped at the local country stores. Thirteen customers, over 7 percent of the clientele of the Murdoch store, owned more than 1,000 acres of land. One customer, Walter Coles, owned over 7,000 acres; four other customers owned over 3,000 acres. Almost 9 percent of the customers owned over twenty slaves; Coles owned 126 slaves and Paul Carrington had seventy-six. The largest landholder of the Dromgoole clientele had over 4,000 acres. Both stores also counted several members of the counties' political elites among their customers. The Dromgoole store had two current or past justices of the county court and one sheriff as patrons; and the Murdoch store, because of its location near a ferry and the junction of three counties, had thirteen present or former justices, six current or former sheriffs, and one current and two former members of the House of Burgesses among its customers. The latter included Carrington, one of the few well-known Southside politicians during the eighteenth century.

These two small groups of people were a microcosm of two different eighteenth-century societies. The more western Halifax County of 1774–75 was more of a frontier area than the eastern-located Brunswick County of 1791–92. In the former, land was more accessible to the population and holdings were larger because of its abundance, cheaper prices, and its function in speculation. Although possessing some commercial agriculture, as evidenced by the presence of a Scottish store, Halifax County had greater economic opportunity and the more diverse population associated with a frontier region. Not only is this indicated in land and slave holdings, but also in the greater population mobility. Over one-half of the Murdoch customers in 1770–71 were not customers in 1774–75. Brunswick County was more thoroughly dominated, or perhaps decimated, by a long history of commercial tobacco production. More individuals were landless and properties were smaller except for the few large planters who likely owned over half of all land. The Dromgoole trade area, because of its more eastern location, had become more like the Tidewater counties on its eastern border.[18]

A primary staple economy offered considerable opportunity for the local consumer. Country stores were both scattered across the landscape and clustered at selective sites. Along the more traveled roads, itinerant merchants literally brought goods to the customer's door. Local ordinaries also provided a small range of store goods. Periodic markets were available at courthouse sites and estate sales. Consumers in the Southside were more restricted by great travel distance, by lack of centralization of a large number and variety of business establishments, and by linkages between tobacco and store trade. Southside consumers had to travel farther because of more dispersed establishments and poorer road conditions, and had to be more creative because of the practices of acquiring credit and avoiding debt in this cash-poor society. Southside consumers, because of the tobacco marketing system, were more likely to regularly patronize stores at distant locations.

Country Trade and Central-Place Trade-Area Geometry

In the theoretical evolution from dispersed settlement to a well-developed urban network, the trade areas of central places passed through two general phases of circular shapes before attaining the climax trade-area shape of a hexagon. Initially, small central places had broadly circular trade areas that did not fill completely the trading landscape, thus leaving in-between locations with unserved or poorly served demand. As population and business expanded, increased competition between service centers created overlapping circular trade areas where in-between shoppers could patronize either of two competing central places. The hexagon was developed as the ideal shape for the trade area by bisecting all areas where circular trade areas overlapped. This assured that all customers had a single, nearest central place for shopping.

Certain aspects of country-store trade areas broadly conformed to some of the general assumptions of central-place trade areas. As revealed by the Murdoch and Dromgoole stores, a clear distance-decay factor was present as most of the business came from customers located near the establishments and declined with increases in distance. Located in a region with a highly dispersed population and an incomplete settlement system, the trade areas of Southside stores corresponded strongly to the unserved or underserved demand of the incomplete trade area where more remote and underdeveloped areas did not have easy access to stores or did not have sufficient purchasing power to support stores. Perhaps more important for the Southside, especially later in its development, was the overlapping of trade areas. This pattern was especially prominent in tobacco-producing areas, with their high level of mobility, and near ferry and courthouse sites, where the many stores patterned in an open-neighborhood type of country clustering functioned as distinct and separate retail and service establishments rather than operating as components of a single central place. The greater importance of peddlers and periodic estate sales would also create more trade-area overlap in this spatially competitive trading milieu.

The residences of the Murdoch store customers suggest a particular trade-area geometry that might be applicable to many of the ferry-site and crossroads-oriented stores in the region. The major concentrations of Murdoch customers were in northeast Halifax County and across the Staunton River in Charlotte County. An additional smaller group of customers came across ferries from Bedford County. Fewer customers came from comparable distances upriver and downriver from the store. The road network, with its orientation from fall zone to backcountry, trended northeast to southwest, crossing rivers rather than following their courses. The resulting trade area for ferry-based stores, and also for those at crossroads, was a sector arrangement in which cone-shaped trading areas expanded with increased distance from the store and sectors with large numbers of customers were interspersed with sectors containing sharply reduced numbers of customers. This trade-area geometry suggests overlap with other stores with increased distance and unserved demand along rivers between stores or along inferior roads leading to a crossroads location.

This particular geometry is reminiscent of August Lösch's modification of Christaller's trade-area homogeneity. Lösch suggested, in a more real-world context, that there were variations in urban development that took the pattern of alternating city-rich, city-poor sectors around a central city. For the dispersed Southside, this translates to alternating consumer-rich sectors along main highways leading to ferry and crossroad sites and consumer-poor sectors along rivers and inferior roads more poorly focused on these sites (Figs. 5-3 and 5-4).

Any discussion of country-store trade areas in the context of central-place trade-area geometry must not deviate too far from the obvious difference between the decentralized character of one and the centrality of the other. Similarities as perceived in an evolutionary interpretation do not alter the fact that the Southside was a region essentially devoid of central places where decentralized country stores dispensed goods and services.

Consumer Behavior in Decentralized Trade Compared to Consumer Behavior in Central-Place Theory

Although there were certain similar patterns between consumer behavior in decentralized and centralized trading contexts, specifically the factors of distance-decay (or least effort) and the heterogeneity of the shopping population at small places, contrasting behavioral patterns were more the general rule. Consumer behavior in decentralized trade varied from the norm in four ways: (1) lack of access to different trading levels within the region, (2) uneven distribution of

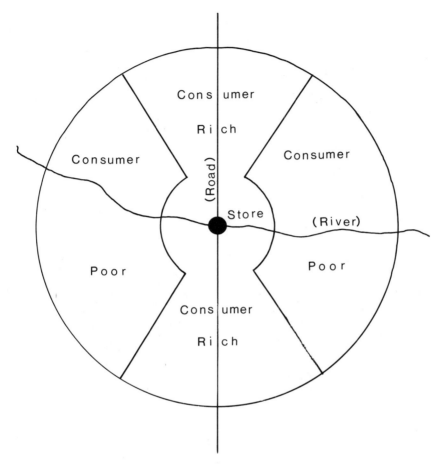

Figure 5-3. Idealized trade area, ferry location, 1791–92.

customers, (3) greater customer travel time to the lowest-level places, and (4) the greater significance of the multipurpose trip. Unlike a system of central places, Southside customers did not have access to the different trading levels of a hierarchical system. Without these several levels, Southside consumers shopped at a much greater number of lower-level places, or country stores, and made the long trading ascent directly from the lowest-order shopping places to the highest place in the trading system. The presumption of central-place theory was that customers responded to only one place at a given level and that each successive place up the trading ladder provided an adequate supply of increasingly higher-order goods.

With only one regional level at which to shop, Southside consumers were more motivated by gaining advantages through beating the

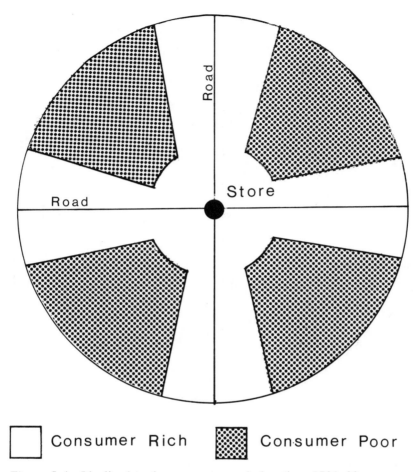

Figure 5-4. Idealized trade area, crossroads location, 1791–92.

system in the store-customer relationship than in the level of need, frequency of purchase, or cost of a good. Although the availability and quality of goods were important considerations, the fact that all stores offered similar products gave impetus to obtaining the best credit opportunity, higher prices for tobacco and other farm products, highest volume of third-party transactions and cash advances, and the increased opportunity to participate in debt avoidance. In response to this consumer behavior, store trade areas overlapped in several directions that defied conformity with the more rigidly defined trade boundaries prescribed by central-place theory.

Central-place theory assumes that there is an even distribution of population or purchasing power around a service center. Farming areas of the American Midwest during the mid-twentieth century had a high level of conformity with this particular aspect of central-place theory, but frontier areas, especially in the American South, were not likely to follow suit. In the Southside, with the westward advance of settlement, population was always unevenly arranged. The quality of soil, the level of involvement in tobacco cultivation, the quality of overland transport, and the availability of ferries to cross major streams were among the more important factors that created variations in consumer access to country stores. Also very critical was the high mobility level of the population. This tended to disrupt the presumed close association between low-level trading places and the neatly managed consumers attached to their trade area.

Because of the poor quality of roads, the scattered and uneven distribution of country stores, the number of low-level place alternatives for the consumer, and the long-distance trade of the tobacco marketing system, Southside consumers traveled for longer periods of time to reach their retail objectives. Although this was a fact of life in all early frontier areas, it persisted beyond this early period in the Southside because of the varied trading alternatives at the local level and the greater opportunity to shop at distant wholesale-export centers that were part of the tobacco marketing system.

The multipurpose trip is ironically a late twentieth-century phenomenon in which consumers bypass local retailers for travel to more distant retail centers, where a greater quantity and diversity of goods are purchased. This new consumer practice has been encouraged by a combination of better highways, fewer time constraints on consumers, the location of easily accessible shopping malls on the fringes of larger cities, and sharp increases in materialism. The result of this consumer travel to larger and more distant centers has been the rapid decline of hamlets and villages, the lower-order places in the central-place system. In the eighteenth-century Southside, the multipurpose trip was focused on the fall-zone ports that received, inspected, and shipped the region's tobacco. Although it was a true higher-order place for the wealthy to shop, primarily through the personal attention given planters by their factors, it was just a larger country store, in terms of the goods purchased, for the many and varied Southsiders who participated in the various aspects of the long-distance tobacco trade. The modern multipurpose trip has caused the decline of local and smaller central places. However, in the Southside, because the tobacco inspection system was an original component of regional trade, the multipurpose trip was an important part of the larger trading system that was the main obstacle to the development of service centers in the region.

Notes

1.   For Cunninghame, see Letter from James Robinson to John Turner, October 6, 1777, William Cunninghame and Company Letterbook. At both Murdoch and Dromgoole stores, percentages are based on customers who could be located, not the entire store population. At the Murdoch store, 182 of 407 customers were located; at the Dromgoole store, eighty-nine of 145 customers were located. The Murdoch daybook is found in Manuscripts, Library of Congress, Washington, D.C.; the Dromgoole daybook is in the Southern Historical Collection, University of North Carolina, Chapel Hill.

2.   For both Wooding and Owen, see Halifax County Judgments, March, August, 1755.

3.   Shopping patterns based on debt avoidance were determined from county judgments and order books, account books, and "British Mercantile Claims."

4.   Thomas M. Devine, "Glasgow Merchants and the Collapse of the Tobacco Trade, *The Scottish Historical Review* 52 (1973), 60.

5.   Charlotte County Court Cases, August–September 1771 (part II) and August 1772.

6.   Soltow, "Scottish Traders in Virginia, 1750–1775," 85.

7.   Halifax County Pleas 2:102.

8.   Pittsylvania County Accounts Current 3:100–101.

9.   Richard R. Beeman, ed., "Trade and Travel in Post-Revolutionary Virginia: A Diary of an Itinerant Peddler, 1807–1808," *Virginia Magazine of History and Biography* 84 (1976), 174–88.

10.   Ibid., 179.

11.   Dudgeon's business transaction is found in Halifax County Judgments, February, March, 1753; his estate inventory is in Halifax Will Book 1:172.

12.   Mitchell and Hofstra, "Town and Country in Backcountry Virginia."

13.   For Munford, see Mecklenburg Will Book 3:21–23. The Amelia County sale is from Amelia Will Book 1:47.

14.   The Crenshaw Account Book is in Manuscripts, Library of Congress. Because a few critical early pages are missing from the document, the given name of Crenshaw is missing.

15.   Mitchell and Hofstra, "Town and Country in Backcountry Virginia."

16.   In addition to the Halifax County store, the company operated a store in Pittsylvania County and may have been associated with the Dreghorn and Murdoch store in Prince Edward County. Among the various partners in the firm were James Murdoch, John Murdoch, James Peadie, George Murdoch, and George Yuille, all of Glasgow, Gabriel Matthie of Greenock, and Thomas Yuille of Halifax County. Yuille came to Virginia as the supercargo for the company and later was the managing factor. After a stay in Richmond, Yuille moved to Halifax and settled near the store. John Smith and Don McNicholl, who later became Thomas Yuille's son-in-law, were the storekeepers. See Halifax County Deed Book 9:393–401.

17.   Dromgoole purchased the fifty-acre site from Isham and Frances Randle in 1787. See Brunswick County Deed Book 14:350–51. The name "Sligo" is the name of the county in Ireland from which Dromgoole emigrated. The most important subsequent store site was Canaan, located in the southern part of the county where Dromgoole maintained his residence. Dromgoole was noted more for his work as a Methodist minister and as the leader of that church in eastern Southside Virginia.

18.   Discussion of the characteristics of frontier and commercial societies is based loosely on Jackson Turner Main, *The Social Structure of Revolutionary America* (Princeton, N.J., 1965), 44–59.

6

Functions of Country Trade

The functions of country trade are revealed in the relationships between country stores and their customers. As the primary focus of country trade and the only full-time, fixed-location mercantile operation in the Southside, country stores provided a great variety of manufactured goods, services associated with marketing agricultural commodities, credit, cash advances, and payments to customer's creditors and, because of the shortage of cash and the lack of banking institutions, functioned as the clearinghouse for the local debt network. Country trade functions provide an additional component to central-place theory that complements the broader spatial aspects of the model. As the disperser of imported manufactured goods and as the exporter of a local product destined for distant international markets, country stores were positioned critically within a vast international trade network that belied their backcountry locations.

Retailing

The country store was first and foremost a retailing institution. Of the primary store functions of retailing, providing services, providing cash, and granting goods, cash, and services to third parties, the former function clearly dominated. The percentage by value of store business that was transacted for the sale of goods ranged from a high of 82 percent during the 1750s to a low of 70 percent during the 1780s (Table 6-1).

The most important pattern in the retailing process was the variation in store patronage during the course of a year. Based on the

Table 6-1.
Country Store Functions (percentage of
business in each category by value)

Time Period	Retailing	Cash	Cash/Goods/Services to Third Party
1750–59 (126 accounts) (40 stores)	82	4	14
1760–69 (249 accounts) (27 stores)	80	5	15
1770–75 (405 accounts) (26 stores)	74	4	21
1784–89 (74 accounts) (31 stores)	70	13	17
1790–1800 (82 accounts) (28 stores)	76	5	19

Source: Court judgments: Counties of Halifax, Mecklenburg, Charlotte, and Pittsylvania.

transactions at four Southside stores, ranging in time from 1774 to 1800, a greater volume of business was transacted during the late fall and early winter months of November, December, and January, while the lowest volume of business took place in midsummer, primarily the months of July and August (Fig. 6-1). John Morton sold £680 of goods from his Charlotte County store in November of 1797, or 22 percent of his 1797–98 yearly sales.[1] The Scottish firm of James Murdoch and Company concentrated 48 percent of its total sales for 1774–75 in the three-month period from November through January at its Halifax County store. August sales of £57 made up only 2 percent of their total yearly sales. Stores also had a secondary surge of business during one month of a period extending from March through June, apparently in response to the upcoming planting season. The monthly variations in retailing were also reflected in the number of customers. During November the number of daily customers at the Murdoch store ranged from three to forty-three for twenty-six shop-

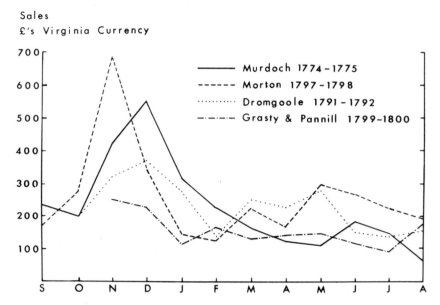

Sales
£'s Virginia Currency

——————— Murdoch 1774-1775
- - - - - - Morton 1797-1798
················· Dromgoole 1791-1792
—·—·—· Grasty & Pannill 1799-1800

Figure 6-1. Business patterns of four country stores.

ping days, or an average of eighteen customers per day; for August the range was one to eleven, or a daily average of four customers.

The variations in monthly sales were primarily related to the seasonal rhythms of an agrarian society. The warmer months were the most active and most structured, and the most confining in terms of travel and consumer decision making. All levels of Southside society were influenced by the work demands from the period of planting preparation in spring to harvesting time in late summer. Even tobacco inspection warehouses either closed or operated with reduced personnel during this period in order that workers could tend to their crops. The secondary business peak experienced during the spring months came primarily as a result of preparation for planting season (Fig. 6-1). The Murdoch store sold seventeen hoes on two consecutive days in March of 1775 and a total of sixty-seven during the two months of March and April. Almanac sales also increased during this period. As the demands of agriculture were reduced during the fall and winter seasons, the region turned to activities that increased store sales. These were the seasons to market tobacco, construct and repair clothes, cure beef and pork, and ward off the cold with the assistance of one's favorite libation. The sale of tobacco reduced the debt to the store and created new optimism and opportunity for the consumer to purchase the cloth, salt, and rum that formed most of the support for country stores.

Daniel Thorp discovered a similar seasonal regimen at a rural tavern in the Piedmont of North Carolina that also sold store-goods.[2] Unlike the Southside, where the seasonal demands of tobacco cultivation kept consumers away from stores, the operators closed the tavern-store to tend to the demands of their own crops. Smaller planter-merchants in the Southside probably followed this practice during earlier periods of settlement. Thorp also found that in the Moravian trading village of Bethabara, located in the same general area, merchant activity was not strongly linked to an agriculturally imposed seasonality of trade. While this might be true of the more diversified wheat and livestock economy of central North Carolina, this separation from agricultural production may not have occurred in the larger fall-zone entrepôts of Virginia, where the demands of the primary staple economy drew no boundary between town and country.

Not all temporal variations in country trade were geared to agricultural patterns. An additional factor in the lower sales during the warmer months was the character of the fiscal year. Because the business year operated from September to the following August, some of the reduced activity of customers was because their purchases had greatly exceeded their payments and the store had begun the process of reducing or terminating credit purchases. Variations in supply also occasionally could reverse the dominance of the normal patterns. The Murdoch store, for example, sold more than 220 ells (more than 238 yards) of rolls, an inexpensive cloth, on one day in August. On one day in June, seven of eleven customers of the store purchased bar iron.

Merchandise Sold

Because country stores were the only establishments to sell goods on a full-time basis from a fixed location, the range of merchandise was by necessity quite extensive. Personal items such as hair ribbon, mirrors, and lace handkerchiefs vied for attention along with large quantities of cloth, shoes, shot and powder, cross-cut saws, saddles, frying pans, barrels of rum, and bags of salt. Based on a sevenfold classification of merchandise sold in country stores, fabrics and notions easily dominated the purchases of customers. This category of purchases was followed in order by food and drink, hardware, clothes and accessories, household goods, personal goods, and miscellaneous items that did not fit into the other six groups (Table 6-2).

Sales in fabrics and notions were dominated by a great variety of

Table 6-2.
Sales of Country Store Merchandise
(percent of sales by value)

Time Period	Fabrics & Notions	Food & Drink	Hardware	Clothes & Accessories	Household	Personal	Misc.
1750–59 (90 accounts) (32 stores)	40	20	15	7	10	3	5
1760–69 (200 accounts) (40 stores)	65	11	8	6	6	4	<1
1770–75 (292 accounts) (28 stores)	61	13	10	7	5	3	1
1790–1800 (132 accounts) (5 stores)	46	20	17	9	5	2	1

Source: Court judgments: counties of Halifax, Mecklenburg, Charlotte, and Pittsylvania; James Murdoch Daybook, 1774–75; John Morton Daybook, 1797–98.

cloth, ribbon, lace, bed ticking, thimbles, needles, pins, and buttons. Sales in this category ranged from a high of 65 percent of store retailing during the 1760s to a low of 40 percent during the 1750s (Table 6-2). Merchant inventories also revealed greater quantities of these items. During the 1790s fabrics and notions accounted for 66 percent of John Field's inventory, 36 percent of Matthew Robertson's stock, and 44 percent of the goods in David Pannill's store (Table 6-3).

Fabric was the most-purchased item at the country stores. The cloth generally reflected the style of life that the settlers lived. Coarse, inexpensive, practical fabrics were needed for their long wear and durability. Most fabrics were some coarse form of cotton, linen, or wool. Oznaburg, an inexpensive cotton, was the most purchased fabric and was used for both white and slave clothing. Buckram, roll, and dowlass were other frequently purchased coarse materials. Drill was purchased for work clothes, gingham for dresses, brown holland for children's clothes, shalloon for linings, lasting for shoe uppers, and sheeting for the obvious function. The stores also provided finer-quality cloth such as muslin, cambric, broadcloth, duffel, drab, velvet, and cashmere. These were purchased frequently by the wealthier planters, but usually in small quantities. The most expensive items in this category were broadcloth, usually selling for over £1 per yard; cambric, as high as 11s. per yard; and calico and duffle, reaching 10s. and 8s. 6d. per yard respectively. Some fabrics indicated the large trade network in which the Southside participated. Many fabrics—holland, cambric, cashmere, Irish linen, Indian cotton, Russian duck and sheeting, and German oznaburg, for example—were identified by the areas in which they had originated.

Food and drink were usually the second most purchased items in the country stores, although always closely followed by hardware products (Table 6-2). Food and drink sales of 20 percent during the 1750s ranked highest and sales of 11 percent during the 1760s were the lowest for the category. Food items were not usually finished products or edible goods in the form in which they were sold. Salt and sugar dominated sales of food items, but pepper, allspice, ginger, molasses, and cloves also were purchased frequently. The high volume of salt and sugar sales in part was related to their use beyond the kitchen. Salt was used to cure meat and sugar was an ingredient in the making of whisky and brandy. Chocolate and mustard were the most common items in the category that were consumed directly as food. Although infrequent in their occurrence, local items such as meat, butter, corn, and flour were also included in this category. These items appeared more often in the post-Revolutionary period. Local farm

Table 6-3.
Merchandise in Mercant's Inventories
(percent by value)

Time Period	Fabrics & Notions	Food & Drink	Hardware	Clothes & Accessories	Household	Personal	Misc.
John Field Inventory (1795) (£508 6s. 7d.)	66	9	10	6	6	3	1
Matt Robertson Inventory (1798) (£429 9s. 9d.)	36	20	14	12	12	3	3
David Pannill Inventory (1803) (£2,143 16s. 12d.)	44	11	23	5	10	4	3

Source: Mecklenburg Will Book 3, 282–301; Amelia Will Book 5, 442–55; Pittsylvania Accounts Current 3, 305–23.

products probably comprised a greater percentage of store goods in secondary staple-producing regions of the South because of the reduced export trade in these more diversified economies.[3]

Rum was the most common drink of the Southsiders and was purchased in quantities ranging from shots to barrels, although most purchases were for a pint, a quart, or a half-gallon. Merchants who operated ordinaries on the store premises sold greater quantities. Wine was purchased infrequently, although the Robertson inventory listed an unusually large quantity that was in excess of sixty gallons. Brandy, usually of local origin, was a distant second to rum in popularity, and another local product, whisky, only rarely was purchased from stores. In contrast to the heavy consumption of rum in the Southside, Thorp's analysis of consumer behavior revealed that locally distilled whisky was the drink of choice in the North Carolina Piedmont.[4] The greater availability of rum in the Southside reflected the region's participation in a larger trading system. However, more brandy and whisky were consumed than the accounts would indicate because of their production and consumption outside the store network. An occasional beer and even the odd bottle of gin were also sold at the stores. Neither coffee nor tea, almost always identified as either bohea (dark) or hyson (green), was in heavy demand during the 1750s and 1760s. Coffee, clearly the preferred beverage, began to appear more frequently during the 1770s, and its acceptance increased after the Revolutionary War.

The hardware category was composed of a variety of goods that dealt with construction, agriculture, hunting, and animal husbandry (Table 6-2). The most frequently purchased items were nails, shot and powder, bar iron, gun flints, hoes, scythes, saws, files, adzes, gouges, locks, window glass, hinges, stirrup irons, saddles, bits, bridles, spurs, girths, curry combs, rope, pocket knives, and sheep shears. Hardware sales ranged from a high of 17 percent during the 1790s to a low of 8 percent during the 1760s. The most expensive hardware items were guns, as high as £5 each, and a woman's sidesaddle, usually priced over £3.

In the context of the needs of an expanding frontier society geared to livestock and agriculture, it is initially surprising that hardware items made up such a small part of store merchandise. But much of the hardware business was performed by local blacksmiths who, in addition to repairing tools, were among the leading manufacturers in the region. Individual planters, farmers, and slaves also performed as subsistence practitioners. Items such as hoes, which appeared relatively infrequently in store accounts, apparently were also kept for long periods of time and were maintained by frequent repairs.

Clothes and accessories ranged from 6 to 9 percent of store sales and included hose and stockings, shoes, boots, gloves, hats, bonnets, and cloaks (Table 6-2). Accessories clearly dominated this category. Coats, trousers, and dresses rarely appeared in store accounts unless the merchant also operated a tailor shop. Other than these practitioners and the few independent tailors in the Southside, and the greater number at the fall zone, most clothes were constructed at home from a variety of fabrics. The John Morton store sold more shoes because the firm also operated a shoe-manufacturing business on or near the store premises. The clothes and accessories category contained several relatively expensive items. A satin bonnet was priced at £1 10s., a man's "fine" hat at £1 2s., a woman's hat at 10s. 6d., a "fine" pocketbook at 10s., and children's pumps sold for 12s. 6d. The most expensive single item was probably a cardinal, or cloak, that usually sold for £2 to £3.

Household goods made up 5 to 10 percent of the purchases from country stores (Table 6-2). Kitchen items, primarily pots, pans, bowls, dishes, eating utensils, mugs, glasses, and canisters, were purchased more frequently than goods for other rooms. Matthew Robertson's small store in Amelia County carried an unusually large number of kitchen items that included eighty-seven bowls, fifty-three pewter basins, seven dozen pewter plates, five teapots, and over four dozen cups and saucers. Blankets, rugs, and bed cords were the most commonly purchased items for the remainder of the house. Furniture was not sold in country stores. The most expensive household items were rugs, usually over £1 and as high as £3, Dutch blankets at 8s., and large iron pots for just under £1.

Purchases of personal items, primarily handkerchiefs, razors, combs, writing paper, spectacles, hair ribbon, and tobacco products and containers, comprised from 2 to 4 percent of store sales (Table 6-2). A Barcelona silk handkerchief sold for 10s., and a printed handkerchief could be purchased for 8s. Miscellaneous merchandise included mainly books and medicines. The best illustration of this category came from the David Pannill inventory of 1803 that contained twelve bibles, thirteen testaments, six books on medicine, five Morse's *Geographies*, twelve cyphering books, thirty-three spelling books, eight history books, twelve primers, one-hundred twenty-two almanacs, and three dictionaries.

The sale of slaves was a rare occurrence in the country-store trade. The bulk of the backcountry slave trade was carried on at a trading level above the country store. Although many of the mercantile firms that operated the backcountry stores traded heavily in slaves, the location for this activity was Norfolk or the fall-zone ports. At the local level, slaves were more likely to be purchased at estate sales or from planters raising funds to pay their debts. But occasionally country stores were used to market slaves. John Hook of nearby Bedford County requested twelve or fifteen slaves from Neil Jamieson, the Norfolk-based factor for the Glassford mercantile firm, by the middle of March to supply some of the labor needs for the planting season.[5] Andrew French, the storekeeper for the Prince Edward store of Alexander Speirs, advertised a parcel of choice slaves for sale at the courthouse in October of 1768 that included house carpenters, sawyers, "house wenches," and "ground Negroes."[6] Whether French was acting for Speirs or involved in a separate business venture is not known.

Price Structure

The price structure of country trade was determined by both general influences that were common to all mercantile activity during the eighteenth century and specific factors unique to backcountry retailing. The broader influences were the costs of operating on credit, exchange rates, tobacco prices, wars, and supply problems. The primary Southside influence was distance from fall-zone wholesalers. The expected price variations between Scottish stores and local planter-merchants also must be considered.

The costs of operating on credit forced merchants to raise the prices of goods to help offset the losses from accounts that were never paid and from escalating accounts where purchases exceeded payments over long periods of time. If interest were charged on the latter accounts, that was also incorporated into the price of goods. John Glassford "estimated that the average investment took four years to come back" and doubted it would ever be less than three years.[7] Prices not only reflected the credit system of Virginia and the Southside, but also financial arrangements in Britain. To finance their operations, Scottish mercantile companies borrowed money from sources in London. Interest and fees on these loans cost at least 8 percent annually.[8] These costs were also passed on to the consumer in the form of increased prices of goods.

The influences of sterling exchange rates on prices were complex and will be discussed only in a general context. If the sterling exchange rate, the value of Virginia money compared to £100 sterling, were £130, it would require £130 of Virginia currency to purchase goods valued at £100 sterling. It would appear that when the exchange rate rose, because manufactured goods were purchased from Great Britain, the prices of country trade goods would increase accordingly if the merchant wished to continue making a profit. Joseph Ernst, however, has indicated that prices in the American colonies did not always follow changes in the exchange rate and suggested that gluts, credit shifts, and demand factors were perhaps more important.[9]

The exchange rate was especially high during the first half of the 1760s and low during the first half of the 1750s, late 1760s, and early 1770s. The average rate for 1764 was £160.73; for 1754, the rate was £127.55; and for 1766 and 1770 it was £128.48 and £118.00 respectively (Appendix B). Prices on four selected store goods during these periods very generally corresponded to those rate variations. The median annual prices for a bushel of salt, a gallon of rum, an ell of oznaburg, and a pound of sugar were significantly higher during the early 1760s, when the exchange rates were high, than during the late 1760s and in 1770, when the exchange rates were low. The decline in the price of sugar throughout the entire period from 1762 to 1770, however, represented a deviation from a total positive correlation with exchange rates.

More significant for the Southside were the variations in prices within short periods of time because of factors that were not related to the exchange rate. During the years 1766 and 1767, the beginning of a period of low exchange rates, the price of a yard of Irish linen ranged from 2s. 9d. to 6s. 9d. at various Southside locations west of the Staunton River. Between 1761 and 1765, a period of high exchange rates, John Smith of Pittsylvania County purchased rum at the fall zone for prices that ranged between 4s. 3d. and 8s. 1d. per gallon. Between 1763 and 1765, he paid from 3s. to 8s. for a bushel of salt at the same location.

One of the most important influences on prices of goods would appear to be tobacco prices. These prices would in part also reflect changes in the exchange rate. Since tobacco was the primary means of paying for goods, the prices of goods should have reflected changes in the price of tobacco. This pattern, however, did not always occur. Tobacco prices increased slowly and sporadically between 1758 and 1769 and dramatically between 1792 and 1798. During the period 1758 to 1769, the median annual price of oznaburg increased slightly; the prices of sugar and salt rose significantly and then dropped; and the median prices for rum dropped over the entire period. During the period from 1792 to 1798, median annual prices of all four goods increased. Tobacco prices declined slightly from 1770 to 1775, and declined more sharply between 1784 and 1792 and between 1798 and

1800. During the former period, the price of salt declined and then increased in price; oznaburg remained the same; and sugar and rum increased. During the 1784–92 period, sugar, oznaburg, and rum increased in price while salt increased and then decreased. The prices of all four items increased during the 1798–1800 period of declining tobacco prices.

The highest prices for all four goods occurred during wartime. For example, in 1779, the price of a bushel of salt reached £3 10s. These higher prices reflected the high inflation rates created by the issuing of paper currency to finance the war and the supply shortages caused by the reduction in commercial shipping. In 1778 David Ross wrote John Hook that all dry goods were scarce.[10] And conversely, prices often declined sharply immediately following a war. Prices for salt and rum fell sharply after the French and Indian War despite the sharp rise in exchange rates. In some unusual instances, impending war could force down the price of goods. In September of 1775, a mob of 100 armed men forced Petersburg (Scottish) merchants to sell goods at specified low prices.[11]

Supply difficulties during nonwar periods that created temporary shortages of store goods probably increased prices, but this cannot be documented over long periods of time at this scale of inquiry. These shortages could have been caused by a number of factors associated with manufacturing and finance in Britain and other supplier locations, and transportation from these locations to Virginia. Evidence of shortages in goods came primarily from the fall zone. During 1764, for example, a number of wagons used to transport tobacco to the fall zone returned to the backcountry without the customary backloads that were often in excess of 3,000 pounds per wagon.[12] At other times the available wagons appeared to be overwhelmed by the volume of goods to be transported to the backcountry. Reflecting the new trading structure between Britain and the newly independent United States, prices increased after the Revolutionary War. Although the price of rum almost doubled between 1776 and 1800, the largest price increase was for a particular group of goods was in hardware, specifically metal goods such as implement blades and nails, and gunpowder. But conversely, one observer noted, from his fall-zone location, that Virginia had goods sufficient for eighteen months and that sales were so slow that many items were being sold at public auction.[13]

The single most important cause of price variations within the Southside was the distance between fall-zone wholesalers and backcountry retailers. It was not only the number of miles traversed that created high freight costs and unpredictable contacts with suppliers, but also the greater travel time created by bad roads, inclement weather, accidents that damaged transportation equipment and store goods, and unreliable wagoners. During the 1790s freight rates to carry backloads from Petersburg to more eastern Brunswick County were 2s. and 3s. per hundredweight, or a maximum of £3 for a load of 2,000 pounds.[14] In more western Pittsylvania County during the same period, rates were usually 5s. per hundredweight, or £5 for a backload of similar weight. Consumers in western counties, by virtue of freight rates 67 to 150 percent higher than Brunswick County's, paid higher prices for goods than did consumers in other parts of the region.

As a result of higher transport costs alone, the prices of store goods were 100 to 150 percent higher in the area west of Staunton River than at the fall zone. In 1762 the price of an ell of oznaburg was usually 8d. at the fall zone, but was as much as 200 percent higher in the Southside.[15] In 1766 Irish linen was 10 to 350 percent more expensive in the backcountry. Throughout the year 1770, Crenshaw and Company of Petersburg sold a bushel of salt for 2s., while in the Southside it sold for 4s. 6d. to 6s., or as much as 200 percent higher.

Backcountry planters who bypassed the local stores to trade directly with fall-zone companies should have benefited from the cheaper prices offered by the distant mercantile firms. For John Smith, who traded initially with William and James Donald and then with Alexander Speirs, both based at Manchester, prices on most goods were considerably below those at the local level. But at times, Smith paid backcountry prices, especially for rum. In 1771 the Murdoch store in Halifax County sold rum for as much as 3s. per gallon less than Smith paid at the fall zone. Any advantages or disadvantages that Smith had in trading directly with the fall zone were complicated by his costs for transporting the goods from Manchester and by his credits realized from wagoning store goods from fall-zone warehouses to backcountry stores for his factor.

Scottish mercantile companies, having close relationships with manufacturing and shipping firms, and with high-volume purchasing, would appear to have been more likely to offer lower prices for goods than the local merchant-planters. Actual prices revealed that goods purchased at Scottish stores usually were slightly lower in price than those from locally based stores, but often were similar to local stores, and on occasions were actually higher than Southside-based companies. The less-than-expected price differentials likely reflected the dominance of Scottish stores that had severely reduced the local competition, the Scots' need to recoup losses created by the large volume of generous credit granted to planters, and the recognition by merchant-planters that parity in prices was the only means of survival. Table 6-4 shows specific examples of price variations that were representative of general trends. The factor of variable distance from fall-zone suppliers has been reduced by selecting stores with generally similar locations with relation to distance from those dominant wholesalers. All annual price comparisons in the table reflect goods sold in the same month of that year. Comparison prices do not include any differences in quality of goods or length of stay in the store stock.

Although not usually apparent in the store accounts, stores may have varied prices to some individuals based on the perception by the merchant of their ability to eventually pay for the goods, their distance from the local community, or other personal factors. For example, John Morton of Charlotte County charged one customer 2s. for a pound of coffee and another customer 2s. 3d. for the same item on the same day in 1797. If there was a difference in quality, it was not noted in the account, and not one Southside account ever mentioned different varieties of coffee. In 1770 a fall-zone merchant charged a Brunswick County customer 8d. for an ell of oznaburg. Two months earlier he had charged a North Carolina customer 1s. 3d., almost double the earlier price for the same item and considerably more than the prevailing price in the Southside at the time.

Purchases of large quantities of a particular item usually resulted in a lower charge. In 1770 rum cost 3s. 6d. and 4s. 2d. per gallon when purchased by the barrel. The price of a single gallon of rum ranged from 5s. to 6s. during the same period. In 1789 Susanna Murray of Mecklenburg County purchased a bolt of oznaburg, or 145 yards, for £7 5s. or 1s. per yard.[16] She saved 12s. 1d. over the prevailing price of 1s. 1d. per single yard purchased.

The markup on store goods was usually about 100 percent, but varied depending on the merchant, the goods, and the time period. In August of 1751, Andrew Martin, a small merchant and ordinary-keeper in Halifax County, bought a hogshead of rum for 4s. per gallon.[17] During this period most merchants in the area sold a gallon of rum for 8s. retail and an additional merchant sold the item for 12s., a markup of 100 to 200 percent. If Martin sold his sugar for the prevailing price at the time, he would have realized a 33 percent profit. Being both a small merchant and also the operator of a tippling place, he probably exceeded that norm. Based on the Halifax County court judgments, the markups on oznaburg and Irish linen were 122 and 65 percent respectively in 1762. In 1763 the profits on rum ranged from 78 to 122 percent. In 1770 the markup on rum was just under 100

Table 6-4.
Comparative Prices at Scottish and Merchant-Planter Stores

Merchant	Sugar (lb.)			Salt (bu.)			Oznaburg (ell)			Rum (gal.)
	1760	1770	1772	1760	1766	1769	1760	1770	1772	1771
Buchanan & Hastie (S)					6s. 6d.				1s. 2d.	5s. 6d.
J&R Donald (S)		7d.				4s. 6d.		1s. 4d.	1s. 1d.	
C. Duncan (S)								1s. 6d.		
J. Murdock (S)	1s.			6s.			1s. 6d.			
Speirs (S)						4s. 6d.		1s. 2d.		
Calloway (MP)		9d.				6s.		1s. 4d.		
M. Marable (MP)			7d.		6s.				1s. 2d.	
McDaniel (MP)	1s.						1s. 6d.			
Muter (MP)						6s.				
Stokes (MP)				6s.						
Wimbish (MP)										5s.
Field & Call (FZ)			6d.					1s. 2d.		

Source: Halifax County judgments.

Stores are located at relatively similar distances from the fall zone. (S) Scottish; (MP) Merchant-Planter; (FZ) local store of fall-zone company.

percent. Profits in the post-Revolutionary period were similar to those before the war. Lewis Atherton has calculated that Pittsylvania County merchant Philip Grasty, operating around the turn of the century, usually added 100 percent to the wholesale price of goods before selling them.[18]

Credit

Most retail transactions at country stores were credit sales. Cash was not readily available in the region, with only 9 percent of all eighteenth-century inventories listing that item. In 1774–75 only 7 percent of retail sales at the Murdoch store in Halifax County were cash sales, and in 1799–1800 only 4 percent of purchases at the Stony Hill store of Pittsylvania County merchants Grasty and Pannill were by cash. A much greater percentage of the Southside country-store trade was on credit compared with stores in the American South during the antebellum period. Atherton has calculated that the cash to credit ratio in the American South ranged from 25–75 to 33–67.[19] The greater importance of credit in the Southside may be traced to the greater impact of an export staple in which mercantile companies operated primarily through a barter system that traded store credit for tobacco.

Merchants generally granted easy credit to most Southsiders, whether or not they were tobacco producers, although this practice varied with economic conditions. The post–Revolutionary War collectors for prewar debts owed to British merchants, primarily Scottish merchants in the Southside, time and again commented on the practice of merchants giving credit to virtually anyone, no matter what their economic situation. Among the numerous examples of this practice were the accounts of Richard Wilkins, John and Daniel May, and Robert Sebley (Selby) with the firm of Robert Dinwiddie and Thomas Crawford. According to the debt collector, Wilkins "was never able to pay the sum of more than £93 while he resided in the county." As for the May brothers, who owed over £164, they "were not possessed of sufficient property to justify a credit of this sum." Sebley, who owed more than £27, "at the time of this account was in very indigent circumstances."[20]

Many customers were probably not even aware of the size of their debt because it was the general practice not to ask for receipts. One postwar collector in Lunenburg County remarked that "not one man in twenty ever required a receipt from his merchant in this part of the country."[21] This easy credit policy can also be seen in the total debts owed to Scottish mercantile companies. At the end of the colonial period, the total Virginia debts owed to the firm of William Cunninghame were almost £130,000. As previously indicated, the debts at the company's Halifax County store totaled over £6,100.[22] Although not in the high debt category of Tidewater planters, there were nevertheless many large individual debts in the Southside. Alexander Gordon of Mecklenburg County owed Alexander Speirs over £2,100 and Nathaniel Terry of Halifax County was in debt to the same company for almost £1,000.[23]

Local merchants paralleled the credit practices of the Scottish companies. William Hendrick, a Mecklenburg County merchant, was owed over £4,600 in unpaid accounts in 1800. The individual accounts ranged from a high of over £390 to a low of 3d.[24] The monthly pattern of customers' debts and credits have been calculated for one Southside store (Fig. 6-2). In 1774–75 the Murdoch store had only two months, June and August, when cash purchases and payments to accounts exceeded goods purchased on credit. Credit purchases exceeded payments by the largest margin, over £339, during December, the height of the winter shopping season. For the year, goods purchased on credit totaled over £2,500 and cash purchases and payments to accounts were £1,022.

The greatest threat to generous credit was, like the economy, based in external locations. The Southside was a small part of a vast house

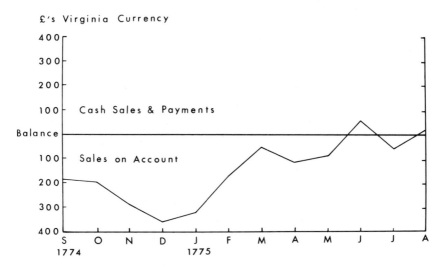

Figure 6-2. Balance between sales on account and cash sales/account payments.

of cards. Financial crises elsewhere in the world of British trade forced Southside merchants to tighten credit and call in debts. In 1772 and 1773, as a result of a British bank crisis, merchants filled the court dockets with suits. Some merchants went door to door to collect debts during hard times and might accept anything to cut their losses.[25] Hard times for the Scottish firm of Buchanan and Hastie came during the Revolutionary War. Unable to collect from its debtors and unable to sell more goods, the firm went bankrupt in 1777.[26]

Within this milieu of easy credit, there was, however, a greater complexity. Perhaps the most revealing evidence of this complexity was revealed in the debt structure of the Murdoch firm's Halifax County store. During the business year of 1770–71, 40 percent of the 196 customers increased their accounts while making payments to those accounts; 20 percent increased their accounts while making no payments; 23 percent decreased their accounts by payments; and 17 percent paid off their accounts.[27] Moza Hurt increased his debt by £44 without any payments to his account. He apparently paid some of that debt, for he was still a customer in 1774–75 when he purchased over £21 of goods. Individuals who marketed tobacco through the store had substantially larger accounts. The median value of their purchases in 1770–71 was approximately £21, while the median value of annual purchases for the entire store clientele was just under £9.

Two general types of accounts were more likely to be the object of court suits. The first type involved credit purchases over several years where small payments to maintain the account had been dwarfed by large purchases. This occasionally resulted in suits to collect debts of several hundred pounds. The second type was the single visit to the store followed by no additional contact. This type of account was especially prominent during the 1750s and 1760s, when potential settlers paused briefly before continuing on to some other place. These also occurred during later years because of the continued high mobility of the Southside population and the unfulfilled economic opportunity of many of the region's inhabitants.

Because the customer usually did not have the cash to pay the debt if he lost the court suit, assuming that he could be found, he had to guarantee payment with a bond. If another party could not be found to guarantee the bond or if the interest on the bond was not paid, the debtor might have to mortgage all or part of his land. Although land ownership was transferred by this process, most suits were settled without such drastic measures. Among the larger mortgages were those of Archibald Gordon of Pittsylvania County, the well-traveled Thomas Tunstall of Halifax County, and Abraham Maury of Lunenburg

County.[28] Gordon mortgaged over 1,000 acres of land to satisfy a debt of £515 to Petersburg merchant Patrick Ramsey. Tunstall mortgaged two separate plantations that totaled 750 acres to satisfy a debt of £500 to Buchanan and Hastie. Maury mortgaged 130 acres that contained a grist mill and a sawmill to pay a store debt of £241 to Speirs, Bowman, and Company.

A final method of collecting past due debts was the attachment of property. To satisfy part or all of a debt, merchants attached various items of personal property that might include livestock, slaves, and tobacco. For most debtors in this dilemma, the objects were usually rather ordinary but critical household items such as beds, pots, pans, rugs, furniture, and dishes. James Norrell of Halifax County was ordered by the court to pay the Murdoch store his debt of £150 plus interest before July 1, 1768, or suffer the attachment of his entire personal estate of wagon, gear, team, three beds, ten head of cattle, six sheep, ten hogs, household furniture, kitchen utensils, hoes, skins, and all of his crops for the year 1766.[29] He apparently was able to come to some agreement with the store, for he was a customer in 1770–71 and continued to operate as a wagoner for the firm. In July of 1777, Matthew Marable, for some time absent from these pages, provided some indication of the magnitude of planter debt to country merchants, and in this instance merely a local planter-merchant. Marable held by deed of trust, to secure him payment of large debts, all or part of the land, slaves, and personal property of twenty-six plantations. In less than two months, he planned to offer all of the holdings at public sale.[30] The Scots did not appear to be this ruthless.

Financial Services

All nonretailing functions of country trade came under the umbrella of financial services. These services, direct cash loans, and cash, goods, and services paid to third parties, were necessary because of the scarcity of money in the primary staple economy. It was primarily through this network of financial services, in conjunction with the remittance structure, that the country stores functioned as the clearinghouses for the local debt network. Although this practice was primarily a service for tobacco producers, it filtered down at a lesser scale of financial involvement to non-tobacco-producers as well. These services also had a much greater impact on local trade than is suggested by the retailing to services ratio in Table 6-1.

Cash loans to customers, a common component of the relationship between merchant and customer, accounted for 4 to 13 percent of country store business (Table 6-1). Cash advances were more common in the Southside than the primary staple areas of the American South during the antebellum period. Atherton states that "It [store credit] seems never to have extended to the purchase of slaves and land, and only to a limited extent to the advancement of cash sums to customers."[31] Both local planter-merchants and Scottish firms granted cash advances, but the latter, in part because of their varied activities and greater financial resources, were more likely to provide cash and also to advance larger amounts.

Cash advances were given more readily to individuals who were more likely to market their tobacco through the store. The Scottish firm of Thomas Yuille and Company, before he moved to Halifax County as James Murdoch's factor, gave cash advances to Amelia County planter Edward Moorefield that comprised £11 14s. 9d. of a total account of £31 15s. 3d. during the period 1750–52. Moorefield bartered his tobacco through Yuille's store in each of those three years. Between 1763 and 1766, John Sullivant was given cash advances of more than £42 by Alexander Speirs and Company. During that period he marketed more than £60 worth of tobacco through their store.[32] Cash advances were also available without the linkage to the tobacco trade. In 1771 cash advances comprised over 80 percent of John Chapman's more than £27 account with William Cunninghame without benefit of any tobacco credits.[33] A few shillings were even occasionally advanced to persons of rather frail economic standing.

The granting of cash, merchandise, and services to third parties was primarily to satisfy the external debts of store customers. It was in this capacity that country trade functioned as the primary clearinghouse for the local debt network. This was a more extensive and complex version of payments in kind that have distinguished the trade of cash-poor agricultural economies in varied temporal and geographic settings. Through this arrangement the store paid for the debts of its customers with goods or cash. The cost to the merchant was then charged to the customer's account. Since the store provided most of the non-household-produced goods, was the primary agency for marketing agricultural and natural products, and was responsible for circulating most of the region's money supply, it was the only possible focal point for managing the region's debt network. Payments to third parties was much more prevalent in local store transactions than cash advances because it had the important advantage of operating with little need for cash. Payments to third parties ranged from 14 to 21 percent of the value of store business (Table 6-1).

Accounts were not always clear regarding the type of payment made to the third party. Three types of third-party transactions were indicated: "sundries to a third party," "cash to a third party," and the somewhat ambiguous "to third party" with a currency value opposite the person's name in the debit column of the account. Given the more ubiquitous nature of store goods, it is assumed that this last category of transaction was used more often with reference to store goods.

The highest volume of third-party transactions involved the marketing of tobacco: the costs associated with its transport, inspection, and often reinspection when hogsheads were not properly packed. The merchant assumed the obligations of marketing the product, but the planter always paid for these expenses through his store account. The costs of wagoning one hogshead of tobacco from west of the Staunton River took from £1 5s. to more than £5 from the potential profits of planters during the last half of the eighteenth century. Poor prizing and accidents in transit increased these costs. In 1761 the Scottish firm of Robert Hastie and Company charged John Thomas £2 5s. for the costs of reprizing his tobacco after it failed the initial inspection.[34] John Smith paid an additional £8 12s. to hang and dry his eight hogsheads of water-damaged tobacco.[35] Merchant-planters assumed these duties after the Revolutionary War. In 1798 Beverely Willard of Pittsylvania County had charged to his account at David Pannill's store £12 16s. 3d. for the costs of wagoning and inspecting and, at those prices, apparently reinspecting two hogsheads of tobacco.[36]

Although tobacco-marketing costs dominated payments to third parties, the practice spanned the entire trading spectrum. Merchants paid customer accounts with other stores. The Murdoch store paid £1 2s. 5d. to George Muter and Company for customer Thomas Benjamin and 5s. 6d. to James Smith and Company for customer William Glass. Local Halifax County merchant John Middleton paid William Covington's debt of 1s. 6d. to a peddler.[37] The Murdoch store regularly paid the county taxes and other fees of customers. The store paid 8s. to the parish collector and £1 10s. 4d. to the sheriff for William Pearman. Murdoch and other merchants also paid for customers' advertisements in the *Virginia Gazette*.[38] One of the more unusual types of third-party transactions was the more than £30 that Matthew Marable paid to a carpenter for constructing a building for customer John Foushee.[39] One local merchant in Mecklenburg County paid a third party £1 1s., the amount that a customer owed for losses on his cockfighting wagers.[40]

To illustrate how payments to third parties operated at one store, it is useful to examine the accounts of three customers at the Murdoch store during 1770–71. Because the three customers had businesses of their own, a great deal of potential existed for third-party transactions completely within the framework of store clientele. James Norrell was a wagoner who had at least fourteen accounts with Murdoch customers; William London was a tailor who had at least twenty-six accounts with Murdoch customers; and Henria Booker operated a ferry and had a large but undetermined number of customers with Murdoch accounts. Each of the three provided a service or made a product for Murdoch customers. The Murdoch customers then charged these accounts to their regular store accounts. The three entrepreneurs then used these accounts for credit toward payment of their own accounts at the store. All of this took place without going beyond the store clientele and usually without any cash being involved.

Methods of Paying Accounts

The methods of paying accounts reflected the character of the local economy and changes in that economy over time. Over the last half of the eighteenth century, tobacco and payments by third parties were the primary methods of remittance. The dominance of these two methods indicates the importance of the export-staple economy, with its reliance on one cash crop and the resulting shortage of cash in the economy. Primary changes in payments over time were the sharp decline of skins and furs after the 1760s and the increase in wheat during the 1790s.

Plantation and farm products were the primary means of remittance, ranging from a high of 72 percent by value of total payments during 1784–89 to a low of 25 percent during the 1750s (Table 6-5). Tobacco, although appearing in less than one-third of accounts containing remittances, comprised more than 80 percent of the value of agricultural payments and as much as 65 percent of total payments to appease store debts. Wheat never comprised as much as 1 percent of total remittances in a decade until the 1790s, when it provided 7 percent of such payments. The primary explanation for this was the dominance of the Grasty and Pannill store of northeastern Pittsylvania County in the sample. Of 190 accounts used for that decade, 123 originated from that single store during its 1799–1800 business year. Of the total value of remittances at the store, 12 percent came from wheat. The 18 percent of payments by value attributed to "other products" during the 1790s was also increased by the activity at the Grasty and Pannill store, where 23 percent of payments were in this category.

These payments included corn, oats, fodder, whisky, beef, pork, horses, butter, beeswax, and 212 gallons of locally produced brandy.

Table 6-5.
Payment of Accounts (percent of each category by value)

Time Period	Skins/ Furs	Cash	Third Party	Services Performed	Tobacco	Wheat	Other Products
1750–59 (79 accounts) (22 stores)	10	22	28	16	15	<1	9
1760–69 (247 accounts) (48 stores)	7	9	29	8	38	<1	8
1770–75 (355 accounts) (27 stores)	3	10	30	6	48	<1	3
1784–89 (53 accounts) (24 stores)	0	6	16	6	65	0	7
1790–1800 (190 accounts) (24 stores)	<1	18	18	11	28	7	18

Source: Court judgments: counties of Halifax, Mecklenburg, Charlotte, and Pittslvania; Murdoch Ledger, 1770–71; Murdoch Daybook, 1774–75; Grasty and Pannill Ledger, Mt. Airy Store, 1799–1800.
Third Party: Payment of account by another individual but no indication of whether cash, service, or tobacco. Services Performed: Primarily wagoning, carpentry, and blacksmith work. Other Products: Corn, oats, fodder, whisky, brandy, livestock, beef, pork, butter, beeswax, tallow, and others.

A third party paying the debt of a store customer, comprising as much as 30 percent by value of remittances, was second only to to-bacco as a method for paying store accounts (Table 6-5). Just as merchants paid customers' debts to third parties, customers followed this practice to pay their debts to merchants. Reversing the previous orientation of third-party payments to customers best illustrates how the third-party payments worked. During the year 1770–71 James Norrell, the ever-present wagoner, was credited with £126 17s. from third-party sources toward his account at the Murdoch store. These third-party contributors were Murdoch customers for whom Norrell had performed wagoning services. The store gave Norrell credit for payments toward his account by charging them to the individuals who owed Norrell for services performed.

Cash payments ranged from a high of 22 percent of the value of payments during 1750–59 to a low of 6 percent of the value of payments in the postwar period of 1784–89 (Table 6-5). This was well below the cash remittances, 40 to 73 percent by value, made at three stores in the diversified grain economy of the Shenandoah Valley during the second half of the eighteenth century and the 82 percent at a combination tavern-store in Piedmont North Carolina between 1755 and 1775.[41] This contrast once again strongly indicates the Southside's greater involvement in a primary-staple economy.

Services performed for the merchant by customers to satisfy their debts ranged from a high of 16 percent of the total value of store payments in 1750–59 to a low of 6 percent in 1784–89 (Table 6-5). These services varied, but the larger-volume credits were usually for carpentry, wagonering, and blacksmith work. In 1771 William Osborne was given credit for over £158 toward his £306 debt at the Mecklenburg County store of Robert Donald and Company by building a storehouse, smokehouse, lumber house, and counting room for the company.[42] Wagoners comprised one of the largest tertiary occupations in the region. By all evidence encountered, they were usually paid in store goods. In 1762 a wagoner brought a backload of twelve sacks of salt to Matthew Marable and, for his efforts, lowered his account balance by almost £3.[43] Numerous smaller tasks were also performed to pay store debts. In 1761 James Dyer sawed 160 feet of plank for the firm of McCaul and Lyle for approximately seven shillings worth of credit at their Halifax store.[44] Other smaller tasks, especially for plantation-located stores, included mauling rails, plowing corn, cradling wheat, manufacturing shoes, and making chairs.

Deerskins and furs were used to pay store debts before the Revolutionary War and, during the period 1760–69, accounted for 10 percent by value of payments to store accounts (Table 6-5). Reflecting the decreases in wild animal habitats because of population growth and agricultural expansion, skins and furs were insignificant after the war period, with only occasional occurrence. Most of the individual skin and fur credits were small. The larger operations were either no longer active in the Southside after the 1750s or the trade bypassed the local country stores.

The dispersed settlement system and the primary-staple economy of the Southside were evident in the types of transactions performed at the country stores. While the large number of store functions, the variety of goods sold, and the methods of paying accounts indicated the importance of the country stores in pre–central-place settlement structure, the diversity and scale of operations was the result of the powerful influence of the primary staple economy and its vast trading linkages. The country store had all the ingredients of a small frontier town—dry goods store, spirits and food shop, hardware, book store, bank, transportation business, commodities exchange, and pawn shop–finance company. But it also dealt in illusion. It was not a town, and its dominance in the backcountry was overshadowed by the external economic forces that created and guaranteed its prominence.

Notes

1. The business year began on September 1 and ended on the last day of August of the following year.
2. Thorp, "Doing Business in the Backcountry," 398–99.
3. Ibid., 399.
4. Ibid., 398–99, 403.
5. Letter of January 20, 1769, Neil Jamieson Papers.
6. *Virginia Gazette*, Rind, October 27, 1768.
7. Price, "The Rise of Glasgow," 197.
8. Soltow, "Scottish Traders in Virginia," 197.
9. Joseph A. Ernst, *Money and Politics in America, 1755–1775* (Chapel Hill, N.C., 1973), 3–17.
10. Letter from Ross to Hook, October 24, 1778, John Hook Papers.
11. Ibid., September, 1775.
12. Letter from Alexander Stewart to John Smith, December 21, 1764, Pocket Plantation Papers.
13. J. Rives Childs, "French Consul Martin Oster Reports on Virginia, 1784–1796," *Virginia Magazine of History and Biography* 76 (1968), 35.
14. Freight rates are from county judgments and merchant account books.
15. Price information is from Halifax and Pittsylvania Judgments, Southside account books, and Petersburg-based Crenshaw and Company. The majority of fall-zone accounts actually come from the backcountry judgments.
16. Mecklenburg County Loose Papers, March 1792.
17. Halifax Judgments, March 1758.
18. Atherton, *The Southern Country Store*, 170.
19. Ibid., 53.
20. For Wilkins, see "British Mercantile Claims," 16 (1972), 180; for the May brothers and Selbey, see ibid., 181.
21. Ibid., 18 (1974), 281.
22. McMurran, "The Virginia Claims of William Cunninghame and Company," 95–96.
23. For Gordon, see Mecklenburg Will Book 3:358; for Terry, see Halifax Judgments, March 1774.
24. Mecklenburg Will Book 4:194–218.
25. Letter of David Ross to John Hook, January 25, 1776, John Hook Papers.

26. Devine, *Tobacco Lords*, 178.

27. This was probably only one of several ledgers for the Murdoch store for that year. This is based on a list of over 600 names of customers in the particular ledger that held only 196 accounts.

28. For Gordon, see Mecklenburg Will Book 3:125, 500; for Tunstall, see Halifax Deed Book 3:410; Maury's problems are detailed in Lunenburg County Deed Book 11:197.

29. Halifax Deed Book 6:182.

30. *Virginia Gazette*, Rind, July 22, 1773.

31. Atherton, *The Southern Country Store*, 53.

32. For Yuille and Moorefield, see Halifax County Judgments, 1757; for Speirs and Sullivant, see Charlotte County Court Cases, March–September 1769.

33. Halifax County Judgments, May 1772, A to D.

34. Ibid., June 1762.

35. Pocket Plantation Papers, Box 1.

36. Pittsylvania County Judgments, August 1800.

37. Halifax County Judgments, July 1761, H to Z.

38. Ibid., March–August 1755; May 1758.

39. Ibid., May 1772, A to M.

40. Mecklenburg County Loose Papers, 1793–96.

41. Mitchell, *Frontier and Commercialism*, 212; Thorp, "Doing Business in the Backcountry," 405.

42. Halifax County Judgments, May 1772, A to D.

43. Ibid., June 1763.

44. Ibid., May 1762; June 1763.

7

A Final Ensemble

In 1789 François Xavier Dupont, a French visitor to Petersburg, observed that "from Norfolk on for about 120 miles there is nothing but woods. They say it is the same thing all the way to Boston. If this is the case these United States are nothing but a vast forest where bears will be roaming in a thousand years."[1] Dupont's perspective on the settlement pattern of the early United States was strongly influenced by his European environment, with its heavily populated and highly developed cultural landscapes. It is likely that other individuals with similar backgrounds would have expressed similar views.

The contemporary Virginian may have countered these observations by suggesting that the relatively undeveloped cultural landscapes of Virginia were the result of a short period of settlement and economic development in the Tidewater. He or she, perhaps to the puzzlement of the Frenchman, could have pointed out the large number of ports and the complex settlement history of the region, especially revealed in its reduced soil fertility, its rapid population turnover, and its function as a source for much of the population in interior parts of the American South. European views were generally of limited perspective, victimized by the traveler's imperative to infer from a limited range of geographic observation, in this case the lower James River area, conclusions not representative of the geographic whole of the United States or even of the state of Virginia.

In the writing of both geography and history, like the view of Dupont, perspective is everything. Studies in the historical geography of North America during the past thirty years have emphasized settlement evolution in the context of regional economic development.

The primary theoretical approach has been that of the prevailing view of contemporary regional settlement geography, Walter Christaller's central-place theory. The application of central-place theory has emphasized the central locations of places in relation to population, or purchasing power, and the hierarchical position of places in a settlement system. The contention that regional economic development would lead to a well-defined urban network has been the primary assumption of the application of central-place theory to evolving settlement systems.

Central-place theory, however, does not work in Southside Virginia. During a settlement history of approximately seventy years, the region did not follow the expected evolutionary path exhibited by other developing regions of North America. Settlement evolution did not follow economic development. As the region progressed rapidly toward a commercial agricultural economy, its regional settlement structure remained in the inertial mold associated with the predominant early pioneer economy. As the Southside developed into an important component of the world economy, with its tobacco marketed in Great Britain and continental Europe and with its settlers granted access to manufactured products from all over the world, the original frontier-mercantile trading system remained intact. A system of central places, composed of dominant regional center, lesser towns, and smaller service centers such as villages and hamlets, did not replace the decentralized places (primarily plantations, ferry sites, and courthouses) that comprised the old settlement order. No dominant regional trading town, or towns, emerged to organize the Southside's trade and to provide linkages between the region and its external markets. Tobacco and other regional exports continued to move from plantations to fall-zone ports. Manufactured goods continued to move from fall-zone ports to country stores.

In the absence of towns, Southside trade was focused on country stores. Whether located at a solitary site, usually on a plantation as either the only business or as one of several activities, or loosely clustered in an open-country neighborhood pattern on adjacent plantations in areas of greater trading potential (primarily ferry and courthouse sites), country stores were the most important focal points in the region. Country stores functioned as the towns, villages, and hamlets of the Southside. They dispensed a variety of retail goods that included cloth and other clothing-construction materials, food and drink, housewares, hardware, ready-made clothes, and personal items. Easy credit purchases and a barter system that exchanged store goods for a variety of local natural and farm products, predominantly tobacco, were the primary components of the trading structure.

But there existed within that general structure a myriad of complex business relationships. The provision of services, such as the marketing of tobacco, the advance of cash, and the dominant retailing function, was a relatively simple linear transaction if carried out between merchant and customer. But if placed within the context of the country store as the primary banking institution of the region, or rather the clearinghouse for the local debt network, these simple transactions became complex business entanglements in which store customers used the goods, cash, and services provided by the merchant to both pay debts to and collect debts from third-party interests.

Although a central-place network did not evolve in the Southside, certain aspects of Christaller's model were generally present in the decentralized trade of the region. Stores had distinct trade areas that were based on the range of a good, or distance-decay principles. As in central-place theory, customers located near the store, despite the high level of consumer mobility within the region, provided the greatest support for the store. Although there was no structured hierarchy within the region, certain stores did greater volumes of business because of their more strategic locations. These higher-volume stores also included those of the more aggressive Scottish mercantile companies that dominated the country-store and tobacco trade before the Revolutionary War. Some aspects of threshold size were also present in the region. Other than the obvious requisite number of customers to make a store financially viable, tobacco producers provided the primary support for the local stores. In recognition of that support, they were provided with greater access to credit, cash advances, and support for payments of debts to third parties.

The Southside experience suggests greater accord with August Lösch's less-structured interpretation of central-place theory. Overall, in contrast to Christaller, Lösch was concerned more with smaller places in the settlement network and with the construction of the central-place system from the bottom, or from the smaller places. Lösch's assumption of variation in the shape and size of the retail and service trade area and diversity of behavior of the customers within that trade area is more applicable to the Southside's trading patterns. The high degree of mobility of Southside consumers—the product of the frontier in conjunction with the long-distance marketing of tobacco and the endemic debt avoidance—created, as a regional norm, overlapping store trade areas. Notions of hierarchy and range were reduced in favor of a general consumer free-for-all in which customers patronized numerous stores within a relatively large geographic area with seemingly little regard for the dictates of distance and size of establishment.

It is also Lösch's alternative trade-area geometry of consumer-rich and consumer-poor areas that best represents the reality of country-store trade areas in the Southside. At both ferry and crossroad sites, the preferred locations for high-volume merchandising, store customers tended to be drawn from areas adjacent to the dominant highways. At crossroad locations customers originated primarily from the area adjacent to the four main highways, the four different directions created by the two roads comprising the crossroads, while fewer patrons came from the more poorly served areas between the four dominant roads. At ferry locations store customers were concentrated along the two roads, the two different directions of the one road crossing the river, while fewer customers originated from the area adjacent to the river. In the area near the store, where no such transportation shadow existed, customers came from all directions.

The factors that created such variations in trade-area geometry may also have favored the store patron in the merchant-customer business relationship, a view held by Lösch that was in sharp contrast to the merchant orientation embraced by Christaller. With their accessibility to easy credit, their playing merchant against merchant in the practice of debt avoidance, and their frequent migration beyond the region to new settlement frontiers, the customers seemed to have the advantage over the local merchants. But this interpretation must also be tempered by the high cost of backcountry store goods, the manipulation of tobacco prices and transport costs by the merchant, and the merchant's right to bring suit in the court system.

Because economic development did not give rise to a central-place network in the Southside, the theoretical focus then must be shifted to James Vance's long-distance trade model, with its orientation to a frontier-mercantile trading structure. In the context of the Southside's long settlement history and well-developed commercial agricultural system, the suggestion of close association with Vance's model continues the regional paradox that is Southside Virginia. The frontier-mercantile trading structure implies scattered, primarily subsistence-directed settlers shipping a few surplus items, such as furs, deerskins, livestock, or a barrel of corn whisky, over crude trails or down dangerous streams to a distant market town, usually an entrepôt that handled trade between developing frontier regions and their markets in developed economic areas. Commercial agricultural production and population growth were not postulated as components of the model. They were not part of the same linear trading structure that supported the rudimentary market orientation of the pioneer economy. Nevertheless, after more than seventy years of economic development and with one of the most commercially oriented agricultural economies in North America, Southsiders continued to ship tobacco and other products directly to the fall zone, primarily the entrepôt of Petersburg.

The critical part of Vance's model is the rapid development of a regional central-place network that, stimulated by the greater demands of a well-developed market economy, supplants the entrepôt–country store exchange system. Southside development then is even more profound in that the trading model that best represents the region's experience throughout the eighteenth century, and into the early nineteenth century, is only the formative component of a model whose primary orientation is toward the central-place system that is assumed to follow rapidly on the heels of the initial linear trading system.

Based on the perceptions of the Southside population, the physical environment was a component of long-distance trade. The fall zone, where continuous ocean navigation was terminated, deprived the region of potential port development. This landlocked location strengthened the position of long-distance trade in the region. The clay roadbeds that often brought transport to a standstill gave the region an infrastructure that was positioned at a level more commensurate with the difficulties expected in a pioneer economy. Southsiders were "alarmed and distressed" by the economic stagnation created by their landlocked position. Efforts at regional reform were based on the construction of a vast network of internal navigational improvements that would permit the cheaper transport of backcountry agricultural products to more favorable external markets. The numerous legislative petitions for such change, many written with great emotion and rhetoric, reveal their belief that the ultimate cause of regional inertia, as indicated in the lack of a town network and the continued agricultural dominance of the "ruinous" tobacco, was the economic restriction created by the region's landlocked position.

An important functional addition to the long-distance trade model, gleaned from the Southside experience, is the retail-trade component. Numerous Southsiders, primarily in the service of the tobacco trade, purchased goods at the distant fall-zone ports, where the staple was inspected and shipped to foreign markets. Although some of these purchases were hierarchical, represented by the conspicuous consumption of some well-to-do planters, the great majority of this trade, from wealthy planter to lowly wagon attendant, dealt with common goods that were also available at stores in the backcountry.

The continued dominance of long-distance trade in a region with a long settlement history suggests a strong correlation with the leading principles of Carville Earle and Ronald Hoffman's staple theory of settlement and economic development. Indeed, it would appear that the Southside was the regional archetype for the primary-staple component of their thesis that linked urban development to agricultural production. In the Earle and Hoffman scheme, primary-staple production, or crops grown primarily for the export market, made few demands on the production region for handling, processing, or marketing. Without these demands, an urban network was less likely to develop. Tobacco, the basis of economic development and population growth in the Southside, did not require an elaborate infrastructure or any special handling. The Southside participated in the tobacco trade only as the primary producer and in the rudimental transport of the crop to the fall-zone market. Tobacco inspection warehouses, wholesalers, exporters, brokers, and manufacturers—the occupational bases of urban development—were located outside the region.

The failure of commercial wheat production to expand beyond the narrow geographic bounds of highly localized Southside markets appears also to be linked to Earle and Hoffman's interpretation of the staple thesis. The infrastructure that supported the dominant tobacco trade was unable to meet the requirements of the wheat trade. Because of the limitations of the regional infrastructure, commercial wheat production did not develop beyond a narrow strip of territory adjacent to the primary fall-zone market.

Additionally, the Southside experience offers evidence to expand the principles of Earle and Hoffman's interpretation of the staple thesis. The large slave population that was the basis of labor in the production of tobacco effectively worked against the establishment of central places in the region. Increasing to almost one-half the regional population by 1800, this population seriously restricted the level of consumer demand needed to support towns. A regional population in excess of 125,000 and some county population densities in excess of thirty persons per square mile did not translate into requisite figures for support of urban development when half of those people were not independent consumers. The real support of urban development, the white population who were the consumers, never reached fifteen persons per square mile in any of the counties.

Although the evidence from Southside Virginia strongly supports Earle and Hoffman's staple thesis, it also suggests that some aspects of the model are too rigid. Their proposition that wheat production was associated primarily with free labor does not hold together under scrutiny from the viewpoint of the Southside experience. Wheat was produced on tobacco plantations with slave labor throughout the region. The use of slave labor also occurred in regions where wheat was the prevailing commercial crop. In the central and northern Piedmont regions of Virginia during the antebellum period, slaves clearly dominated the labor force.[2]

The spatially limited market available to Southside wheat suggests associations kindred to those of Johann von Thunen.[3] Von Thunen developed a system of commercial agricultural land use that emphasized increased extensive activities with increased distance from a single market center. In von Thunen's assumptions, wheat production took place at considerable distance from market because of its relatively lower yields per acre that required greater amounts of cheaper land. However, in relation to the primary market at the fall zone, Southside wheat occupied the inner-ring location of more intensive cultivation because of the poor support provided by the regional transport system and the strong competition from tobacco culture. Because of its ease of movement in a variety of modes and conditions of transport, tobacco occupied land-use rings that ranged from close proximity to market, if soil fertility could provide that support, to distant rings that were only surpassed in distance from market by the most extensive land use of livestock economy. Wheat, however, did remain a viable crop in the backcountry because of the many decentralized local markets and the more subsistent character of the crop on large landholdings.

If Monsieur Dupont had traveled through Southside Virginia, perhaps pursuing his interest in purchasing land in the backcountry, he would have found an even greater level of decentralized settlement. Unlike the more experienced travelers, John Smyth and Congressman William Loughton Smith, who interpreted the region's decentralized settlement landscape as just a slightly eccentric version of the Southern backcountry character, Dupont would probably have had some difficulty in understanding a region that did not contain any towns despite having replaced the many roaming bears with a well-developed cultural landscape. Although he would not have realized it, the locational key to understanding the Southside was Petersburg, his destination. Although Petersburg was located on the Southside's eastern border, it was the region's functional center. Petersburg contained the region's tobacco inspections, its wholesale warehouses, its interregional traders, its shipping docks, and a considerable quantity of its retail and service functions, and it was the focus of its road system. As Dupont toured Petersburg, he was well aware of the importance of tobacco to the prominence of the town. It is unlikely, however, that he could imagine the powerful influence of tobacco on the absence of towns in Southside Virginia.

Notes

1. Nall, "A Letter from Petersburg," 148.
2. Irwin, "Tobacco, Wheat, and Slaves in the Virginia Piedmont, 1850–1860."
3. Hall, ed., *Von Thunen's Isolated State: An English Edition of "Der Isolierte Staat,"* Carla M. Wartenberg, trans. (Oxford, 1966).

Appendix A

Database for Analysis of Country Trade (No. of Individual Accounts)

Time Period	From Court Judgments	From Account Books	From Will Books	Total
1750–1759	197	0	13	210
1760–1769	452	17	9	478
1770–1775	295	956	32	1,283
1784–1789	126	95	25	246
1790–1800	116	948	10	1,074
Total	1,186	2,016	89	3,291

Appendix B

Tobacco Prices, 1732–1799, and Exchange Rates, 1732–1775, Pence per Pound

Year	No. of Accounts	Highest Price	Lowest Price	Average Price	Average Exchange Rate[1]
			Sterling		
1732	1	1.64	1.64	1.64	121.00
1733	2	1.99	1.66	1.83	120.00
1734	1	1.67	1.67	1.67	120.00
1736	1	1.96	1.96	1.96	122.70
1738	1	1.45	1.45	1.45	123.75
1739	2	1.54	0.97	1.26	122.50
1740	2	1.58	1.58	1.58	119.17
1742	3	1.83	1.58	1.69	120.00
1743	4	1.58	1.00	1.19	120.00
1744	3	1.97	1.15	1.49	121.88
1745	2	1.40	1.22	1.31	127.60
1746	2	1.35	1.35	1.35	131.87
1749	2	1.60	1.60	1.60	123.75
1750	12	1.92	1.52	1.71	125.94
1751	18	1.87	1.17	1.49	128.42
1752	3	1.54	1.54	1.54	129.92
1753	4	1.39	1.31	1.35	129.50
1754	4	1.56	1.40	1.52	127.55
1755	9	1.85	1.16	1.40	129.38
1756	2	1.56	1.40	1.48	128.44
1757	3	1.73	1.58	1.63	139.71
1758	7	1.75	1.17	1.33	137.92
1759	4	1.73	1.30	1.55	139.97
1760	14	1.70	1.07	1.52	141.43

Year	No. of Accounts	Highest Price	Lowest Price	Average Price	Average Exchange Rate[1]
1761	16	1.68	0.98	1.55	143.72
1762	8	1.70	0.92	1.48	152.40
1763	11	1.64	0.95	1.36	159.88
1764	4	1.49	1.49	1.49	160.73
1765	9	1.49	0.93	1.18	160.36
1766	6	2.11	1.56	1.83	128.48
1767	5	2.40	1.76	1.98	125.54
1768	10	2.40	1.68	2.07	124.99
1769	19	2.71	1.80	2.29	121.97
1770	56	2.61	1.91	2.14	118.00
1771	18	2.43	1.62	1.90	123.60
1772	10	2.43	1.54	1.87	123.59
1773	4	2.31	1.23	1.69	129.75
1774	12	2.08	1.54	1.71	130.00
1775	6	2.49	1.66	1.97	120.00

Virginia Currency

Year	No. of Accounts	Highest Price	Lowest Price	Average Price	
1776	2	1.56	1.50	1.53	
1777	5	4.20	1.20	3.05	
1778	4	9.07	4.32	7.10	
1779	2	26.40	6.00	16.20	
1780	1	1.92	1.92	1.92	
1781	3	3.90	2.16	2.74	
1782	9	3.00	2.40	2.70	
1783	2	4.32	2.58	3.45	
1784	3	4.56	3.60	4.16	
1785	24	4.32	2.64	3.32	
1786	22	3.60	1.92	2.64	
1787	18	3.60	1.80	2.67	
1788	50	3.12	2.16	2.44	
1789	21	2.64	2.16	2.34	
1790	10	3.12	1.44	2.38	
1791	5	2.76	1.92	2.20	
1792	7	2.22	1.56	1.89	
1793	9	2.52	1.80	2.01	
1794	10	3.60	1.92	2.62	
1795	5	3.60	1.80	2.87	
1796	2	2.40	2.40	2.40	
1797	3	4.08	2.88	3.32	
1798	15	8.28	4.80	6.51	
1799	4	5.40	4.32	4.95	

Source: County court judgments, merchant account books, and will books (1730s and 1740s). Exchange rates are from John J. McCusker, *Money and Exchange in Europe and America: A Handbook* (Chapel Hill, N.C., 1978), 205–14.

1. Virginia currency equivalent to £100 sterling.

Index

Abingdon, Pa., 75
aboriginals, 33; *see also* Indians
Africa, 16
agriculture, *see* economic activities
   (primary)
Albemarle Sound, 29, 58
All Hallows Parish, Md., 17, 20
Amelia County: cattle and hog
   holdings, 72–74; close proximity to
   fall-zone merchants, 145; country
   store goods, 167; courthouse, 63;
   flax, 78; flour mills, 85; fodder,
   73; inventories, 102, 104, 106; lack
   of towns, 5; land ownership, 107;
   merchants, 52–53; part of peddler
   circuit, 140; population expansion
   and distribution, 41–42; road
   conditions, 96; sheep, 74; slave
   population, 45–46, 107; stock marks,
   73; tobacco and tobacco notes, 79,
   92; topography, 19; wealth
   structure, 102–4, 106–7; wheat, 86
American Midwest, 14, 16, 18, 20–21,
   155
American South: cash advances at
   country stores, 178; cash to credit
   ratio, 174; few towns, 2; persistence of country trade, 11; population source region, 185; primary

staple production, 14; society, 18;
   uneven distribution of purchasing
   power, 155
Anglican Church, 37, 42, 147
Anglican parishes, 35
antebellum, 14
Appalachian Mountains, 2
Appalachian region, 49, 71
Appomattox River: access to tobacco
   inspection warehouses, 79; flour
   mills, 88; focus of Indian trade
   (skins and furs), 71; interruption of
   continuous navigation, 29; navigational improvements, 88; northern
   boundary of Southside region, 4;
   settlement expansion, 41; tobacco
   trade, 92, 96
artisans, 12
Atherton, Lewis, 18, 20, 174, 178
Atkinson, Roger: English merchant
   (factor), 115; observations on
   wheat and tobacco, 87; owner of
   town of Peytonsburg, 67n42
Augusta County, Va., 104, 106

backcountry: hinterlands, 59; New
   England, 49; posts and stations, 16;
   Southern, 18, 20–21, 62, 75; trad-
   ing connections with entrepôts, 15

197

About the Author

Charles J. Farmer, a product of the small town and rural environment of the North Carolina backcountry, is associate professor of geography at Frostburg State University, Frostburg, Maryland. Although he is interested in a variety of past and present North American landscapes, his research interests are focused primarily on the historical geography of the American South. He earned his Ph.D. from the University of Maryland, College Park.